Becoming Mr Nice

Becoming Mr Nice
The Howard Marks Archive

Amber Marks

NO EXIT PRESS

First published in 2021
by No Exit Press,
an imprint of
Oldcastle Books Ltd,
Harpenden,
Herts, UK
noexit.co.uk

A CIP catalogue record for this book is available from the British Library.

ISBN:
978-0-85730-393-6 (hardcover)
978-0-85730-394-3 (ebook)

2 4 6 8 10 9 7 5 3 1

Design by Ben Weaver Studio
Printed & bound by Ozgraf, Poland

Copyright © 2021, Amber Marks

The right of Amber Marks to be identified as the author of this work has been asserted in accordance with the Copyright, Designs and Patents Act 1988. All rights reserved. No part of this book may be reproduced, stored in or introduced into a retrieval system, or transmitted, in any form or by any means (electronic, mechanical, photocopying, recording or otherwise) without the written permission of the publishers.

Any person who does any unauthorised act in relation to this publication may be liable to criminal prosecution and civil claims for damages.

Contents

References

HT
David Leigh, *High Time: The Life and Times of Howard Marks* (Heinemann, 1984)

HMP
Paul Eddy & Sara Walden (Eds.), *Hunting Marco Polo: The Pursuit of Howard Marks* (Bantam Press, 1991)

MN
Howard Marks, *Mr Nice* (Secker & Warburg, 1996)

SMN
Carlo Morselli, *Structuring Mr Nice: Entrepreneurial Opportunities and Brokerage Positioning in the Cannabis Trade* (École de Criminologie, Université de Montréal, 2000)

JHCH
Thomas Grant, *Jeremy Hutchinson's Case Histories: From Lady Chatterley's Lover to Howard Marks* (John Murray, 2015)

Preface

'It is impossible to control what happens to you. The only thing you can control is your attitude to it.'
– Howard Marks

Becoming Mr Nice tells the life story of Howard Marks through his published and unpublished writings, hitherto unrevealed court transcripts, photographs, the smuggling records missed in police searches, and personal mementos. Every image in this book has been scanned or photographed from Howard's valuables, a biography told by treasured objects. Notwithstanding an unusual and peripatetic lifestyle including two bouts of incarceration, first in the United Kingdom (1980–82) and later in the United States of America (1988–95), several years on the run throughout Europe (1974–88) and multiple bases in the Far East, Howard succeeded, with the help of friends and family, in preserving this collection of artefacts. Howard and I pulled most of these together in the final years of his life, storing it in a large wooden shed in the backyard of his rented apartment in Leeds. It is my pleasure to share many of its highlights in this book. Detailed captions to the images, based on my personal knowledge and archival research, combine with the text of Howard's own writings to guide us through the images chronologically.

The book opens with a telegram from Captain Dennis Marks of the Merchant Navy, welcoming his son Howard to the world in August 1945, some three weeks before the end of World War II. From his childhood thoughts on philosophy and friendship (in scanned extracts from Howard's school books) we move to the rebellious years of his adolescence in South Wales and his surprise acceptance into Oxford University in 1964. Much of the text in this chapter will be familiar to readers of *Mr Nice*. It was originally written at the request of John Jones, Dean of Balliol College, while Howard was serving a prison sentence of twenty-five years in Terre Haute, Indiana, and I have taken the text from this typed manuscript, 'Reminiscences of Balliol'. We follow Howard's activities during the height of London psychedelia and learn of his dismay at the policing of anti-Vietnam protests in a letter to his parents. The smuggling life of a budding entrepreneur takes off in the early seventies with driving licences and passports in multiple identities, including that of film director Donald Nice and TV engineer Mr Tunnicliffe. Howard's headline-grabbing disappearance in 1974 and fugitive years are chronicled with extracts from a hitherto unpublished account, the accuracy of which cannot be vouched for as it was prepared for his court case. This is followed by Her Majesty's Customs & Excise's 'Operation Cartoon', featuring photographs of Howard's involvement in the biggest ever cannabis importation into the United Kingdom, apparently on behalf of the Mexican Secret Service. The first half of the book culminates in hitherto unseen court transcripts of his spy-scandal-riddled trial at the Old Bailey in 1981, where, to the fury of law enforcement, he is acquitted by the jury.

Things become hectic following Howard's release from custody in 1982. His voice is lost in the confusion of the world as we hurtle our way towards the height of the Drug War. Records from the appropriately named 'Operation Eclectic', then the largest international collaboration of law enforcement, and spearheaded by the US Drug Enforcement Agency, piece together Howard's life through graphs, phone tap transcripts and investigative leads. The emotional toll of Howard and his wife Judy's arrests in Palma de Mallorca and extradition to the United States is laid bare through contemporaneous witness statements and correspondence. Previously undisclosed manuscripts reveal the audacious defence Howard would have run, and enjoyed running, had the DEA not succeeded in coercing his partner in crime, Ernie Combs of the Brotherhood of Eternal Love, to give evidence against him.

An intimate look at Howard's time in one of the United States' highest security penitentiaries provides a rare glimpse into the harsh reality of mass incarceration. Sentenced to 25 years, his prison letters show how he secures his miraculously early release in 1995 and reveal the emotional highs and lows of this time. The final chapter relates his conversion in the press from heinous drug baron to the popularly acclaimed cultural icon and celebrated cannabis activist, Mr Nice.

I hope you enjoy his story as much as Howard did and would have wanted you to.

Amber Marks

This book is dedicated to my dad and all of those who loved him, with enormous thanks to the custodians of the Howard Marks Archive for its maintenance and for allowing me to access, research and reproduce selected contents in this keepsake.

1

From the Valleys to the Dreaming Spires

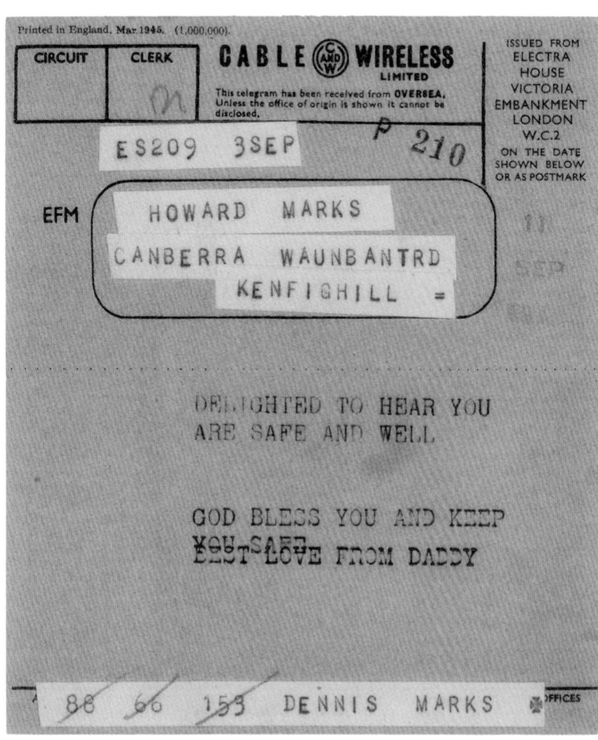

Printed in England. Mar 1945. (1,000,000).

CIRCUIT | CLERK

CABLE & WIRELESS LIMITED

This telegram has been received from OVERSEA. Unless the office of origin is shown it cannot be disclosed.

ISSUED FROM ELECTRA HOUSE VICTORIA EMBANKMENT LONDON W.C.2 ON THE DATE SHOWN BELOW OR AS POSTMARK

ES209 3SEP P 210

EFM HOWARD MARKS
CANBERRA WAUNBANTRD
KENFIGHILL =

DELIGHTED TO HEAR YOU
ARE SAFE AND WELL

GOD BLESS YOU AND KEEP
YOU SAFE
BEST LOVE FROM DADDY

88 66 153 DENNIS MARKS

Captain Dennis Marks sent this telegram on hearing of Howard's birth on 13 August 1945. Shortly after his return home to Wales and towards the end of his 21 years in service, Captain Marks was allowed to take Edna, a school teacher, and their son Howard (aged three) round the world on the *Bradburn*, a 10,000-ton freighter owned by Reardon Smith and Co, Cardiff.

Howard's father, David Thomas Dennis Marks joined Reardon Smith Ships in October 1929 aged 16. He was made Captain in 1944, while serving in the Merchant Navy during WWII.

Fripassagerare i sällskap med 5000 ton till Malmö

Kapten D. Marks med sonen Howard och hustrun Edna.

Så rörligt som det var i Malmö frihamn på tisdagsmorgonen har man knappast skådat motsvarigheten till någon gång tillförne i år. Det stora "numret" var brittiska ångaren Leeds City, som i dagningen anlände med en jättelast vete, kli, solrosmjöl och jordnötsmjöl — sammanlagt 8.000 ton, lastade i Rosario och Buenos Ayres — plus en fripassagerare.

(→) Howard pictured with his parents in Malmö, Sweden, on one of the *Bradburn*'s many stopovers.

(↓) Howard experimented with aliases from an early age, signing this work 'Howardo de Viccin'. He named the boat *The Linda*, after his beloved younger sister.

PS

Headquarters of The I-Spy Tribe

News Chronicle Wigwam
Bouverie Street
London, E.C.4
Telephone: FLEet Street 5000

Redskin Howard Marks
16a Waunbank Road
Kenfig Hill
Nr. Bridgend
Glam.

27th August 1958

How, Redskin Howard !

Thank you for your smoke-signal and photograph. I was MOST interested to hear about the smallest street in the world. I should imagine that it can well claim that title - as well as it's amusing name !

Yes, here is a pen for you. I think you deserve it after sending me such a splendid report. Enclosed with this letter is the photograph as you mentioned in your letter that you would like to have it back.

It was super to hear about the smallest house in the world - which you saw on the I-SPY trail at Conway. AND, of course, the smallest church in the world at Colwyn Bay.

Write again soon, won't you ?
Odhu/tinggo, Redskin
A LETTER FROM BIG CHIEF I-SPY

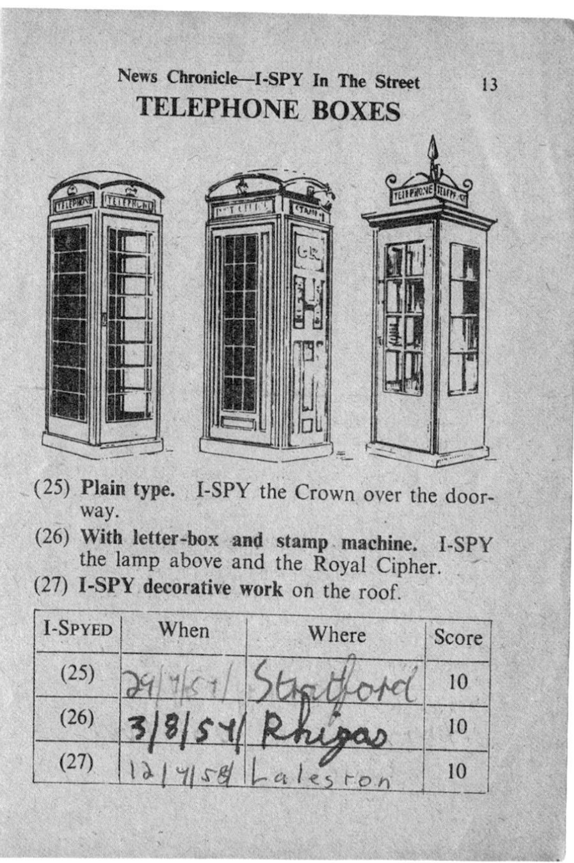

News Chronicle—I-SPY In The Street 13

TELEPHONE BOXES

(25) **Plain type.** I-SPY the Crown over the doorway.

(26) **With letter-box and stamp machine.** I-SPY the lamp above and the Royal Cipher.

(27) **I-SPY decorative work** on the roof.

I-SPYED	When	Where	Score
(25)	29/7/57	Stratford	10
(26)	3/8/57	Rhigos	10
(27)	12/7/58	Laleston	10

(↑↗) The I-SPY books were popular with school children throughout the 1950s and 1960s. Upon completion, the books were sent to the HQ of the I-SPY Tribe and returned with an Order of Merit. Howard completed several dozen of these booklets. In this letter, dated 27 August 1958, shortly after Howard's 13th birthday, the Headquarters of the I-SPY Tribe thanks him for his smoke-signal and for informing HQ of the name that Howard believed to be of the shortest street in the world.

Howard as a young boy.

(→) Marty Langford and Howard grew up together in the small village of Kenfig Hill, in Bridgend County Borough, South Wales. In 1980 Marty pleaded guilty to his role in one of Howard's cannabis ventures. Both keen photographers from a young age, this photo of Howard trainspotting was taken by Marty and developed by Howard in the darkroom he set up at home.

Clear Thinking

Our material progress has outstripped our mental progress. The reason lies in ignorance, suspicion, superstition and ~~[illegible]~~ in prejudice. We need to think clearly.

Politics - Science of Government

Economics - study of man in his quest for living.

It was difficult for new people to change or abandon a habit of mind. They will discard an obsolete weapon, but will cling with in the face of all reason to discard a cherished belief.

" Men fear thought as they fear nothing else in the world."

But thought must be purposeful.

We are too lazy. to think, It is so much easier to accept what we are taught to or to take the opinion of so called authorities and

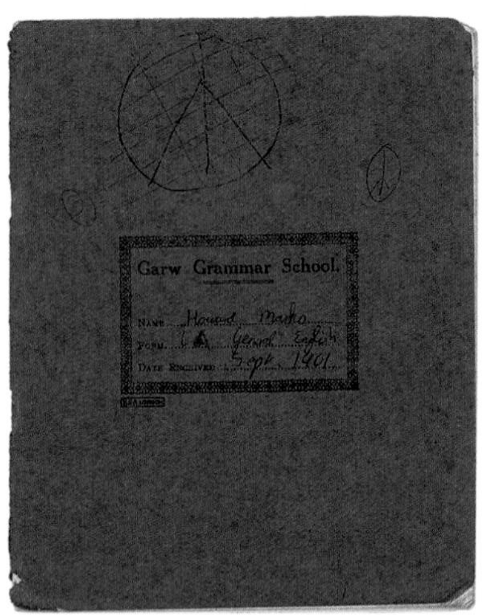

(←) Howard's school books include an essay on the importance of clear thinking. Here he quotes 'Men fear thought as they fear nothing else on earth' from *Why Men Fight* by the philosopher and pacifist Bertrand Russell, of whom Howard was a fan from an early age. Around the age of 13, Howard was given three months detention for leading a strike against the poor quality of the school dinners.

(↗) In Howard's essay on 'A Sense of Humour' he says it is the most important quality in a companion, quite sure he would rather be cheered up than sympathised with.

a tidal wave for instance. And of course no scientist has been able to create life, ~~something~~ which is due to nature

(4) Unnatural is used in this passage to mean abnormal or extraordinary. ~~Most~~ All men are expected not to betray their country.

~~On~~ A Sense of Humour.

When we think of humour, ~~we~~ it brings to mind gaiety and happiness. Life on earth does not mean anything if we are not happy. Of course being happy does not mean that you make a fool of yourself wherever you go. What I think is really meant by happiness is contentment. What is the good of having any virtues if we are not content with them. ~~If we are~~

If we are contented, we feel like smiling, we have a sense of humour, we are optimists.

If I was asked to choose a companion for any exploration or voyage I would be likely to do, the first quality I would look for is a sense of humour. One would much rather be cheered up rather than sympathised with I am sure.

If we have a sense of humour we are contented, we cannot be

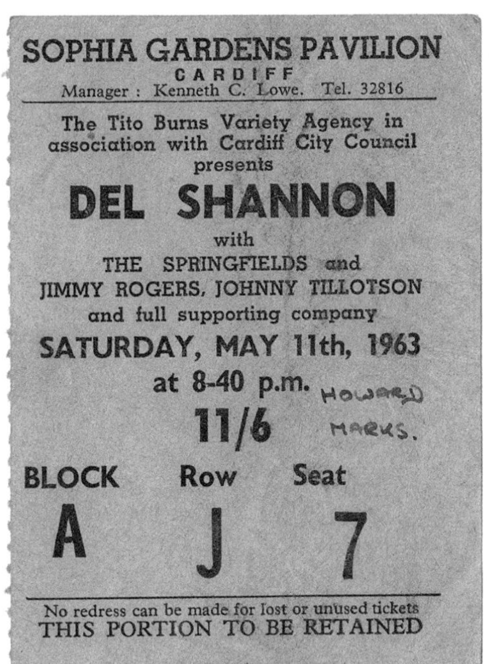

SOPHIA GARDENS PAVILION
CARDIFF
Manager : Kenneth C. Lowe. Tel. 32816

The Tito Burns Variety Agency in association with Cardiff City Council presents

DEL SHANNON

with
THE SPRINGFIELDS and
JIMMY ROGERS, JOHNNY TILLOTSON
and full supporting company

SATURDAY, MAY 11th, 1963
at 8-40 p.m.
11/6

HOWARD MARKS.

BLOCK	Row	Seat
A	J	7

No redress can be made for lost or unused tickets
THIS PORTION TO BE RETAINED

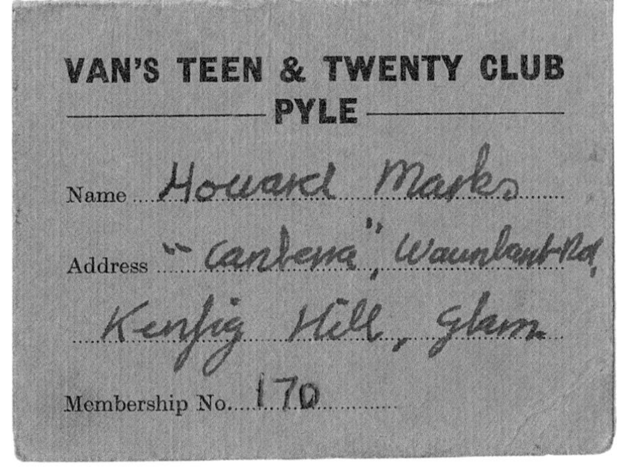

VAN'S TEEN & TWENTY CLUB
PYLE

Name Howard Marks
Address "Canberra", Waunbant Rd, Kenfig Hill, Glam.
Membership No. 170

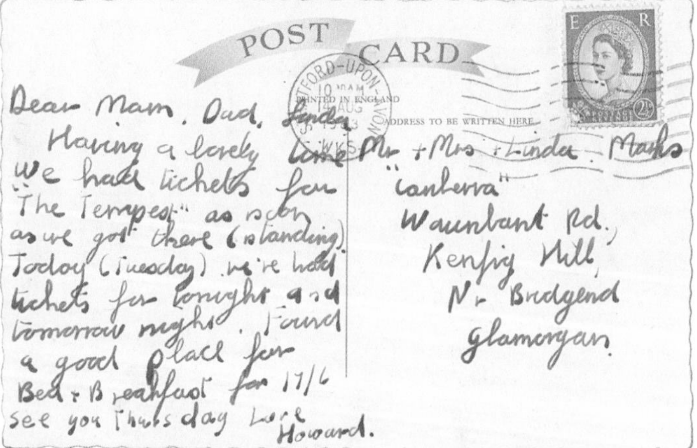

POST CARD

Dear Mam, Dad, Linda
Having a lovely time
We had tickets for "The Tempest" as soon as we got there (standing). Today (Tuesday) we've had tickets for tonight and tomorrow night. Found a good place for Bed & Breakfast for 17/6
See you Thursday Love
Howard.

ADDRESS TO BE WRITTEN HERE
Mr + Mrs + Linda Marks
"Canberra"
Waunbant Rd,
Kenfig Hill,
Nr Bridgend
Glamorgan

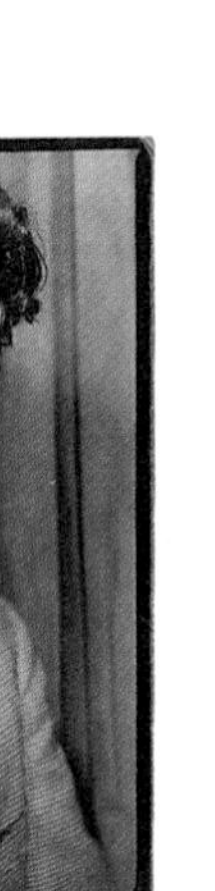

Howard in his Teddy Boy years.

(↖↑) Chief amongst Howard's interests were music and Shakespeare's plays. Howard was allowed to pursue these after obtaining good results in his O Level examinations. A music venue, Van's Teen and Twenty Club, opened up in Kenfig Hill and Howard occasionally sang rock 'n' roll songs there.

Valley Boy
1945-64

'Garw' is a Welsh word meaning 'rough', and Pontycymer is the penultimate village in what used to be a coal mining valley terminating in a dead end. The radius of the school's catchment circle was about fifteen miles. I lived precisely eleven miles away from the school gates, but the school bus took almost an hour to make the journey. The bus was jokingly referred to as 'yellow dog' on account of its propensity to stop at every lamp post. There were no extra-curricular activities of any sort.

A school uniform existed, but very few pupils wore it. The school playground and classrooms were subject to frequent invasions of sheep meandering off the mountainside. One illustrious Old Boy could be boasted of – Daniel Davies, the Queen's Physician.

My 'A' level subjects were Pure and Applied Mathematics, Physics, and Chemistry. Although competent in these subjects, I had little or no interest in them and absolutely no interest in any other academic discipline. My interests overlapped my obsessions and were limited to sex, alcohol, and rock 'n' roll music; all of which were vigorously and passionately pursued.

It was an overwhelming surprise when my headmaster, H J Davies, took me aside one day and said that he wanted me to sit the Oxford Entrance Scholarship Examination. It had been at least eight years since anyone from the Garw Grammar School had attempted to get into Oxford. The person who had attempted it had been successful and was, in fact, the headmaster's son John Davies, who read Physics at Balliol. Accordingly it was suggested that I try to do precisely that.

Sometime during the autumn of 1963, I attended at Balliol for a preliminary interview. I remember little about the train journey from Bridgend to Oxford. I sat opposite a man holding a pair of handcuffs, and for the first time, I saw the dreaming spires. A couple of hours later, I was waiting outside to be 'generally' interviewed. Also waiting was another interviewee who asked me which school I came from. I told him. 'Where's that?' he asked. I answered. 'Oh Wales!' he said very scornfully. I asked him which school he came from. 'Eton,' he said, looking down at the floor. I couldn't resist asking, 'Where's that?' but he didn't reply. In fact I did not know Eton's geographical location, but I must admit that I had heard of it. Eventually I began talking to another grammar school boy who was from Southampton. He too intended to read Physics and also seemed to feel as out of place as I did. His name was Julian Peto, and he has remained absolutely my best friend ever since. □

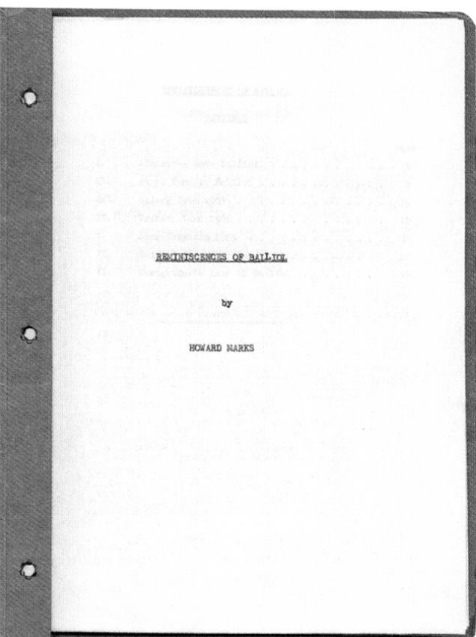

REMINISCENCES OF BALLIOL

by

HOWARD MARKS

The text for this chapter is taken from a bound typescript written by Howard while serving a 25-year sentence in United States Penitentiary, Terre Haute, Indiana. It was completed at the request of John Jones, Dean at Balliol, to whom Howard sent his recollections in separate instalments over the course of the year between 1991–2. In a letter to John dated 7 July 1991, he writes, 'You can probably infer from its output that this typewriter is mechanical and is not blessed with anything approaching a word-processing facility. It was recently manufactured in Brazil and resembles those popular in Welsh villages during the early fifties.'

SOUTHAMPTON ~~49506~~ 49275.

30, Bitterne Way,
~~22 BRYANSTON ROAD~~
BITTERNE
SOUTHAMPTON
HANTS.

16th Jan. 1964

Dear Howard,

I am glad to hear you got in. Balliol has always been the college which admits foreigners, but they seem to be going to ridiculous extremes.

Please excuse the notepaper. It may appear that I bought an assortment of printer's errors cheap, but in fact I am writing from my mistress's house.

I have just found this letter after over a week. I would have written another, only your address was with it. (in my pocket). Last Monday I started work as a technician at Southampton University. I am working for a professor who is studying helicopters. He works out the equations, and he has put me in charge of a £17,000 analogue computer to solve them for him. It's very interesting, but I only get £6 " 15 " 0 a week. I shall probably do it until about June.

I shall see you in March at the Prelims. Still, I suppose it can't be helped.

Your ever affectionate

Julian.

ME

A Welsh bastard playing the harp. (The national sport)

P.S. I haven't got Martin's address, so if you hear from him let me know.

Howard befriended Julian Peto while being interviewed for a place at Balliol College. Both were grammar school boys and came from very different backgrounds to most of those interviewed. They were surprised by their own and each other's admission into Balliol, having been convinced by the derision of other candidates that neither stood a chance. In January 1964 they wrote to inform and congratulate each other on their news. This is Julian's letter to Howard. Julian Peto is now Professor of Epidemiology at the London School of Hygiene and Tropical Medicine.

First Year at Balliol 1964-65

During early October 1964, the big day arrived and I began life as a fully enrolled Balliol undergraduate. I was assigned a small, poky, and drab room on the ground floor of Staircase XXI overlooking St. Giles and vulnerable to inspection by passers by. The gloom of my immediate environment was quickly shattered by an elderly gentleman wearing a white jacket. He knocked on the door, opened it, walked in, and said, 'Be your scout, George.' George and I spent a long time talking to each other, and he explained that his duties included making my bed, cleaning my room, and washing my dishes. This information I found totally astonishing.

Although having little, possibly nothing, in common with my fellow Physics students (always, of course, excepting Julian Peto), there was certainly no feeling of animosity in any direction. Other Physics freshmen were courteously friendly towards me and came to comprehend my heavy Welsh lilt. I gradually began to meet Balliol students outside of the Natural Science faculty and formed the opinion that arts undergraduates, particularly historians and philosophers, were a far more interesting and non-conforming bunch than scientists. Some of them had long hair and wore jeans. Ones that come to mind are: John Adams, Arnold Cragg, Henry Hodge, Chris Fagg, and John Rhodes. A nodding acquaintance with such individuals began to develop.

After a couple of weeks of my first term, a notice appeared in the Porter's Lodge announcing that: 'The following gentlemen will read essays to the Master on the subject of "The Population Problem".' My name then followed along with about six others whose surnames also began with L, M or N. Also present at this essay reading were freshmen John Minford and Hamilton McMillan, both of whom had a very significant effect on my life. John Minford was convinced that I was a talented actor and persuaded me to join the Balliol Dramatic Society. Hamilton McMillan, many years after graduation, was convinced that I would make a talented espionage agent and persuaded me to work for MI6.

Henry Hodge was one of the immediate neighbours of mine with whom I had a close personal friendship. He was one of the users of my window with removable bars; his girlfriend then being Emma Rothschild. Henry often spoke of his friend Denys Irving, who had been rusticated from Oxford for that particular academic year and had sensibly spent that year visiting exotic parts of the world. He had recently returned from his voyages of discovery and was about to visit, presumably illegally, his friends at Oxford. There were a number of friends of Denys who had gathered at Chalfont Road. I was invited over there to meet him and join in a social gathering. I felt fairly honoured to be invited to join the 'big boys' and looked forward to the engagement.

Denys had brought with him some marijuana in the form of kif from Morocco. Up to that point I had heard the odd whisper of drugs being taken at the University and was aware that marijuana was popular with British West Indian communities, modern jazz enthusiasts, American beatniks, and the British self-styled intellectual wave of 'angry young men'. I still, however, had not consciously retained any description of the effects of marijuana. With a great deal of enthusiastic interest, therefore, I accepted the joint that was offered and took my first few puffs.

I became an active member of the Balliol Dramatic Society and was soon adopted into a group of largely second-year Balliol undergraduates often referred to as 'The Establishment'. These included the long-haired trio of Chris Fagg, John Rhodes and John Adams and others such as John Hamwee, Roger Silverstone, Rick Lambert, Michael Wilkins, Peter Ford and Paul Swain. I greatly enjoyed their company and spent most of the day with them. 'The Establishment' also formed the core of the Victorian Society and invited me to become a member. It was a strange society, to say the least, but the main requirement was to down large amounts of drink – this time port, which I had never tried.

For their Hilary Term production, the dramatic societies of Balliol and Lady Margaret Hall chose Oscar Wilde's *Salomé*. John Minford, the producer, asked if I would play the part of John the Baptist. The part was not a very large one, and most of my lines had to be bellowed from a makeshift cistern constructed in an alcove which normally housed a piano. Minford felt that my Welsh accent might add some authenticity to the evangelical wailings emitting from the cistern. Salomé herself was played by Vivien Rothwell and one of the palace guards was played by Hamilton McMillan. At some stage – mercifully offstage – John the Baptist was beheaded. This required a model to be made of my head and for this model to be adorned with bloody entrails obtained from one of the city's butchers. The end result was placed on a silver platter for presentation to Salomé.

The first and last three weeks of my first long vacation were spent at my parents' house in Wales, while the intervening ten weeks were spent hitch-hiking fairly randomly around Great Britain and Europe. My European travels included a visit to Copenhagen, where I ran completely out of money. Luckily, I had made friends with members of a Danish rock and roll group, who very kindly allowed me to sing with them on a few occasions thereby earning enough money to leave the country. The route back to the United Kingdom took me through Hamburg, where my friend Hamilton McMillan lived. Mac had given me his particulars, and I telephoned him from a sordid bar in the Reeperbahn. (I was looking for the Star Club where the Beatles had been discovered.) He was delighted to hear from me, insisted I stay a few nights at his home, and came to pick me up. □

30, Bitterne Way,
Southampton,
HANTS.
(Tel. Southampton 49275)
28.12.64

Dear Howard,

I hope you enjoyed Christmas in the usual drunken Welsh fashion of which you gave me such a graphic description. As I threatened, Richard and I might turn up to terrorise the Rhondda Valley for a couple of days. As he has to go back to Cambridge on January 4th we'd probably turn up the 1st or the 2nd and then go straight to Cambridge if it's convenient for you. If we did come we'd stay in bed & breakfast places so as not to inconvenience your mother. Could you let me know whether or not you'll be around, and if so if it's convenient for us to turn up then? I'm sorry I left it so late to let you know, but I didn't realise how early Richard had to go up to Cambridge. I don't know how long the post takes, but if you

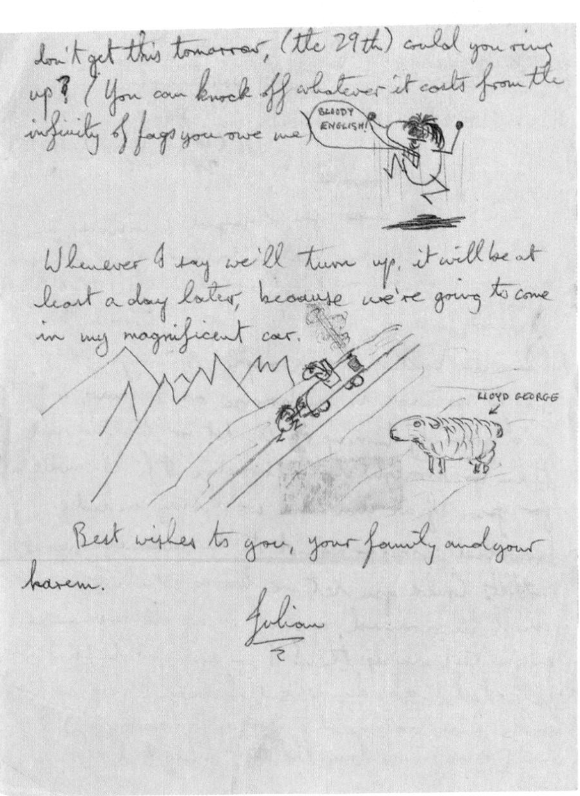

don't get this tomorrow, (the 29th) could you ring up? (You can knock off whatever it costs from the infinity of fags you owe me)

Whenever I say we'll turn up, it will be at least a day later, because we're going to come in my magnificent car.

Best wishes to you, your family and your harem.

Julian

Letter to Howard from Julian Peto on 28 December 1964 proposing a visit to Wales by Julian and his brother Richard.

Howard in thespian mode in his parents' garden in Kenfig Hill.

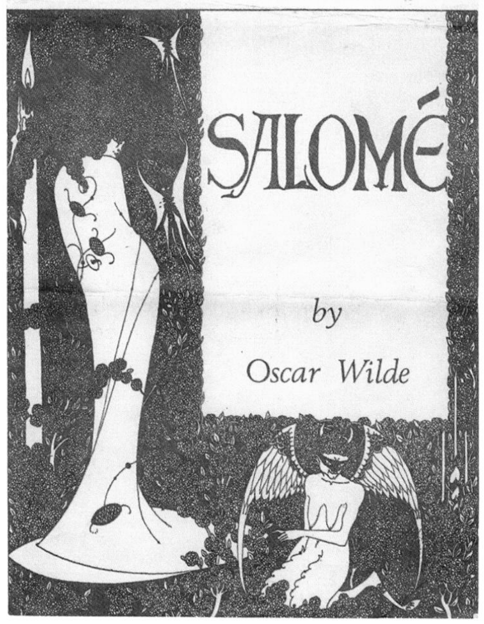

Howard played the part of John the Baptist in this production of Oscar Wilde's tragedy *Salomé*.

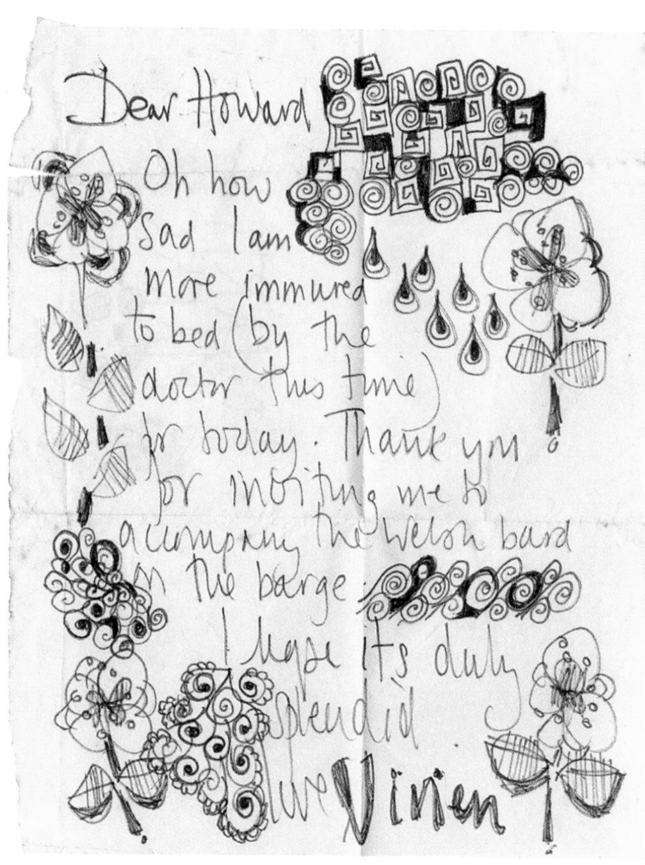

Dear Howard

Oh how sad I am more immured to bed (by the doctor this time) for today. Thank you for inviting me to accompany the Welsh bard on the barge. I hope it's duly splendid

love Vivien

Howard

PAINTINGS & DRAWINGS
VIVIEN ROTHWELL

OXFORD UNION CELLARS
17th—24th OCTOBER, 65

preview Sunday 17th 6pm RSVP

(↑) Letter and invite from Howard's college friend, Vivien Rothwell.

MARIJUANA (2)

When I entered Oxford University, I encountered a great variety of people from widely differing sovial and cultural backgrounds. My inability to find common ground on which to communicate with them severely inhibited me, and I became rather withdrawn and reclusive. Occaisonally, however, when very drunk, I would do Elvis Presley imitations at various functions which together with my then outrageous long haired appearance and 'primitive animal' projection endeared me to the non-conformist student element with whom I began to vaguely associate.

One day in June, 1965, while at an informal gathering at one of these newly found friend,s lodgings, a joint of marijuana was passed to me. Someone had produced it, ready rolled, from his pocket, smoked some, passed it to another friend who gave it to me. Between my first hearing about marijuana and first trying it, I had learned some more about its use. I knew that it was popular with the British West Indian communities, jazz enthusiasts, American beatniks, and the British self styled intellectual wave of 'angry young men.' I still, however, had not consciously retained any description of the affects of marijuana. It was, therefore, with a great deal of interest that I took my first few puffs.

The effects were surprisingly mild but quite long lasting. At first, after just a couple of minutes, I started having a sensation akin to 'butterflies' in the stomach but without the customary feelings of trepidation. This led to a desire to laugh followed by my interpreting most of the conversation as amusing enough for me to do so. I then became acutely aware of the music that was being played and of the aesthetic qualities of my immediate environment. Each of these experiences was completely new to me and very much enjoyed. My next awareness

MARIJUANA (3)

was of the slowing down of the passage of time, presumably incurred by the increase of rate of sensory input. Finally I became hungry, as did everyone else in the room, and after eating a welcomed meal, the effects wore off having been present for about three to four hours. There was no detectable hangover effect.

The whole experience had been stimulating, exciting and pleasurable; and I had no reservations about repeating it. For the next six months or so, I smoked marijuana approximately twice a week. Although my use of it was purely hedonistic, I found that for the first time in my life, I began enjoying classical music and viewing works of art. Initially, this newly discovered pursuit was limited to the occaisons that I was under the influence of marijuana but soon extended to occaisons when I was not. It is my sincere belief that my appreciation of classical music and art would not have come into being without the 'trigger' of marijuana. It was not a case of suddenly, for the first time, being exposed to new material; for many years my parents, teachers, and some of my friends had tried to encourage me, in the kindest possible way, to develop an interest in the arts, but to no avail.

Inhibitions presumably caused by my feelings of social and cultural inadequacy gradually disappeared. I became far more gregarious and participated in a host of college activities such as dramatic and debating society functions.

Like many others, I have found marijuana a welcome addition to virtually any informal social gathering. It helps to break down social barriers such as class

In 1991, while serving a 25-year sentence of imprisonment in United States Penitentiary Terre Haute, and at the request of Dr Lester Grinspoon of Harvard Medical School, Howard wrote an 11-page narrative of how he found marijuana useful in his life and his experience of it. These are the second and third pages, where Howard describes his first experience of marijuana.

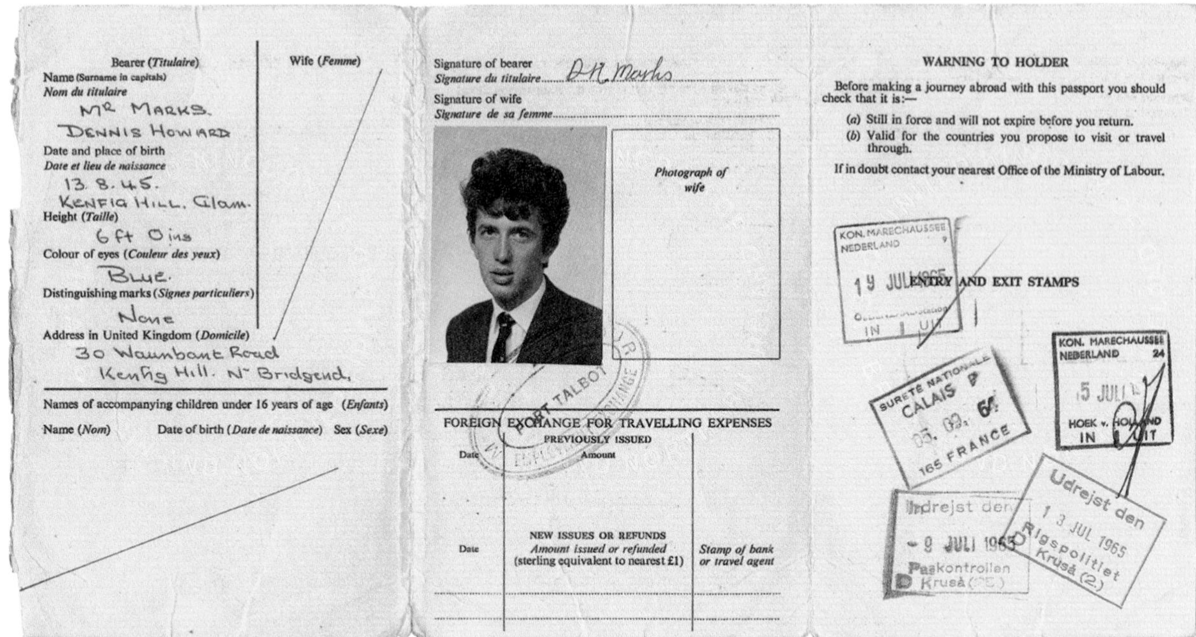

Bearer (*Titulaire*)
Name (Surname in capitals)
Nom du titulaire
MR MARKS.
DENNIS HOWARD
Date and place of birth
Date et lieu de naissance
13. 8. 45.
KENFIG HILL. Glam.
Height (*Taille*)
6 ft 0 ins
Colour of eyes (*Couleur des yeux*)
BLUE.
Distinguishing marks (*Signes particuliers*)
None
Address in United Kingdom (*Domicile*)
30 Waunbant Road
Kenfig Hill. Nr Bridgend.

Wife (*Femme*)

Names of accompanying children under 16 years of age (*Enfants*)

Name (*Nom*) Date of birth (*Date de naissance*) Sex (*Sexe*)

Signature of bearer
Signature du titulaire D.H. Marks
Signature of wife
Signature de sa femme

Photograph of wife

FOREIGN EXCHANGE FOR TRAVELLING EXPENSES
PREVIOUSLY ISSUED
Date Amount

Date NEW ISSUES OR REFUNDS
Amount issued or refunded
(sterling equivalent to nearest £1)
Stamp of bank or travel agent

WARNING TO HOLDER

Before making a journey abroad with this passport you should check that it is:—

(*a*) Still in force and will not expire before you return.
(*b*) Valid for the countries you propose to visit or travel through.

If in doubt contact your nearest Office of the Ministry of Labour.

ENTRY AND EXIT STAMPS

KON. MARECHAUSSEE NEDERLAND 9
19 JUL 1965
IN UIT

KON. MARECHAUSSEE NEDERLAND 24
5 JUL
HOEK v. HOLLAND
IN UIT

SURETE NATIONALE
CALAIS P
05. 09. 64
165 FRANCE

Indrejst den
- 9 JULI 1965
Paskontrollen
D Kruså

Udrejst den
13 JUL 1965
Rigspolitiet
Kruså (2)

(↑) The British Visitor's Passport was a simplified version of the standard passport, introduced in 1961. It could be obtained from any Post Office on provision of the applicant's birth certificate. It was only valid for one year and intended simply for holiday, or similar purposes not exceeding three months in duration. It was withdrawn in 1996 on account of security concerns.

Howard on his summer vacation in Malmö (Sweden), August 1965.

Second Year at Balliol 1965-66

During my continental episodes of the long vacation, I had picked up a varied assortment of ethnic rubbish, pretentious objets d'art, gimmicky knick-knacks, and other hippie software with the intention of using them to decorate my room. These included a 400 sq ft net (used to protect fruit trees from birds), a road sign stating 'Mind the Hose', a very large Cezanne poster, and rolls of aluminium foil wallpaper. I suspended the net from the room's ceiling, papered the walls with aluminium foil, and nailed the Cezanne poster to the floor. Some home-made lamps (orange boxes containing low-wattage coloured bulbs) were carefully placed in corners, and my newly acquired record player was set up with extension speakers dotted around the walls.

All and sundry were welcome to visit my new quarters and bring their friends, records, alcohol and supplies of marijuana and hashish. My rooms rapidly became the location of a non-stop party with music blaring and dense clouds of marijuana smoke billowing out of the door and windows. Terry Deakin, a Merton Egyptologist, actually lived there and the constant sight of the net, which he spent many days gazing at while lying on the floor, inspired him to write a poem (appropriately called 'The Net'), which was later published both in Richard Branson's magazine, *The Student*, and a Deakin anthology of poems entitled *Testament of a Roach Eating Saint*. Various 'townies' would also visit, as would the odd member of the London 'underground' and the occasional student from other universities. The fame of this dope-smoking haven, enshrined and protected by College and University, had spread far and wide.

Balliol, in conjunction with St John's College, Cambridge, occasionally produced a satirical magazine called *Mesopotamia*. Apparently, the Cambridge proponents of the first issue went on to produce *Private Eye*. The Balliol side of the enterprise was controlled by The Establishment. I was appointed Business Editor and was responsible for raising advertising revenue and organisation of sales. For some reason there were some nude photographs of me featured in the magazine, but I cannot remember why. Life became quite hectic during this Hilary Term: an abundance of parties; lots of dates; and a never-ending sequence of Dramatic Society and Victorian Society

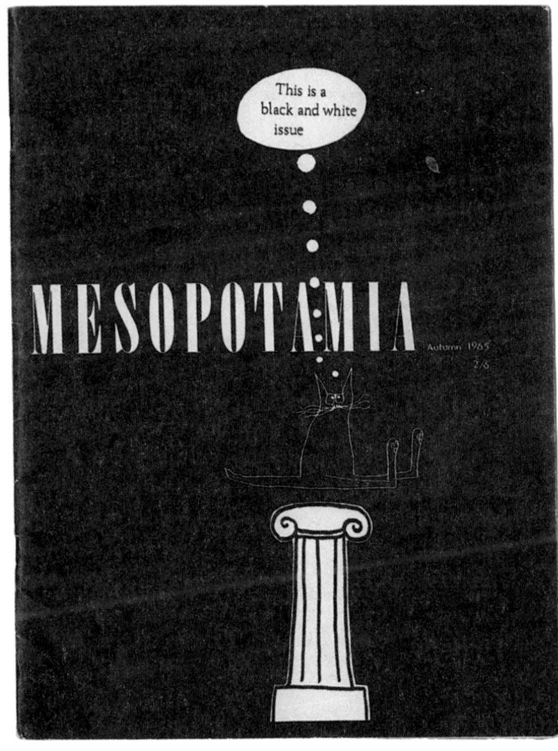

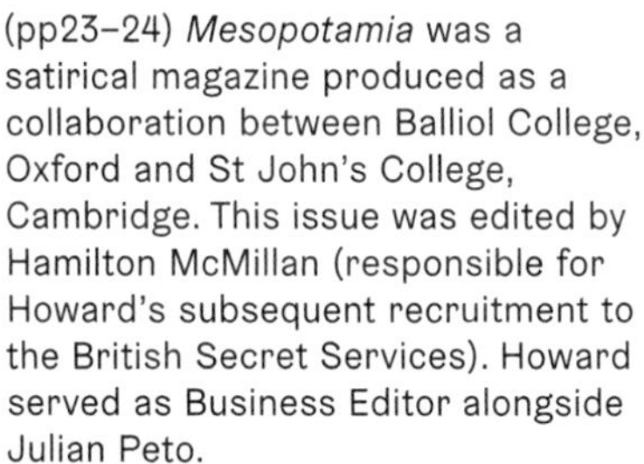
(pp23–24) *Mesopotamia* was a satirical magazine produced as a collaboration between Balliol College, Oxford and St John's College, Cambridge. This issue was edited by Hamilton McMillan (responsible for Howard's subsequent recruitment to the British Secret Services). Howard served as Business Editor alongside Julian Peto.

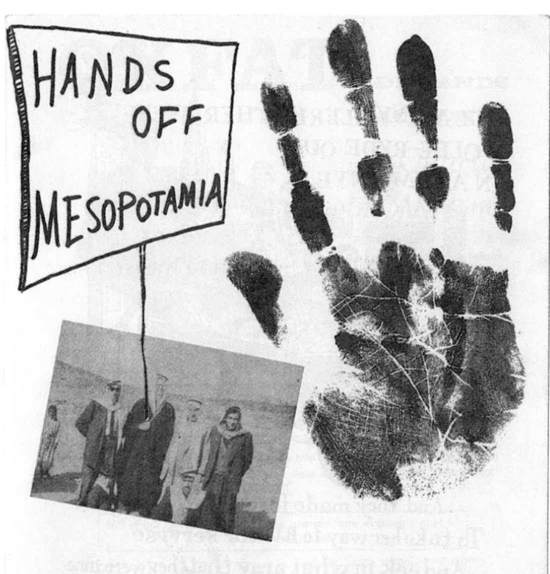

Editors
Biff Harrison
Hamilton McMillan

Business
Howard Marks
Julian Peto

Contributors
Adrian Benjamin
Louis Burnard
Paul Drayton
Chris Fagg
Keith Holman
Susan Inglis
Robert Litman
Edward Mortimer
Chris Moxon
Nigel Rees
Paul Swain
James Turner
John Windsor

Designers
Tom Carter
John Rhodes

Photographs
John Pett
Oxford Mail

Printed at The Kilburn Press Ltd., Wallingford-on-Thames and published by Mesopotamia, Balliol College, Oxford.

However, when we re-examined the rules as they stood we found that we could not in all conscience equate them with the spirit, as opposed to the letter, of our principles, and so accordingly we formulated the following final and overriding rule thus: that any undergraduate found guilty of a deliberate, consistent, and unnecessary observation of any or all college rules, should be brought before a college meeting in order to discuss the question of his future residence in college, the decision of the college meeting on the matter to be in no way final, or even enforceable.'

Finally we discussed the role of the Master himself; Brannigan was frank: 'Yes there were voices raised in protest when I spent half of the original appeal fund on a complete new wardrobe for myself, but this was a completely deliberate and considered step.

Popular Brannigan. Growth is pictured here at a typical get-together between dons and undergraduates, "It's all strictly informal, definitely something to be dressed down to rather than up for."

The sporting image. "It's as much a part of college life as anything else", says Brannigan, "although we aim to introduce drag-racing when the Meadow Road is completed."

Obviously if I am to provide the main focus of undergraduate aspirations my image must be the best and my clothes the trendiest in college, and as any pop singer will tell you living up to the fans' image of you is an expensive business. After all Masters of other colleges have been doing it for years with port and cigars, so why shouldn't I do it with floral ties and epaulettes?'

Brannigan knows that what he has set out to do will make great demands on his natural vigour and trendsetting ability, that he himself will fall in time to his own great principle of built-in obsolescence - 'No one can be a Master after he's thirty unless he's Elvis Presley' - and until then we can only answer with the rest of the world - "Who cares?"

Eden Constitution Suspended

U.D.I. LIKELY IN FEW DAYS?

Ur of the Chaldees, Oct. 25th

A state of martial law was declared in the Eden Protectorate, this morning, according to reliable reports, and the constitution has been formally suspended. These moves represent a prompt and unequivocal response by the British Government to the final breakdown on Monday of the talks between the Edeni Chief Minister, Mr. Adam Smith, and the Secretary of State for Commonwealth Relations, Lord God. Other emergenc measures are believed to include th deportation of Mr. Smith, along with his 'lieutenant', Miss Eve Lardner-Burke, to a plantation in the Seychelles, and the posting of three battalions of the Queen's 99th Northumberland Light Infantry (the "Cherubim") to guard Eden's valuable eastern frontier.

Our Commonwealth Correspondent writes: These troop movements throw a good deal of light on the underlying motives behind the British Government's new 'tough' line in the Eden crisis. There is undoubtedly an increasing apprehensiveness in Whitehall that an independent Eden might immediately fall prey to Mesopotamian irredentism. References in recent speeches of Editorissimo Macmillan to "The achievement of Mesopotamia's natural and historic frontiers" have been received with considerable alarm, since historically the frontiers of Mesopotamia were the Rivers Tigris and Euphrates, both of which have their sources within the present Eden Protectorate.

Viewed in this light, the internal crisis in Eden may be only a by-product of Mesopotamian policy, and certainly the British Government's determination to get rid of the existing Edeni ministry must have been stiffened by Miss Lardner-Burke's remark in her speech last Friday, that the South Armenian Federation was not an acceptable solution since "Eden's natural links are not to the north but to the south-east."

It may however be doubted whether the deportation of Mr. Smith will not have the exact opposite of the effect intended. Although his demands for 'independence now' have become increasingly strident in the last few days, there are signs that within his own party his role has been that of a moderate trying unsuccessfully to contain mounting pressure from the left. That the immediate agent of such pressure has been Miss Lardner-Burke is not in doubt, but it is also probable that she herself was merely reacting to even stronger pressure from an extremist group within the party. The leader of this group has so far successfully concealed his identity, but is probably an elusive figure known to Edenis as "the Serpent" This mysterious personality is believed to have important conections in Mesopotamia, and also to be a prominent figure in the fruit-farming industry—an interest group particularly hard hit by the recent British attempts to limit private consumption in the interests of a planned economy.

"The Serpent" is said to be still at large in the Protectorate, although suffering from a bruised head as a result of his participation in the rioting over the weekend. In these circumstances the deportation of the former ministers seems likely to achieve little except to facilitate the spread of extremism and violence throughout the country.

SANCTIONS?

Dar-es-Salem, Oct. 25th

There are persistent rumours here of a sudden drop in Edeni standards of living. It is even said that an acute butter shortage has resulted in the use of sweat as a substitute in many areas, and in some the peasants have resorted to cultivating 'thorns and thistles' Whether this means the British Government has already imposed economic sanctions is not clear. Informed circles in Dar confirmed late last night that they had not been informed of any such development.

Mr. Adam Smith and Miss Eve Lardner-Burke are greeted at Gatwick Airport.

MORE TROOPS?

Our Defence Correspondent writes:

"It seems highly probable that more British troops will be posted to Eden in the course of the next few days. The government is determined not to let this key strategic site fall into unfriendly hands. Influencial groups in the City are also said to regard British preferences in Eden as of the highest commercial importance. Apart from the country's considerable horticultural potential, there are the interests of British Bdellium Ltd. in the important mining belt of Havilah Province. This company at present holds a monopoly of the gold and onyx mines, said to be worth several million pounds a year to British investors. Needless to say, these groups have welcomed enthusiastically the firm tone adopted by Lord God during the negotiations, and particularly his speech of last Friday emphasising the dependence of Eden's inhabitants on British commercial enterprise. "These people were naked savages before we moved in here," he is quoted as saying. "I would go so far as to say they owe their very existence to us."

Mr. Smith arrives at Chequers for talks with the Premier.

Mr. Smith addresses the Annual Dinner of the Linen Guild.

SOUTHERN ARMENIA
(Brit. Mandate since 1919)
HAVILAH
R.Gihon
R.Pishon
TRUCIAL ASSYRIA
R.Tigris
REP. OF MESOPOTAMIA
R.Euphrates
JORDAN

Map of the Eden Protectorate and surrounding territories, showing position of Havilah Province and the Garden National Park (shaded).

LORD GOD FLYING BACK TODAY

London Oct. 26th

The Secretary of State for Commonwealth Relations, Lord God, is expected back in London this afternoon after his abortive negotiations with the Edeni government. In a brief interview with agency reporters in Carchemish late last night, Lord God said that the Constitutional walks in the Garden National Park had been finally abandoned on Monday evening, and that the atmosphere had been 'cool'.

A representative of Mr. Smith the deposed Prime Minister, said in London last night that Eden was likely to be declared independent unilaterally 'within the next few days'. Asked who would make such a declaration in the absence of Mr. Smith, he replied: "The British Government. Until we are independent they cannot legally declare war on us. After all that is what George III did in 1775."

It is certainly true that the present moment would be an unpropitious one for independence as far as Edeni nationalists are concerned, in view of the apparent impossibility of reconciling the two main nationalist parties, the Edeni Socialist Solidarity Organisation (E.S.S.O.) and the 'Socialists for a Happier Eden' Loyal League (S.H.E.L.L.). Differences of policy between the two parties are minimal, and concerned principally with the measures to be adopted if oil should be discovered on Edeni territory; but the personal antipathy between their leaders are deep-seated and long-standing.

evenings. I was thoroughly enjoying myself and was not looking forward to returning home to Wales. I stayed on at Balliol for as long as the rules permitted, seeking out and attending every possible social occasion. Eventually, the college closed and I returned home, where I spent Easter drinking, sleeping and missing what had now become a truly exciting student life.

I was elected to organise the entertainments for the forthcoming 700th anniversary commemorative ball. My primary duty was to engage groups to supply the musical entertainment and I had a budget of £1,000. As far as I can recall, the ball was an outstanding success. I wasn't able to participate in much of it as I had to spend most of the time ensuring the entertainers were properly catered for and able to perform at the scheduled times. It was, nevertheless, a big thrill for me to smoke marijuana, drink whisky and talk to famous pop singers.

Trinity Term, 1966, was the only term that I really enjoyed to the fullest extent. I'd come to grips with my work, was delighted to be asked to organise a commemorative ball, maintained my hippie existence, drank plenty, smoked loads of marijuana, had abundant sexual adventures and was still able to find time for walks in Christ Church and Port Meadows. After term I stayed on at college until it closed and completed the work that had been set for the long vacation. The third year was to be spent in lodgings, but I postponed the search for suitable accommodation until the following September. □

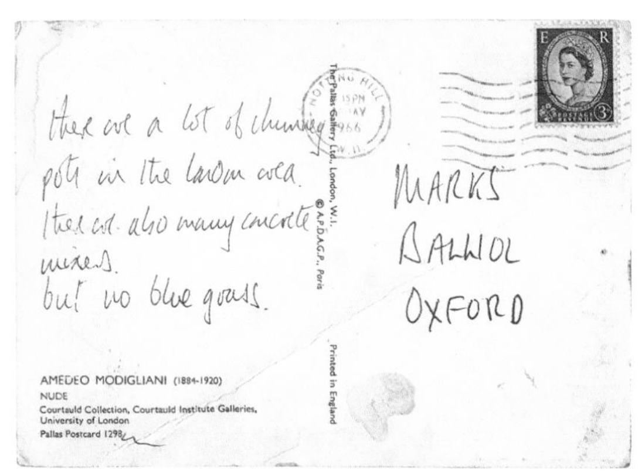

This postcard to Howard was posted in May 1966. The sender is unknown.

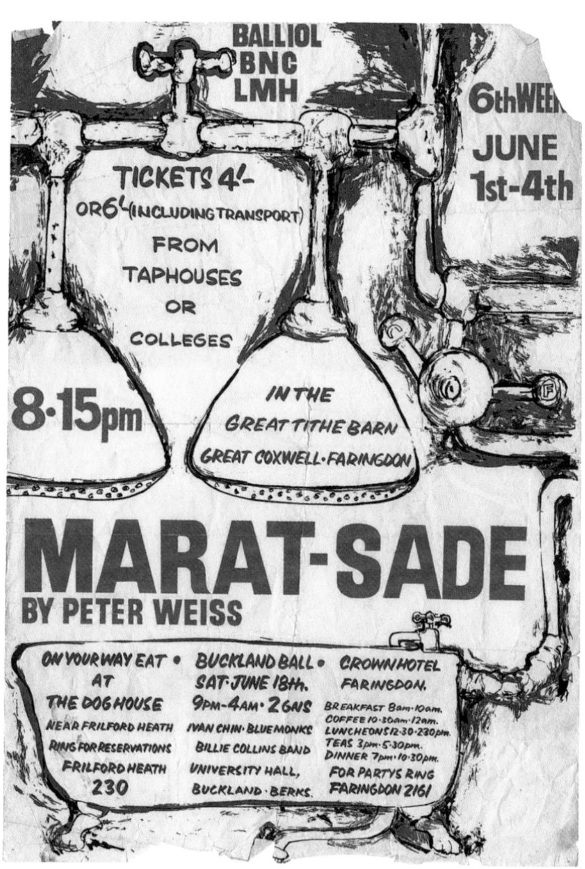

Howard found release from an LSD-triggered depression in his role, custom-designed for a mind-blown Welsh hippy in *Marat-Sade*.

THE NET

for Howard

How often have we lain, my friend,
Under this net which watches us
Through spaces in infinity?
The net sees all we do: laughter;
a passing hangup; chocolate scoffed;
'Who is to roll the next?';
Girls immolated on your manhood;
A little work; drumming of stoned fingers.
The net embraces you and me,
Steve, Julian, other drunkards of transcendence.
Sometimes, a flash
Lights us to understanding:
Friendship-hungry
We gorge ourselves in Xanadu.
The net, weaving us into rhapsodies,
Moves now, and then is still,
Impassive, undulating,
Our scenes recorded in its filaments.
Touching the net, we see
Our other selves sleep by our side,
While mystic flutes lull off our care.
The net has gifted us, my friend,
With amethyst keys
To open arcane doors:
Doors lead to corridors, where
Littered sherds of knowledge
Lie unread.

-b-

Under the net we pick up fragments
Of truth and try to live
Each day as if it were our last.
We fail and we succeed
In psychedelic paradoxes.
And we, Howard, hold knowledge
As our net holds in the rain.

By this net, which has seen us well,
Delighted us and hung us in its spell,
Friend, we must live till all our dues are paid
Knowing ourselves, receptive, unafraid.

18-2-66

Terry Deakin (aka Terence DuQuesne) wrote his poem 'The Net' about a 400-square-foot net (originally intended for protecting fruit trees from birds), which Howard had brought back from his summer vacation in 1965 and draped from the ceiling of his room. Amongst Howard's many guests was Graham Plinston, a politics, philosophy and economics student at St Edmunds Hall, in the year below Howard.

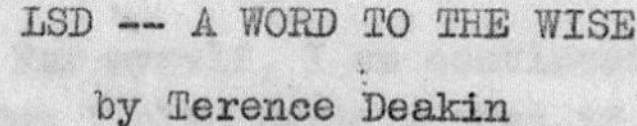

LSD -- A WORD TO THE WISE

by Terence Deakin

It was a couple of years before the newspapers began to publish their lurid and sensational accounts that I first took lysergic acid. I could then foresee some kind of 'psychedelic revolution' in Britain, but in my optimism I hoped that this revolution would not take the turn it has. The very word 'psychedelic' has become so debased that intelligent people can hardly use it meaningfully any more. In London and elsewhere about the country thousands are taking 'trips'. A few do so discreetly in a genuine search for knowledge and enlightenment; yet the majority seem interested only in sensory kicks, in keeping up with Mr Jones, in parading their spurious coolness. The many beneficial attributes of LSD are being submerged in the welter of adverse publicity, from within the Scene and from without. When individuals attempt suicide on their trips; when they claim they have been reborn and remain vicious and petty; when they spend the day after exactly as the day before; when first-timers are abandoned in a difficult phase of the LSD experience by their so-called friends; when the self-conscious type out their incoherent trip-jottings and call them poetry; when adolescents compete to see who can consume the most LSD in the shortest time--who can blame the yellow press for getting the wrong impression? what can we say to the doctors who fulminate against the drug's availability and the egislators who ban it?

(2)

For myself, I am convinced that LSD is widely abused. But I also believe that if it is taken cautiously, in a suitable environment and with trustworthy people, it can be a powerful force for good. It is impossible to generalize about who should, and who should not, experiment with the drug. Whatever I or the authorities or the public may think, many will try it out and on some the effect will be detrimental. Those with psychotic or pre-psychotic personalities should obviously avoid LSD. For most people, however, the success or failure of a trip does not seem to depend on the level of one's neurosis or the degree of general anxiety and frustration. I have seen scores of individuals under the drug's influence: in many cases those of introverted temperament fared better than the extraverts. This is just one reason for urging caution.

Trips with LSD may have either a secular or a religious purpose, maybe both. In my opinion those who undertake such voyages purely for kicks miss the point, and I sometimes become irritated by the often-heard bleat: "Well, where are the hallucinations then?" Watching the walls dissolve or the carpet liquefy may be fun for a while, but such things become boring after the novelty has worn off. It may take only one or two trips before you can see flowers partake of your quintessence, realize that you and your fellow men are God, or feel the heart-beat of the cosmos. Again, some employ LSD in the hope of solving their personal problems. But even if these difficulties are resolved in passing, a whole crop of new and more profound problems may spring up.

Terry sent Howard his essay on LSD, noting that the drug was about to be banned (it was banned in 1966), but that this would not 'deter those who feel entitled to experiment'. Terry developed an academic interest in pharmacology and co-authored *A Handbook of Psychoactive Medicines* in 1982. In 1986, Terry published *Illicit Drugs: Myth And Reality* for the Libertarian Alliance, who presented it as evidence to a House of Commons Home Affairs Committee on the use of illicit drugs. At the same time, with his friend and solicitor Edward Goodman, he published *Britain: An Unfree Country*, a detailed critique of the erosion of personal freedom under the Thatcher regime.

MANAGEMENT COPY

AUTHORISED AGENT UNITED STATES ARMED FORCES ENTERTAINMENT

LICENSED ANNUALLY BY THE City of Westminster.

ARTHUR HOWES (AGENCY) LTD.

EROS HOUSE,
29/31, REGENT STREET,
PICCADILLY CIRCUS,
LONDON, S.W.1.
Telephone : REGent 5202-3-4-5-6-7
Telegrams-Cables : POPSHOWS LONDON S.W.1

This Agency is not responsible for any non-fulfilment of Contracts by Proprietors, Managers or Artistes but every reasonable safeguard is assured.

This Contract is subject to the conditions of the New V.A.E.C. Agreement 1963

Contract No. JEM.1080.

An Agreement made the 29th day of April 19 66. BETWEEN Richard Fyldes. (hereinafter called "the Management") of the one part, and THE KINKS. (hereinafter called "the Artiste") of the other part, Witnesseth that the Management hereby engages the Artiste and the Artiste accepts an engagement to appear as : SEEN AND KNOWN.

(or in his usual entertainment) at the Theatre or Hall and from the dates for the periods and at the salaries stated in the Schedule hereto.

SCHEDULE

The Artiste agrees to appear at 1 Evening performances per night at a salary of £ 300 : 0 : 0d.

......Week
1 Day at The Baliol College, OXFORD. commencing 21st June, 19 66.
Rehearsal at......
......Week
......Day at...... commencing...... 19......
Rehearsal at......
......Week
......Day at...... commencing...... 19......
Rehearsal at......
......Week
......Day at...... commencing...... 19......
Rehearsal at......

ADDITIONAL CLAUSES

1. Artistes to arrive at the venue by 7 p.m., on the night of engagement
2. It is agreed and understood that the artistes shall perform in a maximum of 1 x40 minute spot, as directed by the Management.
3. Settlement shall be by cheque to the artistes on the night of the engagement.
4. It is agreed and understood that the 10% commission accruing from this engagement shall be equally divided between Terry Blood Agency, and the Arthur Howes Agency, Ltd.
5. It is agreed and understood that the Artistes shall not appear within a 10 mile radius of the above venue, either one week prior to or one week following this engagement.

Signature......

Address......

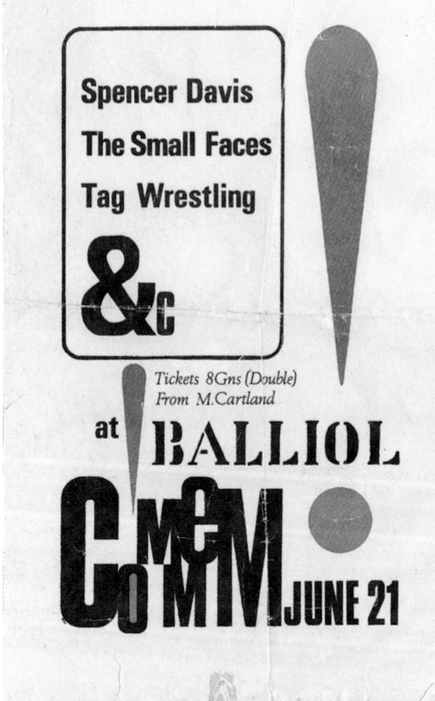

Spencer Davis
The Small Faces
Tag Wrestling
&c
Tickets 8Gns (Double)
From M.Cartland
at BALLIOL
CoMeMM JUNE 21

Poster with original line-up.

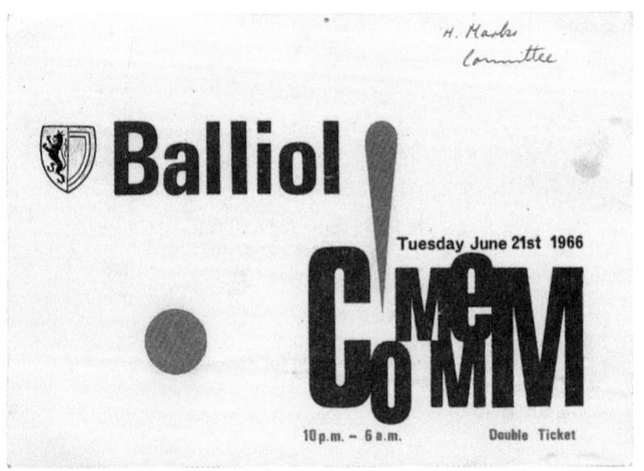

Balliol Ball invite.

Howard booked the relatively unknown Spencer Davis Group and the Small Faces for the ball but within weeks of being booked, they both had Number One hits. The agent offered Howard The Kinks, the Fortunes, Them, and Alan Price (all of whom were already top names) for the same price in exchange for letting the Spencer Davis Group and the Small Faces pull out. These are Howard's contracts for The Kinks and for the Alan Price set.

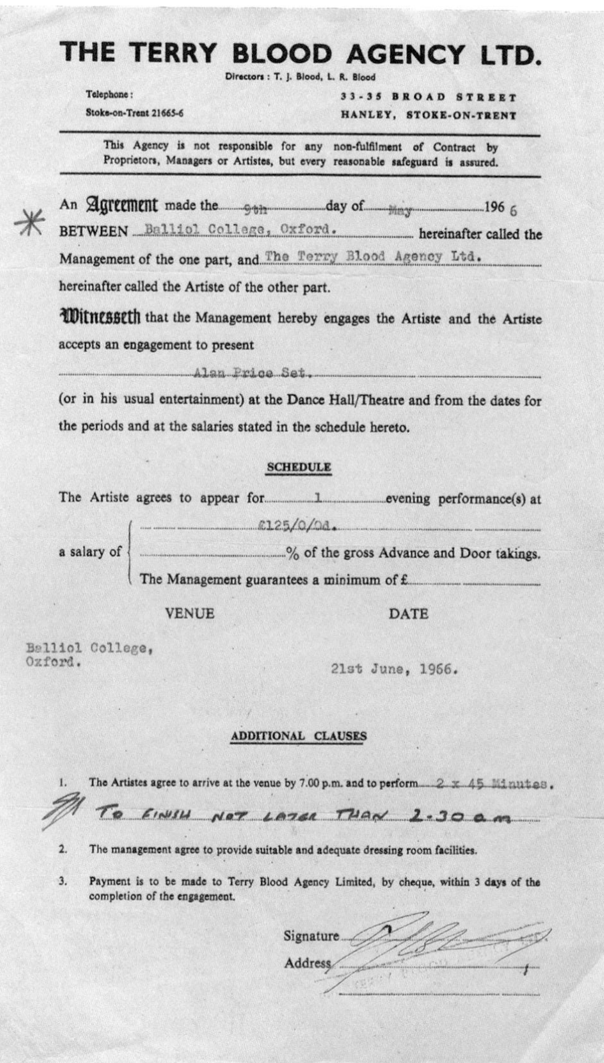

THE TERRY BLOOD AGENCY LTD.

Directors: T. J. Blood, L. R. Blood

Telephone: Stoke-on-Trent 21665-6

33-35 BROAD STREET HANLEY, STOKE-ON-TRENT

This Agency is not responsible for any non-fulfilment of Contract by Proprietors, Managers or Artistes, but every reasonable safeguard is assured.

An Agreement made the 9th day of May 1966 BETWEEN Balliol College, Oxford. hereinafter called the Management of the one part, and The Terry Blood Agency Ltd. hereinafter called the Artiste of the other part.

Witnesseth that the Management hereby engages the Artiste and the Artiste accepts an engagement to present

Alan Price Set.

(or in his usual entertainment) at the Dance Hall/Theatre and from the dates for the periods and at the salaries stated in the schedule hereto.

SCHEDULE

The Artiste agrees to appear for 1 evening performance(s) at

a salary of £125/0/0d.
...% of the gross Advance and Door takings.
The Management guarantees a minimum of £...

VENUE	DATE
Balliol College, Oxford.	21st June, 1966.

ADDITIONAL CLAUSES

1. The Artistes agree to arrive at the venue by 7.00 p.m. and to perform 2 x 45 Minutes.
TO FINISH NOT LATER THAN 2-30 a.m
2. The management agree to provide suitable and adequate dressing room facilities.
3. Payment is to be made to Terry Blood Agency Limited, by cheque, within 3 days of the completion of the engagement.

Signature

Address

Poster with revised line-up.

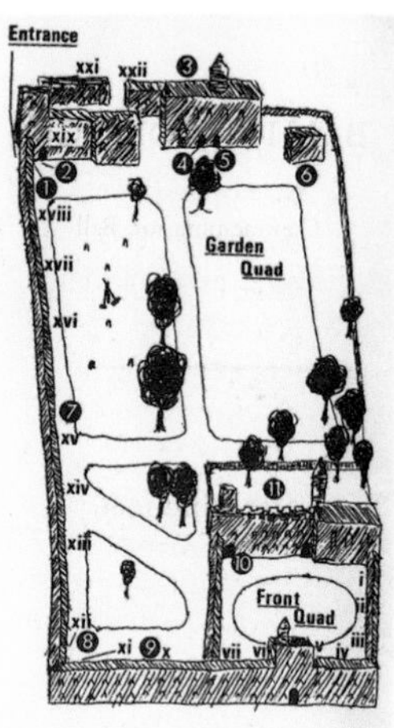

Balliol College

1 Dean's Room and Nurse's Room
2 Massey Room
3 Hall
4 Stores and Buttery
5 Senior Common Room
6 Science Library
7 Junior Common Room and Lindsay Room
8 Staircase XII (sitting out area)
9 Staircase X Cellars
10 Library Staircase
11 Fellows' Garden

Roman numerals refer to staircases

PROGRAMME

Garden Quad

10.00 Them
10.45 The Alan Price Set
11.30 Steel Band
12.00 WRESTLING
12.30 Them
1.00 The Alan Price Set
2.00 The Kinks
2.45 Steel Band
3.30 The Meisterswingers
4.30 Steel Band

Cellars

(Staircase X)

10.30 Bunny Thompson
11.30 The Meisterswingers
12.30 Bunny Thompson
1.30 The Meisterswingers
2.30 Bunny Thompson

At other times there will be a Juke Box.

Front Quad

10.30 Eric Tolley
11.30 The Ram Jam Band
12.30 The Fortunes
1.00 CABARET
1.45 Eric Tolley
3.00 The Fortunes
3.45 The Ram Jam Band
4.30 Eric Tolley

Lindsay Room

There will be a Juke Box and an Amusement Arcade in the Lindsay Room at the bottom of Staircase XV.

First Aid

Any casualties will be attended to in the Nurse's Room by the entrance. These facilities are kindly provided by the St. John Ambulance Brigade.

Coiffure

Ladies' hairdressing facilities will be provided in Staircase I, Room I by Rita Sloan Ltd. from 11 p.m. to 3 a.m.

Dress Repairs

These will be carried out in the basement of Staircase III.

The Committee would like to thank the Bursar and Staff of the College for their co-operation and help.

Committee

Jasper Griffin Esq.
Richard Fildes
Thomas Carter
Michael Cartland
James Cave
Stephen Crew
Howard Marks
John Nicoll
Paul Swain
Eric Wallis

The Committee will be wearing ties with an exclamatory motif . . .

Programme and other graphics by Tom Carter

Printed by the Holywell Press
Alfred Street, Oxford

Music

Provided by

The Kinks
The Fortunes
The Alan Price Set
Them
Geno Washington and the Ram Jam Band
Eric Tolley and his Orchestra
The Caribbean All Steel Band
The Bunny Thompson Trio
The Meisterswingers

A String Quartet from the Royal College of Music may be found in Hall, in the S.C.R. or by Staircase XII.

Cabaret

by

Mick Sadler
Michael Palin
Diana Quick

Food

A Buffet Supper will be served in Hall from 11.00 to 2.30, and Breakfast from 4.00.

Rolls and coffee will be available in the J.C.R. all the time.

Drink

Champagne, other wines and soft drinks will be served from the main bar in the Fellows' Garden. Champagne and wine will also be available until 2.00 from the windows of Staircase XII and from a bar in the front Lodge.

Beer, cider and soft drinks will be served in the Buttery and the Lindsay Bar, where spirits can be bought.

Bottles of champagne and wine, cigars and cigarettes will be on sale in the Stores.

Black Velvet will also be served in the Fellows' Garden.

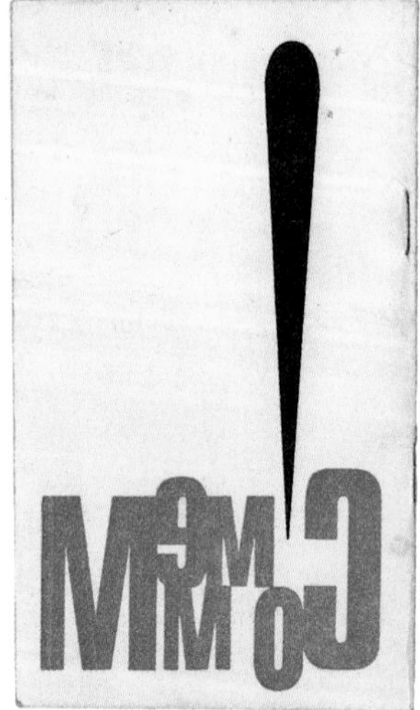

Balliol Ball programme.

Final Year at Balliol 1966-67

46 Paradise Square had the dubious privilege of once having housed both Oxford student Paul Jones, who became the lead vocalist of Manfred Mann, and American 'beat' novelist William Burroughs. Julian, Steve Balogh and I took one room each. People were always on the lookout for cheap rooms to rent in Paradise Square and shortly after we became registered, a couple of pleasant long-haired hippies knocked on our door and asked if we had any space to let. They had a great many friends who gradually began to take over the house, filling it with delightful marijuana smoke and riveting Jimi Hendrix guitar playing. Julian, Steve and I had very little by way of objection to this development and, once again, my home turned into a place where people from far and wide came to smoke marijuana and generally hang out. I have absolutely no recollection of the 1966 Christmas vacation, but do know that I must have spent Christmas Day, at least, at my parents' home in Wales. I do, however, vividly remember the commencement of Hilary Term, which was when I fell madly in love with St Anne's English undergraduate, Ilze Kadegis. Although we had dated each other for about a year, something happened during January 1967 which made us lose our enthusiasm for dating anyone else.

There were some drunken celebrations after finals, some of which took place in the Lindsay Bar. During one of these, I became engrossed in a conversation with the new (actually, by then not that new) Master of Balliol, Christopher Hill. This was the only time I had talked to him outside of handshakings. I've no idea now what we talked about, but I remember leaving the bar with a distinct feeling of sadness that I was soon to be no longer a Balliol student.

Ilze and I had decided to move to London and live together in Notting Hill, which was fast becoming the centre of European psychedelia. We had both been enrolled by London University to do the Postgraduate Certificate in Education and expected to gain teaching positions in London during the subsequent years. We were wrong. □

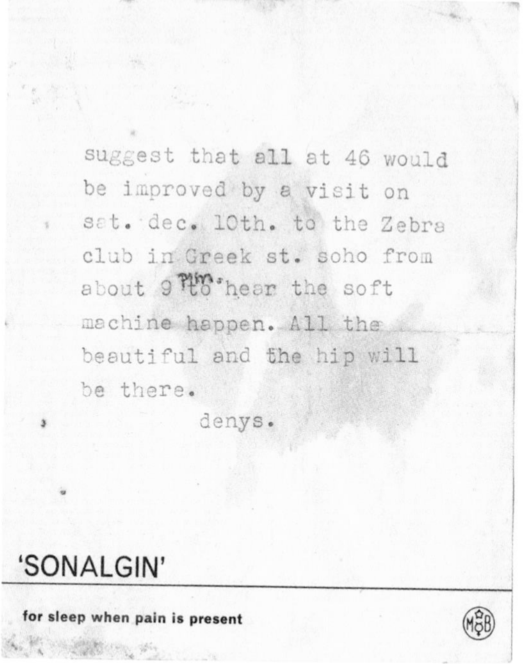
suggest that all at 46 would be improved by a visit on sat. dec. 10th. to the Zebra club in Greek st. soho from about 9 p.m. to hear the soft machine happen. All the beautiful and the hip will be there.

denys.

'SONALGIN'

for sleep when pain is present

Between 10 December 1966 and 14 January 1967, the English psychedelic rock group Soft Machine (Robert Wyatt, Kevin Ayers, Daevid Allen and Mike Ratledge) had a weekly Saturday night residency at the Zebra Club in Soho, London. Mike Ratledge would become a good friend of Howard's. This note is from Denys Irving. Denys Irving had given Howard his first joint. The note was written on what appears to be promotional writing paper for sleeping pills containing butobarbitone, phenacetin and codeine, marketed at the time under the brand name 'Sonalgin'. It was presumably addressed to Howard, Julian Peto and Steve Balogh, at number 46 Paradise Square, Oxford.

Howard larking about in the countryside.

Howard fell in love with Ilze Kadegis, a Latvian undergraduate at St Anne's College, Oxford.

Howard graduated in 1967.

2

Transatlantic Sounds

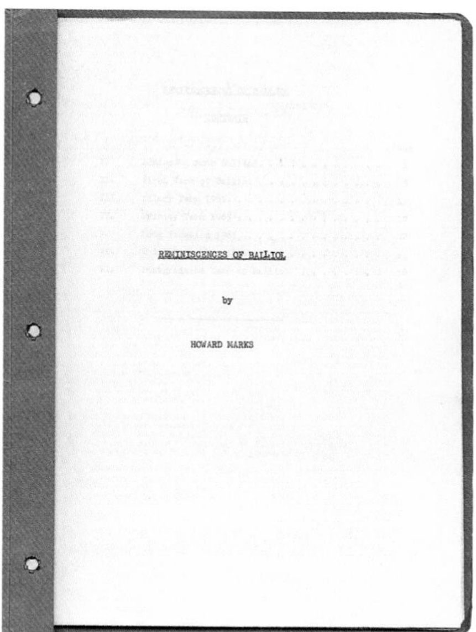
REMINISCENCES OF BALLIOL

by

HOWARD MARKS

The text for this chapter is also taken from the bound typescript written by Howard while in Terre Haute at the request of John Jones, Dean at Balliol.

I lived in London from the summer of 1967 to the summer of 1968. Ilze Kadegis and I took up residence in a third-floor flat at 76 Westbourne Grove, Notting Hill. Julian Peto had also moved to London to pursue an MSc course at Imperial College and he was a regular guest at our flat. Steve Balogh and Hamilton McMillan remained in Oxford to complete four-year degree courses, but often visited us in London. Denys Irving had already been in London for over a year living in an enormous warehouse in St Katharine Dock.

Ilze and I had both been accepted for courses offering postgraduate certificates of education; mine was at the University of London's Institute of Education, while Ilze's was at Cavendish College. After about a week of the first term, I became extremely bored by the course and irritated by the constant berating from lecturers and supervisors regarding my long-haired hippie appearance, which was deemed unsuitable in a budding teacher. I took up other interests, increasing my involvement in the activities of the marijuana-smoking community and concentrating on the ancient Japanese board game of Go. I also began reading the books that my contemporaries had talked about during my undergraduate years.

Bertrand Russell's *History of Western Philosophy* was the most interesting book that I had ever read in my life and led to my reading a variety of works by Plato, Aristotle, Lucretius, Locke, Berkeley, Hume, Aquinas, Leibniz and Spinoza. This reading provoked my sincere and lasting interest in the History and Philosophy of Science. It dawned on me that I'd wasted all the facilities available to me at Oxford and I longed to return there to make use of them.

The powers in charge of History and Philosophy of Science in Oxford were Alistair Crombie and Rom Harré. I wrote to both expressing an interest in doing some postgraduate work and they suggested I came to Oxford to be interviewed. The meetings, held in early December 1967, went very well, and I was accepted to study for the Diploma in History and Philosophy of Science beginning October 1968. Long reading lists were given me.

During late December 1967, Ilze and I got married

at my parents' local Welsh Congregational Chapel. To this day, I have no idea why we took this extraordinary step. We had no intention of having children; we had no money; Ilze was destined for goodness knew what. We took a one-night honeymoon at a bed-and-breakfast establishment in Ogmore-by-Sea.

At the beginning of January 1968, I withdrew from the postgraduate certificate of education course. To make ends meet, I took a five-hour a day teaching job at a London crammer college named Davies Laing & Dick Ltd, and did some private tuition in the evenings.

From January to September 1968, I worked extremely hard at earning money teaching and studying History and Philosophy of Science. I also found time to become a competent Go player and maintain my position in London's underground culture. Ilze and I decided that while I resumed my studies, we should live in a romantic country cottage.

Howard in his parents' living room on the December 1967 morning of his wedding to Ilze Kadegis.

Howard and Ilze were married at a Welsh Congregational Chapel in December 1967.

Howard, Ilze and Julian's then partner in their 'romantic cottage' in Oxfordshire.

While getting drunk at a pub called The Plough in Garsington, we discovered a cottage for rent not one hundred yards away from where we were drinking. The landlords were egg producers called 'Jennings of Garsington', and we rented the cottage for a 12-month period beginning 1 September 1968.

Ilze had found employment at a primary school in Didcot. I had acquired a beaten-up Hillman and we would get up extremely early in order for me to drive Ilze to Oxford railway station in time for the Didcot train. Our daily life was quite conventional in that weekdays were devoted to fulfilling our commitments and weekends were dedicated to pleasure.

One evening, Ilze and I went to a social gathering hosted by one of her colleagues who taught at the school in Didcot. There were two or three other couples present including John and Fanny Stein. John at that time was a general practitioner, while Fanny

only drink was champagne which I don't like. Honestly now Dad. (Incidentally the Thursday before we had been to Auntie Glen's for supper we enjoyed ourselves but Auntie Mairys was in bed with migraine)

Last week passed by fairly uneventfully except that Ilse got inspected by a nun at her school and I caught gastric 'flu.

This Sunday we went to the Vietnam demonstation in Trafalgar square First we listened to a few speeches by people like Vanessa Redgrave and then fifteen thousand of us marched to the American embassy in Grosvenor square where there were two thousand police, some on horseback, waiting for us. All the gang from Oxford were there as you can expect. It was both very exciting and frightening, I expect you saw some of it on T.V. I was very surprised at how ruthlessly violent the police were. They would just charge into the crowd on horses with hooves kicking and truncheons swinging many of the demonstrators got very seriously injured including an old friend of ours from Oxford whom the police, completely unprovoked, smashed over the head with a truncheon and kicked in the face while he was on the ground. If you happened to get face to face with a policeman you were hit, that was it Luckily we were'nt. Things have been very quiet since.

Second page of a letter written by Howard to his parents and dated 1 March 1968.

Howard's boredom and frustration with his nascent teaching career was exacerbated by the revolutionary atmosphere of London in 1968. It was eased by bumping into Graham Plinston, Howard's student friend, rusticated from Oxford (1967–8) for smoking cannabis in a room he rented from Stephanie Sweet. Sweet's appeal against her conviction for 'being concerned in the management of premises used for smoking cannabis' resulted in the famous House of Lords decision *Sweet v Parsley* (1970). The House of Lords cleared her of blame by declaring that unless Parliament had clearly specified to the contrary, proof of a guilty mind, ie, knowledge of the fact that the premises were being used for smoking cannabis, would have to be proven by the prosecution for a person to be guilty of the offence. Graham spent his period of rustication travelling the world. Graham was now back studying at Oxford and became a frequent visitor at Howard and Ilze's Notting Hill flat, sharing his ample supplies of Afghan hashish. Under the influence of high-quality cannabis, Howard became passionately engrossed in reading Philosophy of Science. He decided to abandon teaching and enrol on a postgraduate diploma course in the Philosophy of Science at Balliol.

Howard was a passionate pacifist all of his life. The Vietnam War gets a second mention in his correspondence with his parents, in a letter written to them from Terre Haute Penitentiary, in 1992, 'Last Monday (25 May) was Memorial Day, one of the few holidays that America celebrates. (They don't, for instance, have holidays for Good Friday, Easter Monday and Whitsun Monday – let alone Guy Fawkes day.) Memorial Day commemorates soldiers who have died in the various wars of aggression in Vietnam, Panama, Granada, etc., and the prison authorities expect us to join in this flag-waving glorification of violence by eating our food outside in childish, picnic fashion. Paradigms of American gourmet cuisine – frankfurters and hamburgers – were supplied while we all shivered in the middle of a freak cold spell. Still, it broke the monotony, I suppose. I think I prefer the monotony.'

was a housewife. About halfway through the dinner, I discovered that Fanny's maiden name was Hill and that she was Christopher's daughter. A strong friendship was struck up, particularly between Fanny and me, but we didn't have an affair with each other until long after she and John had separated. John and I also became very good friends and saw each other regularly until my arrest in 1988. Fanny died tragically in a drowning accident in the mid-80s. She was a wonderful person who never failed to inject vitality into any social situation which included her; she is sorely missed.

Shortly after my first meeting with Fanny, I ran into Christopher Hill at a function held in the Lindsay Room. We hardly knew each other, but quickly became engaged in earnest conversation which we both wished to continue when the function drew to a close. Christopher asked if I would be prepared to buy a bottle of whisky and bring it up to his lodgings, where he would immediately reimburse me and continue our discussions. I was delighted to do this. We got on remarkably well and by the end of the evening, Christopher had accepted my invitation to have dinner with us at the cottage in about a week's time.

Ilze was nervous at the prospect of entertaining such distinguished guests and had no idea what kind of meal to prepare. During the previous year in London, I had befriended the chef of the local Indian restaurant and had become reasonably proficient at cooking curries. Christopher had mentioned to me how much he'd enjoyed Indian cuisine while he was in India; accordingly, I agreed to prepare the food. Everyone seemed to get on with everyone else. Christopher was a source of an immense amount of information about Garsington, including the fact that Russell Meiggs lived only a hundred yards away from us (on no occasion did I ever see him in the village) and across an adjacent field, tucked in a hollow, was Garsington Manor, the one-time residence of the Morrell brewery heiress, Lady Ottoline, whom Christopher referred to as Lady Utterley Immoral. Apparently, Bertrand Russell, Aldous Huxley and Lytton Strachey, etc. had all been frequent guests at the manor. My friendship with Fanny Hill led to my meeting her mother, Inez, a remarkable lady with whom I would sit and talk for hours. She was a very special person, who always referred to me as 'that dangerous Welshman'.

My History of Philosophy and Science studies required my using the facilities of both the Bodleian and Radcliffe Science Libraries. This, in turn, led to frequent visits to the King's Arms in Broad Street. My tutors were Alistair Crombie, Rom Harré, Jeffrey St Croix, John North and Michael Dummett. The most interesting of these was Michael Dummett, who became Wykeham Professor of Logic, but was then a Fellow of All Souls and taught me in mathematical logic. He was a devout Christian, excellent Go player and chain smoker. Although most of what he said about mathematical logic went way over my head, I was most interested in his opinions and philosophies.

One topic on which I agreed completely with the revolutionary students was that of racial equality. Enoch Powell was giving a speech, I think at Oxford Town Hall, and I participated in what turned out to be quite a violent demonstration. A few fellow participants had been brutally assaulted by police and, to add insult to injury, had been charged with assault themselves. The next morning, I missed my tutorial with Mr Dummett in order to make myself available at court to speak on my friends' behalf. I hadn't let Mr Dummett know and was feeling a little guilty. Also feeling a little guilty for missing our appointment was Mr Dummett, who had also presented himself at court to speak up for someone who had been arrested during the previous night's demonstration. We burst out laughing at the sight of each other. The same day, he invited me for lunch at All Souls, where I had the privilege of sitting next to John Sparrow. After lunch, Mr Dummett had to hurry off somewhere, and I was taken for a walk around the grounds of the college by Mr Sparrow. I cannot remember much of what we discussed, but, like the Dean of Balliol, he was concerned about revolutionaries and unconcerned about marijuana smoking.

The preponderance of student revolutionaries dominating the quadrangles and bars, and lack of both fellow marijuana smokers and fellow Philosophers of Science, combined with the paucity of books on the History and Philosophy of Science in the Balliol Library led to my spending less and less time in college. By the end of Trinity Term, I would visit Balliol no more than once or twice a week. Ilze was most unhappy with her teaching job in Didcot and we both began to think seriously of leaving Oxford once I'd completed my diploma course. The expectation was for me to continue with a B Phil or D Phil course, but this could easily be done at another university. I read through the prospectuses of colleges throughout the world. Strangely enough, one of the most attractive graduate courses was offered by a university in Indiana very close to where I am now writing. Eventually, I decided on the University of Sussex, which in those days was referred to as 'Balliol by the sea'. Ilze obtained the promise of employment at a convent school in Worthing.

My diploma was acquired without too much difficulty and I was beginning to feel reasonably secure about my ability to pursue an academic career. □

The Paradox of Confirmation

The paradox engendering propositions referring to any hypothesis h = 'All ϕ's are ψ's' are :-

(1) 'All ϕ's are ψ's' is represented symbolically by $(x)(\phi x \supset \psi x)$ and is therefore equivalent to 'All $-\psi$'s are $-\phi$'s', and also equivalent to 'Everything is either ψ or $-\phi$'.
i.e. $(x)(\phi x \supset \psi x) \equiv (x)(-\psi x \supset -\phi x) \equiv (x)[(\phi(x) \vee -\phi(x)) \supset (\psi(x) \vee -\phi(x))]$

(2) Evidence which confirms (disconfirms) a hypothesis also confirms (disconfirms) ~~its~~ all two valued logical equivalents of the hypothesis

(3) An object which is both ϕ and ψ confirms h, an object which is ϕ and $-\psi$ disconfirms h, objects which are $-\phi$ are irrelevant to h.

(1) is referred to as the scientific laws criterion, (2) is referred to as the equivalence condition, (3) is referred to as Nicod's criterion. Sometimes the conjunction of (1) and (2) is jointly referred to as the equivalence condition.

Advocates of the quantitative Bayesian solution to the paradox [Lindenbaum, Peers, Alexander, Mackie, Swinburne, etc.] reject Nicod's criterion, explaining our reasons for accepting its intuitive plausibility as being our tendency to treat weak confirmation as irrelevant. The most simple and rigorous treatment of this solution is that given by Mackie who to obtain his results appeals to a principle which he refers to as the Inverse Principle but has since become known as the Relevance criterion of Confirmation. This can be stated as:-

Principle C: An observation b confirms h in relation to background knowledge k if and only if $P(b/k.h) > P(b/k)$.

Ilze got a job in Worthing and Howard started a PhD in Philosophy of Science at Sussex University. In a letter posted from Sussex on 2 February 1970, Ilze wrote to Howard's parents, 'Howard is very busy too at the moment. He is working on the Theory of Meaning, a terribly exact and mind-boggling part of logic that philosophers have shelved, for its solution is too difficult. Howard has quite a problem there. He has solved the part of Hempel's Paradox where it applies to clearly definable objects and laws, but no one has remotely touched on the part which concerns objects which cannot easily be defined. Howard is now wracking his brains over the problems, which if solved may lead to the solution of Hempel's Paradox! I do have a very clever husband, but he does always get interested in the most absurdly difficult things. Still he seems to need really hard problems to chew, for otherwise he can't get completely involved, and though often puzzled and deep in thought he is in a very contented frame of mind.'

In fact, Howard had become disheartened with his studies and he and Ilze had fallen out of love and started sleeping with other people.

Groups of Vehicles
List 1: Age 21 and over

A Heavy locomotive, light locomotive, motor tractor, heavy motor car and motor car, but excluding any vehicle comprised in group B, F, G, H, J, K or L. (See Note 1).

B A vehicle with automatic transmission which is a heavy locomotive, light locomotive, motor tractor, heavy motor car or motor car, but excluding any vehicle comprised in group F, G, H, J, K or L. (See Notes 1 and 2).

C Motor tricycle weighing not more than 8 cwt unladen, but excluding any vehicle comprised in group E, J, K or L.

D Motor bicycle (with or without sidecar), but excluding any vehicle comprised in group E, K or L. (See Notes 5 and 6).

E Moped (See Note 3).

F Agricultural tractor, but excluding any vehicle comprised in group H.

G Road roller.

H Track-laying vehicle steered by its tracks.

J Invalid carriage.

K Mowing machine or vehicle controlled by a pedestrian.

L Vehicle propelled by electrical power, but excluding any vehicle comprised in group J or K.

LS Vehicle propelled by electrical power if it is a motor cycle, but excluding any vehicle comprised in group J or K.

M Trolley vehicle.

N Vehicle exempted from duty under section 6(6) of the Vehicles (Excise) Act 1962.

P Vehicles comprised in the groups in list 1 except those which a full licence authorises the holder to drive as a full licence holder.

IMPORTANT See Note 4.

Please read Notes 1–6 on page 5. DL 2B(a)

2

D.L.6A № 203168

GLAMORGAN COUNTY COUNCIL
ROAD TRAFFIC ACT 1960
VEHICLE & DRIVING LICENCES ACT 1969

DRIVING LICENCE

Dennis Howard Marks
30 Waunbank Road
Kenfig Hill
Bridgend

is hereby licensed to drive MOTOR VEHICLES of groups A, B, C, E, F, K and L in list 1 from 14 Oct 19 70 until 13 Oct 19 73 inclusive.
This licence has the effect of a provisional licence for vehicles in group P in list 1.

Fee of £1 Received

Local Taxation Officer
County Council Offices
Greyfriars Road, Cardiff

Usual signature of licence holder DHMarks

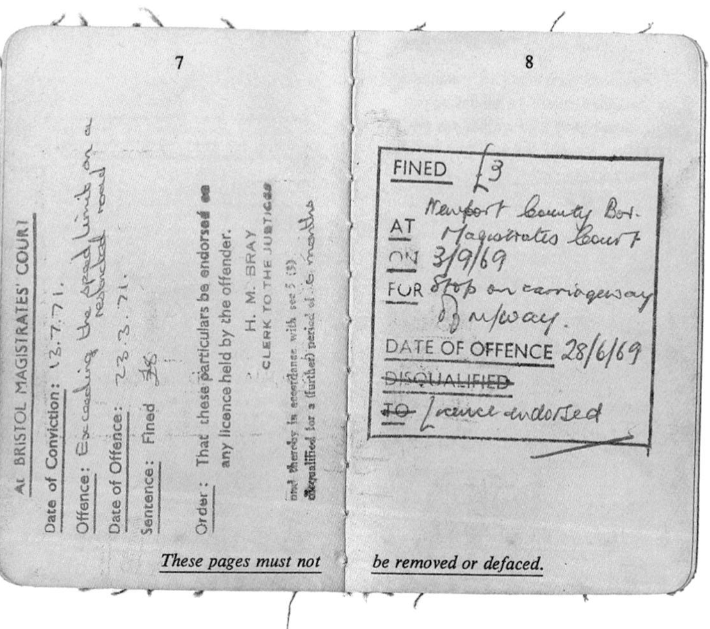

7

At BRISTOL MAGISTRATES' COURT
Date of Conviction: 13.7.71.
Offence: Exceeding the speed limit on a restricted road
Date of Offence: 23.3.71.
Sentence: Fined £8
Order: That these particulars be endorsed on any licence held by the offender.
H. M. BRAY
CLERK TO THE JUSTICES
and thereby in accordance with sec 5 (3) disqualified for a (further) period of ... months

These pages must not

8

FINED £3
AT Newport County Bor. Magistrates Court
ON 3/9/69
FOR Stop on carriageway of motorway.
DATE OF OFFENCE 28/6/69
~~DISQUALIFIED~~
~~TO~~ Licence endorsed

be removed or defaced.

In March 1970 Graham Plinston got busted in Germany with some 45 kilos of hashish. Graham's girlfriend, Mandy, asked Howard to fly out there, find out what had happened, ensure he had legal representation and meet with Graham's business associates on his return:

'Mike Durrani had a brown, hawk-like face, a Savile Row suit, beautiful fingernails and a gold cigarette lighter. He was pouring drinks from a bottle of Johnny Walker Black Label.

"Howard, what a pleasure it is to meet you. Please let me offer you a drink. It is kind of you to come. These are my friends – Sam from Beirut and Nick from Amsterdam. Sam and I have a textile business in Dubai and various other interests. I also have this residence here in London. I am in fact an Afghani by nationality: my grandfather's brother was king. We have been able to get a certain amount of hashish through Europe from time to time, for your friend Graham. How is he managing?" It was a practical meeting. Did he think Graham had named them in his statements? Was the car route "blown"? Was Graham going to be convicted and permanently out of action? If that was to be the case, would Howard ever think of taking over Plinston's smuggling work? "Yes, please," said Howard.' [HT]

Howard accordingly obtained a driving licence and began driving hashish through Europe.

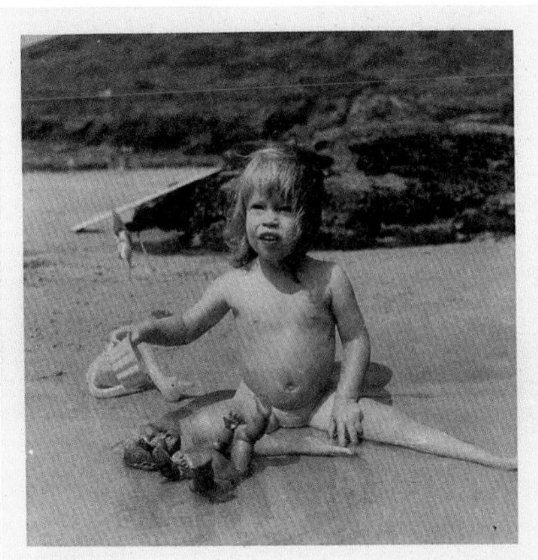

(↑↗) Howard fell in love with Rosie Brindley. Howard abandoned his PhD and dedicated himself to the cannabis trade. Howard and Rosie left their respective marriages amicably and together with Rosie's one-year-old daughter, Emily, moved to Ladbroke Grove, London. Rosie soon became pregnant with Howard's first daughter, Myfanwy Marks.

THE NEVER CHANGE

for Howard

for Howard
as always

My senses are reeling at the real after so many months
But you hot-blooded hound of happiness have not changed
Except perhaps to see the worse and choose the better
Unlike new Pauline gazers into obfuscated views
Scion of bards and beauty mountainously true
Maturity's cloak-like façade is swiftly ripped
When we remember Oxford and tempestuous days
Steady your hand and strike at the inane buffoons
Who yet more bloat our cankered English culture
St George in jeans locked in a breathless fight
With straight great dragons decked in bowler hats
We shall confound them yet my non-capitulating friend
And sally forth where sense and consciousness intend

----

ur friend
Terry Deakin

TD 11-9-70

(→) 'The Never Change' poem by Terry Deakin, November 1970, in which he refers to Howard as a 'hot-blooded hound of happiness'.

(↘→) Graham was released from prison after serving a sentence of six months' imprisonment in Germany. Howard and Graham became partners. Howard and Rosie moved back to Oxford. The jottings in Howard's handwriting on the envelopes (below) and in the memo (opposite), that subsequently featured in the prosecution of Howard in 1980, convey the increasingly international aspects of his work and its contingency on the arrival of money. After Howard and Graham met James McCann the frequency of their importations dramatically increased:

'Alan Marcuson [editor of London underground magazine *Friends*] finally dropped his sensational bombshell at The Warwick Castle. The Plinston crowd needed a way of getting dope down out of the air and into Britain. Right? Preferably by the truckload. Right? Well, he knew a connection who could do it for them.

"This boy," he said emphatically, "can do *anything*."

"Who is he?"

"His name is Jim McCann."

"Where is he?"

"Ballinskelligs."

"Where's that?"

"Ireland."

And Marcuson proceeded to unfold to them a truly amazing story.

One afternoon at the end of February 1971, shortly after his "Britain's Vietnam" issue, Marcuson and his friends were sitting peacefully in their office awaiting the arrival of the American "Yippie" Abbie Hoffman – one of a stream of US pilgrims who were arriving with gratifying frequency to observe the progress of the Irish "revolution".

The door burst open. An alarming apparition manifested itself. It was a plumpish Irishman in his early thirties, with a thick Belfast accent, a pointed nose, and – hidden at first under his cheap leather jacket and then not merely revealed, but waved terrifyingly around – a real gun. It was a sawn-off shotgun of the kind used by bank robbers. It looked as though it might be loaded. With real bullets. Looking around at the aghast expression on the faces of these hippy journalists, it was clear to McCann that his instinctive approach to any new situation had, as usual, succeeded. His audience was off-balance.

"I'm Jim McCann," he told Marcuson, "and what you wrote about the Irish struggle was all shit. Now I'll tell you the real truth."

He unfolded a marvellous tale. Marcuson, enraptured, fumbled for his tape-recorder.

"Every Irishman considers himself a keeper of the Holy Grail," McCann said. "I hate all that fucking linguistic froth they use in the pop culture over here. I fucking detest it."

"Well, what movement are you a member of?"

"Nobody's a member. You don't go and sign here. A group of us were totally disenchanted with fucking politicians and fucking structures... Sartre... We originally called ourselves the Belfast Liberation Front, but now we call ourselves Free Belfast. We only

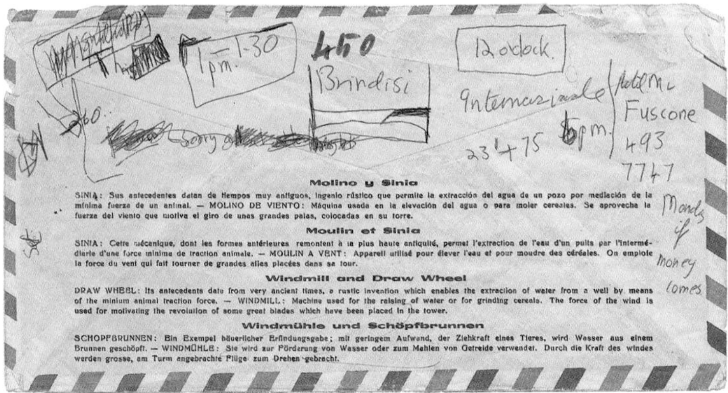

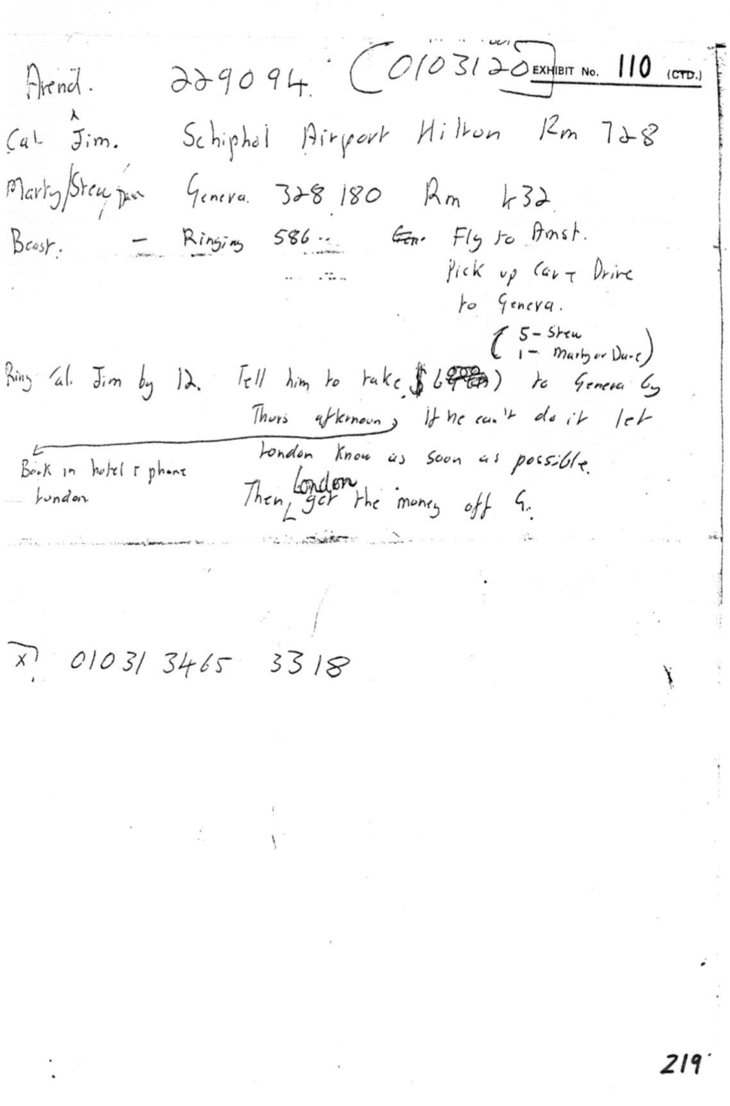

Arend. 229094. (0103120 EXHIBIT No. 110 (CTD.)

Cal Jim. Schiphol Airport Hilton Rm 728

Marty/Stew/Dan Geneva. 328 180 Rm 432

Beast. — Ringing 586... Fly to Amst.
Pick up car + Drive
to Geneva.

(5 - Stew
1 - Marty or Dave)

Ring Cal. Jim by 12. Tell him to take $6000) to Geneva by
Thurs afternoon, if he can't do it let
London know as soon as possible.

Book in hotel + phone
London

Then London get the money off G.

X? 0103 3465 3318

219

interact with the people when they're ready to be interacted with. In our group there are about 100 people to be called. There's about nine in jail at the moment. Pigs, Priests and Politicians, that unholy trinity, are totally barred. We refuse to negotiate on any terms with them. Belfast is like a stunted pygmy wandering in the mist, searching for an awakening..."

"Uh. Are they Maoists?"

"They're not even Maoists: they don't know what they are. They're situationists cum Maoists, cum freaks, cum many, many things. It's a sort of free-wheeling, open-handed situation. British imperialism is trying to shit over the Irish, and the Irish are sticking the big dick of their historical neuroses right up their ass-hole, and they're screaming."

"Well, right on! Is there a, er, heavy criminal element involved in the struggle?"

"No. It's under control. And all the fucking Jean Genets who think stealing's a religious and sacred act. I'm saying to them: 'Don't steal off me! I ain't got nothing! What's mine is yours!'"

"Yeah, um, to what extent do street committees run Free Belfast?"

"They police it, and they defend it. Their main influence comes from the people. You can't say: 'This comes from Che Guevara, and this is the way to dig it, man' and 'This is the way it was done in Chicago.' This guy has a donkey, wouldn't conform; he brings in the best donkey trainer in Ireland, says 'Listen man, I've spent a lot of bread, can you cure it and educate it?' He says 'Of course I can.' So he picks up a big hammer and hits it right between the eyes. And the guy said, 'I asked you to fucking cure it, not kill it!' So the trainer says 'Before I can fucking cure it, I've got to get its fucking attention first!' There you go... We've had to take the sewers in certain parts. *Kanal*. You know. *Ashes and Diamonds* type. 'Kanal' scene... The fucking movies. We're gonna have Great Britain's Sharpeville."

"Wow," Marcuson said.

This rough, bold, instinctively revolutionary account of the Belfast struggle continued in like fashion and warmed Marcuson's heart. He published it word-for-anonymous word in the next issue of *Friends*, under the headline drawn from the Rolling Stones' 1968 hit single: 'Interview with a Belfast Street Fighting Man'.

Actually the whole story was a fabrication from beginning to end, apart from the circumstance that McCann was indeed from Belfast. A tremendous liar, Jim McCann had simply made the whole thing up. Marcuson was not to discover this until much later, by which time McCann had done such genuinely astounding things that he had almost parlayed himself into the position of being a genuine IRA folk hero.

McCann was, in short, a con artist. He was, to those who liked rogues, a likeable rogue. His only real asset was his personality. He used it to generate a hypnotic atmosphere around him in which what he said became somehow regarded as true by otherwise reasonably sensible people. And, as a result, he could from time to time make the most extraordinary things happen. Marcuson was right in a way: "This boy can do anything!"' HT

ANNABELINDA LIMITED
Reg Office 6 Gloucester St
Oxford Telephone 46806

Directors D H Marks
B O'Hanlon Reg No 1030511

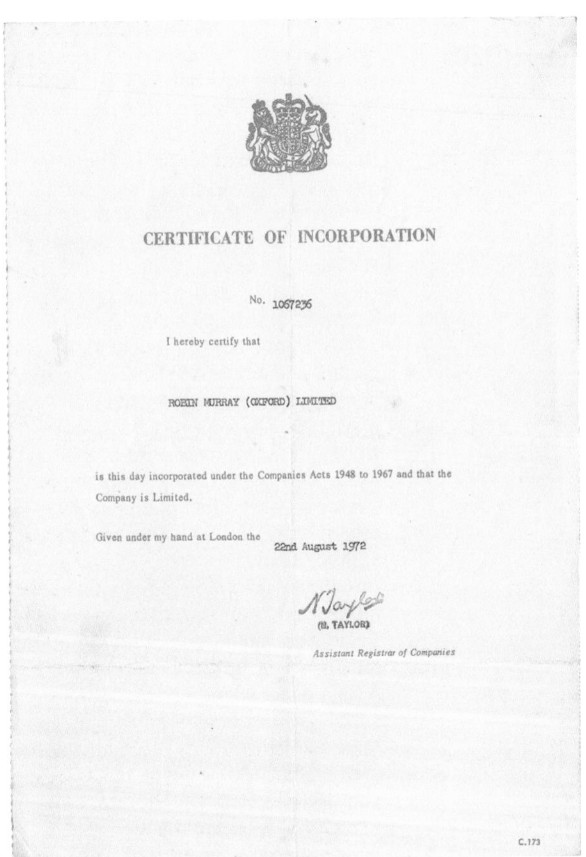

CERTIFICATE OF INCORPORATION

No. 1067236

I hereby certify that

ROBIN MURRAY (OXFORD) LIMITED

is this day incorporated under the Companies Acts 1948 to 1967 and that the Company is Limited.

Given under my hand at London the 22nd August 1972

N Taylor
(N. TAYLOR)
Assistant Registrar of Companies

C.173

Robin Murray certificate of incorporation.

ROBIN MURRAY (OXFORD) LTD
6 Gloucester St Oxford Tel 42428

Directors D H Marks C B O Murphy
R G Murray

(←↓) Howard's most successful venture was AnnaBelinda Ltd, a dressmakers' boutique in Oxford. Around the time it was set up, Hamilton McMillan (the Palace Guard in the Balliol production of *Salomé*) informed Howard that he worked for MI6 and, on learning of Howard's plans to open international branches of AnnaBelinda (he never did) asked if 'the office' would be able borrow it for its own purposes. When McMillan found out that Howard knew James McCann (who had succeeded in convincing everyone other than the IRA that he was a member of the terrorist organisation), McMillan asked if he would be willing to inform on him. Howard agreed, but did nothing of the sort.

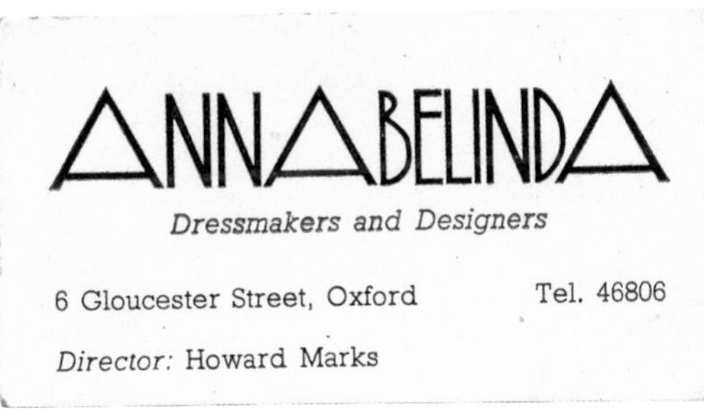
ANNABELINDA
Dressmakers and Designers
6 Gloucester Street, Oxford
Tel. 46806
Director: Howard Marks

ROBIN MURRAY (OXFORD) LTD
6 Gloucester St Oxford Tel 42428
Director DH Marks

(←↗) Howard incorporated Robin Murray Ltd, which was paid to carry out 'refurbishments' at the AnnaBelinda offices. Meanwhile, McCann was putting the funds given to him by Howard and Graham to good use:

'McCann in fact invested only a very small fraction of his newly acquired £500. He had a box of business cards printed. They read "Seamus O'Neill. *Fortune* magazine. New York." Then he rang up Shannon Airport:

"Airport manager's office. My name's O'Neill, I'm an editor for *Fortune* magazine, the top American business weekly. Put me on to the airport manager."

He made his pitch:

"We at *Fortune* are doing a comparative survey of the world's airports, in depth. Advice to our readers – very influential business-men – wouldn't want to omit Shannon: in fact, I've persuaded my colleagues to include it. Didn't want the old country to lose out. Could be worth lots of business. So I've just flown in. If you can arrange a conducted tour of the airport, how it all works, especially the freight side. Yes, as soon as possible – I've just flown in to Dublin and I've only got three days here before going on to Schiphol at Amsterdam. Thursday? Yes, hang on – I think I can manage that..."

Three days later, he was back at Ballinskelligs, beaming. He tossed down document after document on the table in front of a bemused Marcuson.

"International Air Transport Regulations."

Thump.

"More of the same."

Thump

"More ITA rules."

"Here's some maps. Every inch of Shannon."

"And here's all the Customs forms they use. I nicked top copies off all the piles as they were going round. This is the main one. It's an 'Out of Charge' docket – this clears cargo to be released out of the Freeport area on to Irish soil. You just need a Customs man to issue the form and sign it."

Marcuson stared, thunderstruck, at the booty.

"Now, let me see my notes. When the cargo comes in, this is the mark they chalk on the crates, to signify they've been examined and cleared. When they chalk them, they move the crates across the floor of the cargo terminal – let me see the map – from here to just this side here. The main import from Asia – you won't believe this – is cheap religious tracts. They're printed in India. Oh yes, and they have two or three dead bodies coming in from the Middle East for burial here. The point is, they go through in hermetically sealed containers."

"Amazing. What about doing our scam?"

"No problem. I had a little talk to this Customs man. In return for a little financial assistance he'll accept forged 'Out of Charge' dockets."

"Fantastic. How did you do it?"

"Well, he's under a slight misappre-hension. I played the Green Card, you know. The Boys in the North, David O'Connell and all those Provo arms he tried to buy in Amsterdam last year before their ship got busted..."

"What exactly do you mean, Jim?"

"He thinks he's doing it for the ould country, for the North."

"What does he think this stuff is going to be?"

"Well, guns, I suppose. Anyway I can't stay. I've got a plane to catch."' HT

Dennis H. Marks.
International Stamp Dealer.
6 Gloucester Street.
Oxford.
Tel 42428.

DENNIS H. MARKS

International Stamp Dealer

6 Gloucester Street,
Oxford.

(↑↗) Howard set up several businesses in Oxford, including that of International Stamp Dealer.

With the success of the Shannon Airport deals, Howard started making a lot of money fast. He provided the money for Denys Irving (the man who gave Howard his first joint) to press his proto punk LP *Fuck You* under their own record label, Lucifer. It sold 1,500 copies by mail order through *Private Eye*. They made a second single called 'Prick' in 1972. Shortly after building the prototype for a bespoke Amazing Telephone Machine for re-routing Howard's phone calls, Denys Irving died in a tragic hang-gliding accident on the Sussex Downs in 1976.

EXHIBIT No. 106 (CTD.)

2

DESCRIPTION *SIGNALEMENT*

	Bearer *Titulaire*	★Wife *Femme*
Profession / *Profession*	~~[illegible]~~ COMPANY SECRETARY	
Place and date of birth / *Lieu et date de naissance*	KENFIG HILL 13 · 8 · 45	
Country of Residence / *Pays de Résidence*	U. K.	
Height / *Taille*	6 ft. 0 in.	
Colour of eyes / *Couleur des yeux*	BLUE	
Colour of hair / *Couleur des cheveux*	BLACK	
Special peculiarities / *Signes particuliers*	NONE	

PASSPORT OFFICE 26 FEB 1973 LONDON

★CHILDREN *ENFANTS*

Name *Nom*	Date of birth *Date de naissance*	Sex *Sexe*

Usual signature of bearer / *Signature du titulaire* AH Marks

Usual signature of wife / *Signature de sa femme*

(S.312606)

3

Bearer / *Titulaire*

Wife / *Femme*

(PHOTO)

195

Howard's legitimate and illegitimate interests multiplied to the extent that even he seems to have had difficulties deciding what profession best described his activities when completing his passport details.

While the Shannon deals with McCann continued unabated, Graham and Howard branched out into organising boatloads of hashish from Lebanon to Europe as well as suitcases of hashish from Karachi and Beirut to Geneva. With ample amounts coming so easily into Europe, Howard and Graham eagerly agreed to send some of it to the United States after being told of an apparently ingenious method for getting it there from *any* airport in Europe. The soundman who provided the equipment (and stuffed it full of dope) worked for the Californian Ernie Combs, a member of the Brotherhood of Eternal Love. Ernie came from a wealthy family (the first Disneyland resort was built on land purchased from Ernie's father by Walt Disney). This is a copy of a United States Transportation Entry and Manifest of Goods Subject to Customs Inspection and Permit for Musical and Sound Equipment belonging to the Transatlantic Sound Company to Las Vegas.

CUSTOMS FORM NOV. 64 7512

TRANSPORTATION ENTRY AND MANIFEST OF GOODS SUBJECT TO CUSTOMS INSPECTION AND PERMIT

BUREAU OF CUSTOMS

Form Approved Budget Bureau No. [illegible]12.7.

Entry No. IX 7281799
Class of Entry IT (I. T.) (Wd. T.) (Wd. Ex.) (T. E.) (Drawback, etc.)

ACM Entry No. 12505
Port New York
Date September 8, 1973

Dist. No. 12 Port Code No. 01 First U. S. Port of Unlading New York

Port of Las Vegas, Nevada Date September 14, 1973

Entered or imported by Emery Air Freight Corporation to be shipped in bond via Trans World Air Lines consigned to
(C. H. L. number) (Vessel or carrier) (Car number and initial) (Pier or station)
Collector of customs at Las Vegas, Nevada Final foreign destination (For exportations only)
Consignee Trans Atlantic Sound Las Vegas (McCarran International) Airport, Las Vegas, Nevada
(At customs port of exit or destination)
Foreign port of lading Amsterdam B/L No. 343 16866 Date of sailing 9-8-73
(Above information to be furnished only when merchandise is imported by vessel)
Imported on the Pan American Air Lines Flag US on September 8, 1973 via Amsterdam, Holland (N)
(Name of vessel or carrier and motive power) (Date imported) (Last foreign port)
Exported from Netherlands (Amsterdam) on September 8, 1973 Goods now at Trans World Airlines.
(Country) (Date) (Name of warehouse, station, pier, etc.)

Marks and Numbers of Packages	Description and Quantity of Merchandise Number and Kind of Packages (Describe fully as per shipping papers)	Gross Weight in Pounds	Value (Dollars only)	Rate	Duty
One thru Twenty Nine	Twenty Nine (29) Musical and Sound Equiptment Emery Bill No. AMS 51495 to NYC " " " NYC 15958 to LAS Carried to New York on PAA FLT 093 PAA Plane No. N733	3762	EST $3000.00		

G. O. No.

CERTIFICATE OF LADING FOR TRANSPORTATION IN BOND AND/OR LADING FOR EXPORTATION FOR
(Port)

With the Exceptions Noted Above, the Within-Described Goods Were:

Delivered to the Carrier named above, for delivery to the Collector of Customs at destination sealed with Customs seals
Nos.
the packages (were) (were not) labeled, or corded and sealed.
(Inspector or warehouse officer)
(Date)

Laden on the—
(Vessel, vehicle, or aircraft)
which cleared for —
on (Date)
as verified by export records.
(Inspector)
(Date)

I truly declare that the statements contained herein are true and correct to the best of my knowledge and belief.
Entered or withdrawn by Emery Air Freight Corp.

To the Inspector or Warehouse Officer: The above-described goods shall be disposed of as specified herein.
For the Collector.

Received from the collector of customs of above district the merchandise described in this manifest for transportation and delivery into the custody of the customs officers at the port named above, all packages in apparent good order except as noted hereon.
Emery Air Freight Corp.
E.D. Hill
Attorney or Agent of Carrier

(→) In September 1973, Howard went to New York and Los Angeles, his first visit to the United States, to pick up money from Ernie. Shortly after his arrival, one of the speaker loads got busted and featured on the national news. They all scarpered. Howard went on the run through Ibiza, Ireland, France, Germany, Belgium and Amsterdam, where he was arrested in November 1973 and deported to the UK. He was charged with conspiring between July 1973 and September 1973 to import cannabis resin into the United States of America. The prosecution case was that between these dates 'substantial quantities of cannabis resin were smuggled into the United States of America concealed in speakers, which were part of the musical equipment to be used by pop groups touring the United States of America. The equipment was carried by air from various European countries and there were three separate importations. The methods and documents used in each importation have striking similarities. In particular, each was carried out by or on behalf of a fictitious company called Transatlantic Sounds and a document known as a carnet issued by the London Chamber of Commerce used to enable the equipment through the relevant authorities of Europe and into and out of the United States of America without the need for the payment of duty. It is the case for the Crown that the same organisation was responsible for each of the three importations and that on each there was cannabis resin in the speakers.' Opposite is the schedule of movements prepared by the prosecution of musical equipment by Transatlantic Sounds.

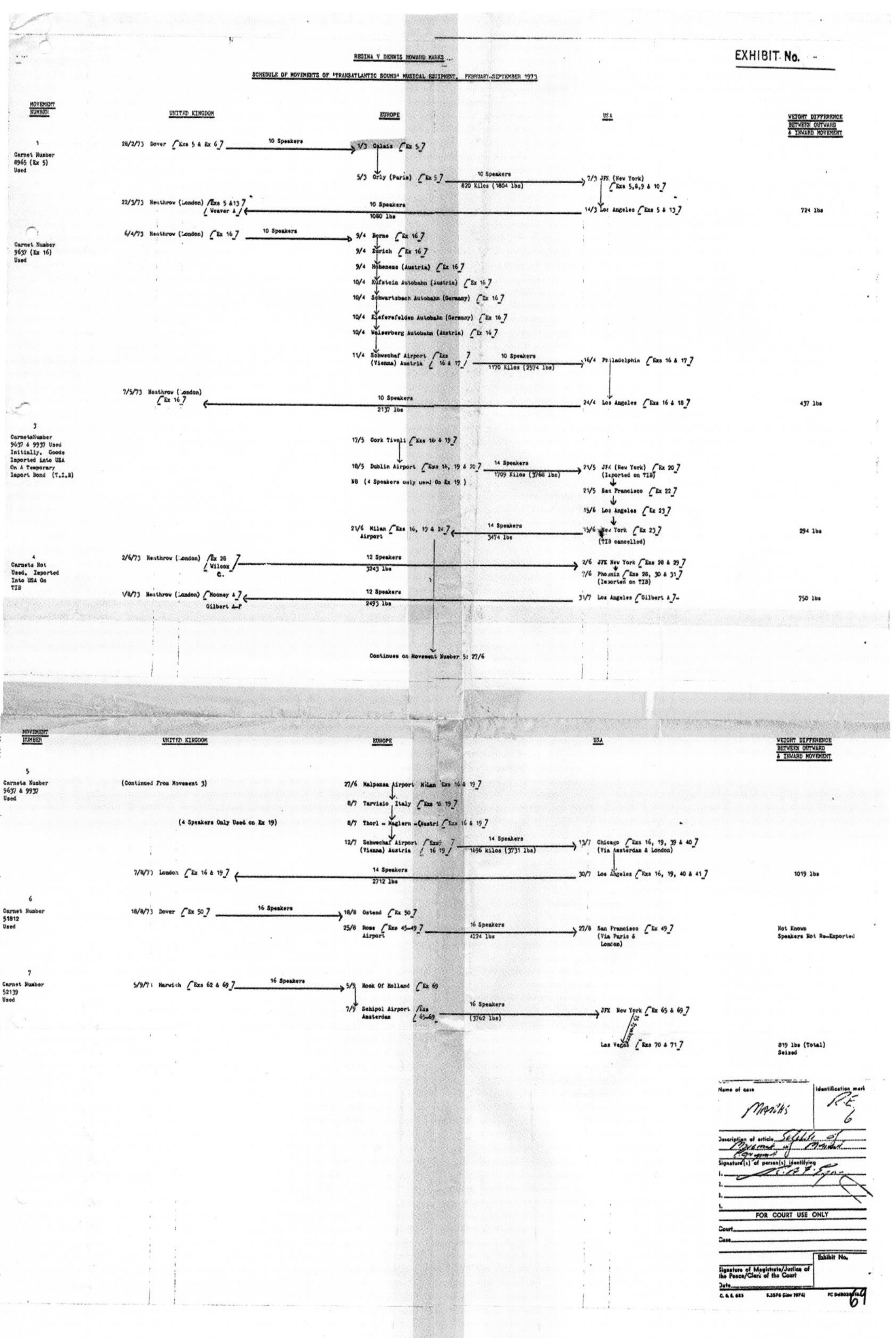

EXHIBIT No.

REGINA V DENNIS HOWARD MARKS

SCHEDULE OF MOVEMENTS OF 'TRANSATLANTIC SOUND' MUSICAL EQUIPMENT, FEBRUARY–SEPTEMBER 1973

MOVEMENT NUMBER	UNITED KINGDOM		EUROPE		USA	WEIGHT DIFFERENCE BETWEEN OUTWARD & INWARD MOVEMENT
1 Carnet Number 8965 (Ex 5) Used	28/2/73 Dover [Exs 5 & Ex 6]	→ 10 Speakers →	1/3 Calais [Ex 5]			
			5/3 Orly (Paris) [Ex 5]	→ 10 Speakers, 820 Kilos (1804 lbs) →	7/3 JFK (New York) [Exs 5,8,9 & 10]	
	22/3/73 Heathrow (London) [Exs 5 & 13 / Weaver A]	← 10 Speakers, 1080 lbs ←			14/3 Los Angeles [Exs 5 & 13]	724 lbs
Carnet Number 9637 (Ex 16) Used	6/4/73 Heathrow (London) [Ex 16]	→ 10 Speakers →	9/4 Berne [Ex 16]			
			9/4 Zurich [Ex 16]			
			9/4 Hohenems (Austria) [Ex 16]			
			10/4 Kufstein Autobahn (Austria) [Ex 16]			
			10/4 Schwartzbach Autobahn (Germany) [Ex 16]			
			10/4 Kieferefelden Autobahn (Germany) [Ex 16]			
			10/4 Walserberg Autobahn (Austria) [Ex 16]			
			11/4 Schwechaf Airport (Vienna) Austria [Exs 16 & 17]	→ 10 Speakers, 1170 Kilos (2574 lbs) →	16/4 Philadelphia [Exs 16 & 17]	
	7/5/73 Heathrow (London) [Ex 16]	← 10 Speakers, 2137 lbs ←			24/4 Los Angeles [Exs 16 & 18]	437 lbs
3 Carnets Number 9637 & 9937 Used Initially. Goods Imported into USA On A Temporary Import Bond (T.I.B)			17/5 Cork Tivoli [Exs 16 & 19]			
			18/5 Dublin Airport [Exs 16, 19 & 20] NB (4 Speakers only used On Ex 19)	→ 14 Speakers, 1709 Kilos (3768 lbs) →	21/5 JFK (New York) [Ex 20] (Imported on TIB)	
					21/5 San Francisco [Ex 22]	
					15/6 Los Angeles [Ex 23]	
			21/6 Milan Airport [Exs 16, 19 & 24]	← 14 Speakers, 3474 lbs ←	15/6 New York [Ex 23] (TIB cancelled)	294 lbs
4 Carnets Not Used. Imported Into USA On TIB	2/6/73 Heathrow (London) [Ex 28 / Wilcox C.]	→ 12 Speakers, 3243 lbs →			2/6 JFK New York [Exs 28 & 29]	
					7/6 Phoenix [Exs 28, 30 & 31] (Imported on TIB)	
	1/8/73 Heathrow (London) [Mooney & Gilbert A–F]	← 12 Speakers, 2493 lbs ←			31/7 Los Angeles [Gilbert A]	750 lbs
			Continues on Movement Number 5: 27/6			

MOVEMENT NUMBER	UNITED KINGDOM		EUROPE		USA	WEIGHT DIFFERENCE BETWEEN OUTWARD & INWARD MOVEMENT
5 Carnets Number 9637 & 9937 Used	(Continued From Movement 3)		27/6 Malpensa Airport Milan [Exs 16 & 19]			
			8/7 Tarvisio Italy [Exs 16 19]			
	(4 Speakers Only Used on Ex 19)		8/7 Thorl – Maglern –(Austri [Exs 16 & 19]			
			12/7 Schwechaf Airport (Vienna) Austria [Exs 16 19]	→ 14 Speakers, 1696 kilos (3731 lbs) →	13/7 Chicago [Exs 16, 19, 39 & 40] (Via Amsterdam & London)	
	7/8/73 London [Ex 16 & 19]	← 14 Speakers, 2712 lbs ←			30/7 Los Angeles [Exs 16, 19, 40 & 41]	1019 lbs
6 Carnet Number 51812 Used	18/8/73 Dover [Ex 50]	→ 16 Speakers →	18/8 Ostend [Ex 50]			
			25/8 Rome Airport [Exs 45–49]	→ 16 Speakers, 4224 lbs →	27/8 San Francisco [Ex 49] (Via Paris & London)	Not Known Speakers Not Re–Exported
7 Carnet Number 52139 Used	5/9/73 Harwich [Exs 62 & 69]	→ 16 Speakers →	5/9 Hook Of Holland [Ex 69			
			7/9 Schipol Airport Amsterdam [Exs 65–69]	→ 16 Speakers, (3762 lbs) →	JFK New York [Ex 65 & 69]	
					Las Vegas [Exs 70 & 71]	819 lbs (Total) Seized

Name of case: Marks
Identification mark: R.E. 6
Description of article
Signature(s) of person(s) identifying
1.
2.
3.
4.
FOR COURT USE ONLY
Court
Case
Exhibit No.
Signature of Magistrate/Justice of the Peace/Clerk of the Court
Date
C. & E. 683 5.3576 (Jan 1974)
69

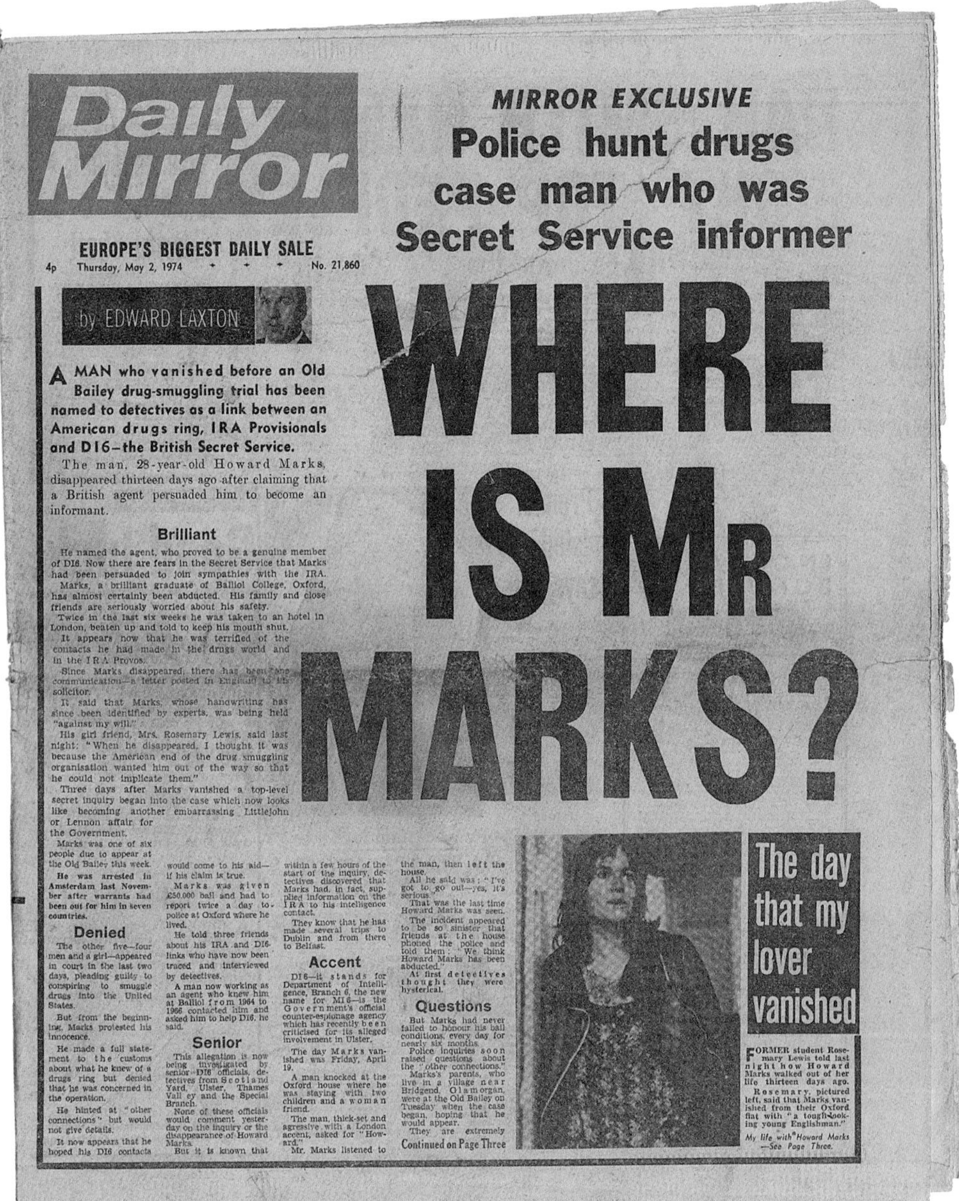

Daily Mirror

EUROPE'S BIGGEST DAILY SALE

4p Thursday, May 2, 1974 * * * No. 21,860

MIRROR EXCLUSIVE

Police hunt drugs case man who was Secret Service informer

WHERE IS MR MARKS?

by EDWARD LAXTON

A MAN who vanished before an Old Bailey drug-smuggling trial has been named to detectives as a link between an American drugs ring, IRA Provisionals and D16—the British Secret Service.

The man, 28-year-old Howard Marks, disappeared thirteen days ago after claiming that a British agent persuaded him to become an informant.

Brilliant

He named the agent, who proved to be a genuine member of DI6. Now there are fears in the Secret Service that Marks had been persuaded to join sympathies with the IRA.

Marks, a brilliant graduate of Balliol College, Oxford, has almost certainly been abducted. His family and close friends are seriously worried about his safety.

Twice in the last six weeks he was taken to an hotel in London, beaten up and told to keep his mouth shut.

It appears now that he was terrified of the contacts he had made in the drugs world and in the IRA Provos.

Since Marks disappeared, there has been one communication—a letter posted in England to his solicitor.

It said that Marks, whose handwriting has since been identified by experts, was being held "against my will."

His girl friend, Mrs. Rosemary Lewis, said last night: "When he disappeared, I thought it was because the American end of the drug smuggling organisation wanted him out of the way so that he could not implicate them."

Three days after Marks vanished a top-level secret inquiry began into the case which now looks like becoming another embarrassing Littlejohn or Lennon affair for the Government.

Marks was one of six people due to appear at the Old Bailey this week.

He was arrested in Amsterdam last November after warrants had been out for him in seven countries.

Denied

The other five—four men and a girl—appeared in court in the last two days, pleading guilty to conspiring to smuggle drugs into the United States.

But from the beginning, Marks protested his innocence.

He made a full statement to the customs about what he knew of a drugs ring but denied that he was concerned in the operation.

He hinted at "other connections" but would not give details.

It now appears that he hoped his DI6 contacts would come to his aid—if his claim is true.

Marks was given £50,000 bail and had to report twice a day to police at Oxford where he lived.

He told three friends about his IRA and DI6 links who have now been traced and interviewed by detectives.

A man now working as an agent who knew him at Balliol from 1964 to 1966 contacted him and asked him to help DI6, he said.

Senior

This allegation is now being investigated by senior DI6 officials, detectives from Scotland Yard, Ulster, Thames Valley and the Special Branch.

None of these officials would comment yesterday on the inquiry or the disappearance of Howard Marks.

But it is known that within a few hours of the start of the inquiry, detectives discovered that Marks had, in fact, supplied information on the IRA to his intelligence contact.

They know that he has made several trips to Dublin and from there to Belfast.

Accent

DI6—it stands for Department of Intelligence, Branch 6, the new name for MI6—is the Government's official counter-espionage agency which has recently been criticised for its alleged involvement in Ulster.

The day Marks vanished was Friday, April 19.

A man knocked at the Oxford house where he was staying with two children and a woman friend.

The man, thick-set and agressive with a London accent, asked for "Howard."

Mr. Marks listened to the man, then left the house.

All he said was: "I've got to go out—yes, it's serious."

That was the last time Howard Marks was seen.

The incident appeared to be so sinister that friends at the house phoned the police and told them: "We think Howard Marks has been abducted."

At first detectives thought they were hysterical.

Questions

But Marks had never failed to honour his bail conditions, every day for nearly six months.

Police inquiries soon raised questions about the "other connections."

Marks's parents, who live in a village near Bridgend, Glamorgan, were at the Old Bailey on Tuesday when the case began, hoping that he would appear.

They are extremely

Continued on Page Three

The day that my lover vanished

FORMER student Rosemary Lewis told last night how Howard Marks walked out of her life thirteen days ago.

Rosemary, pictured left, said that Marks vanished from their Oxford flat with "a tough-looking young Englishman."

My life with Howard Marks—See Page Three.

Front page of the *Daily Mirror*, 2 May 1974. After three weeks in custody, Howard was released on £50,000 bail. Shortly after he was bailed, in April 1974, Howard disappeared, apparently abducted by Mafioso-type associates of Combs, meaning that the bail money provided by his parents could not be forfeited until the circumstances of his disappearance were ascertained. Chief Superintendent Phillip Fairweather of the Thames Valley Police was put in charge of the investigation. Howard stayed on the run for six years. He travelled extensively, particularly in the Middle and Far East, and participated in numerous smuggling adventures from Pakistan, Afghanistan, Nepal, Lebanon and Morocco. He re-established contact with Jim McCann in Vancouver, after bumping into Marty Langford (also on the run) in Vancouver's planetarium. They resumed their former relationship.

3

On the Run

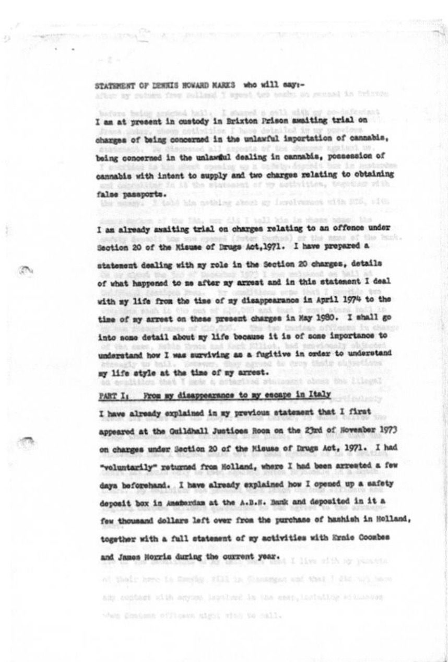

STATEMENT OF DENNIS HOWARD MARKS who will say:-

I am at present in custody in Brixton Prison awaiting trial on charges of being concerned in the unlawful importation of cannabis, being concerned in the unlawful dealing in cannabis, possession of cannabis with intent to supply and two charges relating to obtaining false passports.

I am already awaiting trial on charges relating to an offence under Section 20 of the Misuse of Drugs Act,1971. I have prepared a statement dealing with my role in the Section 20 charges, details of what happened to me after my arrest and in this statement I deal with my life from the time of my disappearance in April 1974 to the time of my arrest on these present charges in May 1980. I shall go into some detail about my life because it is of some importance to understand how I was surviving as a fugitive in order to understand my life style at the time of my arrest.

PART I: From my disappearance to my escape in Italy

I have already explained in my previous statement that I first appeared at the Guildhall Justices Room on the 23rd of November 1973 on charges under Section 20 of the Misuse of Drugs Act, 1971. I had "voluntarily" returned from Holland, where I had been arrested a few days beforehand. I have already explained how I opened up a safety deposit box in Amsterdam at the A.B.N. Bank and deposited in it a few thousand dollars left over from the purchase of hashish in Holland, together with a full statement of my activities with Ernie Coombes and James Morris during the current year.

The text for this chapter is taken from a several-hundred page 'Defence Statement' written by Howard, while on remand in Brixton prison (1980–1) facing charges for the importation of several tons of Colombian cannabis into the UK in 1979. It provides an account of his time on the run between 1974 and his arrest in 1980. The purpose of the document was to assist his lawyers in understanding his defence. It is likely that his lawyers were extremely surprised, and greatly assisted, by its length and detail.

The street into which I emerged was full of market stalls selling everything from food to watches. I now know that the house was located between Genoa Railway Station and the Waterfront. A thunderstorm had just broken and the market traders were busily packing up, while shoppers were fleeing to seek shelter from the rain. I took advantage of the situation to run as fast as my weakened physical condition would allow. I found a public park about two miles from the market street. I stayed there until early the next morning.

I was unkempt. My clothes were filthy and rain-soaked. I had no money and no possessions. I did not speak Italian and I knew no one who lived in Italy, let alone Genoa. I had no idea what had happened during my trial (if indeed it had taken place), or what conclusion my family, parents and friends had drawn regarding my fate. I did not know which way to turn. I considered handing myself in to the nearest police station, but I rejected the idea because the Section 20 charges I would face in England included the movement of cannabis from Italy to the United States and I was afraid that if I gave myself up to the Italian police I might face charges in Italy, followed by extradition to England. I decided to inform my close friend Denys Irving of my whereabouts and to seek his assistance. I had known Denys since 1965 when we were both undergraduates at Balliol College, Oxford. He and Julian Peto were my best friends and apart from my family they were the only people whom I trusted completely.

At about 7.00am on 30 May 1974 I made my way on foot to Piazza di Ferrari and made a reverse-charge call to London. I spoke to Denys Irving, who was very surprised to hear from me. I gave him a brief summary of my predicament. He said that a lot had happened in England that I should know about. He agreed to fly out to Genoa that day, bringing me clothes and money.

After this phone call I walked to Genoa Airport, a distance of about ten miles, to await Mr Irving. He arrived in the late afternoon via Milan. We took a taxi back to Genoa and went to a snack bar. I had not eaten since the previous day. Denys showed me newspaper reports which had come out after my abduction. I was shocked by their contents. Until this moment

This pink file, labelled 'British Secret Service', in Howard's handwriting, contains Howard's news clippings on the activities of MI6. It documents the various scandals in which the Secret Services apparently recruited people to undertake criminal activities in order to gather intelligence for them, supposedly with their protection, only to abandon their recruits when they did get into trouble with the law and to deny having had anything to do with them. Just as McCann referred to the utility of the myth he had created about being an Irish terrorist as the 'Green Card', Howard referred to his recruitment by the Secret Services as his 'Wild Card'.

I had no idea that my activities for British Intelligence were public knowledge and had appeared on the front pages of many newspapers. Most of the reporting was inaccurate, much of it completely false. The consequences were alarming. The main propagator of these falsehoods was a journalist called Edward Laxton, who wrote for the *Daily Mirror*.

Until reading these reports I had intended to return immediately to the United Kingdom to give myself up and establish my innocence in court. I had always been confident of being acquitted of these charges and during my period on bail had worked hard with my barrister and solicitor. I was also intending to carry on with my studies. My supervisor, Rom Harré, was impressed by the original work I had done during this period and I was assured of the fullest cooperation in obtaining an academic post regardless of the outcome of my trial.

Now, however, new factors arose. First of all, I knew that I would be a target for elimination by the IRA. It is remotely possible that my abductors may have belonged to the Mafia, but I had no contact with them myself and knew very little about them. I did, however, assume that publicity was not to the Mafia's liking and if it was the Mafia who had abducted me, my continued existence would be an embarrassment to them.

There had been speculation that I had actually joined the IRA and had political leanings towards the Provisionals. This was complete nonsense and would be known to be nonsense by my MI6 contact, Mr McMillan. However, my existence was already an embarrassment to MI6 and such ridiculous speculation could only increase it. At that time there was a prevalent belief that the Secret Services had eliminated Kenneth Lennon, an Irish Special Branch informer, to avoid embarrassment and I genuinely – although I now believe mistakenly – feared the same thing might happen to me.

Mr Irving also told me about a piece in which it was stated that I had been responsible for the arrest of three IRA members in Hamburg who were caught in an arms/drugs deal. This greatly increased the chance of retaliatory action being taken against me by the IRA. This claim by the *News at Ten* team could well have been true as the people arrested in Hamburg were close associates of James McCann, one being his girlfriend Ann. Their detention and subsequent arrest probably arose from information given by me to MI6.

Given the publicity, I decided that I would have to remain in hiding. I feared for my life from the IRA and possibly the Mafia, and at the very least I felt that the

Americans who had arranged my kidnapping would be on the lookout for me to prevent me giving evidence again. I talked to Mr Irving about these matters well into the night. We now had to find accommodation. I still had no identity papers. Mr Irving went off to find a small hotel where we might be able to stay without registering. He returned in about an hour saying that he had found a *pensione* and had booked us a room. We went to the hotel, had a few drinks at the bar and I stayed the night in his room.

We then discussed how I could obtain some sort of identity papers to enable me to continue hiding abroad. I had no idea how to obtain false documents. We considered the method described in Frederick Forsyth's novel *The Day of the Jackal*, whereby one discovers persons who have died young without making a passport application and one applies for a birth certificate in the name of that person and then a passport. Denys said that he would try to do what he could on his return to England. In the meantime, we decided that the best course of action would be to buy camping equipment, find a crowded site where Denys would register and where I would remain after his departure, using the pass card given to him by the authorities at the campsite.

The plan worked perfectly and Denys left for London. He gave me some money and took some passport-size photographs of me in case he needed them for obtaining a false passport. He also left me with his driving licence and other pieces of personal identity. I arranged to keep in touch with him every few days. After he left I was in a neurotic and distressed state of mind. I had no idea what the future held for me. I was living on the campsite, which was a few miles west of Genoa, but only went there to sleep. I spent my days wandering around art galleries, museums, seeing the sights or lying on the beach. The evenings would mostly be occupied by hanging around bars. I was deeply depressed and could not concentrate on anything.

I spent about two or three weeks in this way. Denys then came over to see me again. There had been no further reports about me in the press. He brought with him a birth certificate in the name of John McKenna, a pair of weak spectacles and an application form for a British Visitor's Passport. His idea was that I should fill in the application form in my own handwriting and he would take it back to London and give it to someone who resembled me and who could take it to a Post Office with two photographs of me and the appropriate fee, giving the impression he had just filled it in. Denys told me that he had found someone to act as my 'lookalike'.

The plan seemed rather clumsy. I was terrified of

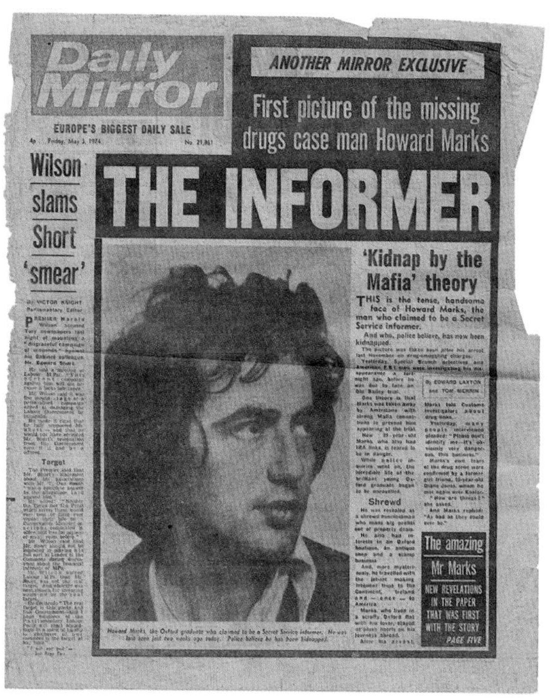

Daily Mirror

EUROPE'S BIGGEST DAILY SALE

4p Friday, May 3, 1974 No. 21,861

ANOTHER MIRROR EXCLUSIVE

First picture of the missing drugs case man Howard Marks

THE INFORMER

Wilson slams Short 'smear'

By VICTOR KNIGHT

Target

'Kidnap by the Mafia' theory

THIS is the tense, handsome face of Howard Marks, the man who claimed to be a Secret Service informer.

And who, police believe, has now been kidnapped.

By EDWARD LAXTON and TOM MERRIN

Shrewd

Howard Marks, the Oxford graduate who claimed to be a Secret Service informer. He was last seen just two weeks ago today. Police believe he has been kidnapped.

The amazing Mr Marks

NEW REVELATIONS IN THE PAPER THAT WAS FIRST WITH THE STORY PAGE FIVE

Daily Mirror, 4 May 1974.

Daily Mirror

EUROPE'S BIGGEST DAILY SALE

4p Thursday, July 4, 1974 No. 21,912

HEALTH CHIEFS IN PLEA TO WILSON

By RONALD BEDFORD Science Editor

MP demands a probe into the strange case of missing informer

THE LONG SILENCE OF MR MYSTERY

Out: Billie Jean King

Out: Evonne Goolagong

Out: John Newcombe

Out: Jan Kodes

The fallen idols

Peter Wilson—See Pages 30 and 31

THE mystery of missing Howard Marks—named to detectives as the link man between the Secret Service, IRA gun-runners and a giant drugs syndicate, deepened yesterday.

Oxford man linked with Secret Service

By EDWARD LAXTON

Private

Escape

Continued on Page Two

Daily Mirror, 4 July 1974.

being asked by the Italian Police for my passport. We took some more passport photographs of me wearing glasses. By now I also had a moustache and a side parting to my hair. Many times I thought of stowing away on a ship, but I always rejected the idea.

I kept in touch with Denys Irving about once a week. The first week of July 1974 he told me that there was important news, but he did not want to discuss it over the telephone. He would be over very shortly with the document that I required.

Denys arrived for a third and last time in Genoa. He told me that Judge Edward Clarke had again postponed the decision on whether my parents' bail should be forfeited. There had been more press coverage about me and someone had even confessed to killing me. The person who had confessed to my murder was unknown to me and later received three months' imprisonment for wasting police time. The press coverage included two more items in the *Daily Mirror* concentrating on my anti-IRA work for MI6. This did nothing to alleviate my worries about becoming a target for IRA gunmen.

Denys had also brought with him the British Visitor's Passport. The signature was obviously not mine, but it was a reasonable copy of my handwriting. We immediately left the campsite and checked into one of the major hotels in Genoa. I used the McKenna passport for the formalities.

It seemed to me futile to carry on in Italy on the run and at the same time maintain contact with the people I loved. If journalists could track me down to Italy with all the precautions I had taken, what hope could there be for me to elude efforts made to find me by the IRA, MI6, British Customs, the Police, etc. I resolved to give myself up to the British authorities and hope that protective custody would be sufficient to keep me from harm.

On the morning of 28 October 1974 I booked a seat on a British Caledonian flight from Genoa to Gatwick, which departed at about 1.00pm. I left the hotel, posted the letter to my parents and took a bus to the airport. I cannot now remember in which name I booked the flight. On arrival at the airport I had a coffee and began a heavy drinking session. After several glasses of spirits I went through the passport check using the McKenna passport. I had no problems with Italian Immigration Officials and I settled down to some more drinking in the departure lounge bar. I also bought some cigarettes and a couple of bottles of Sambuca. The flight was called and I staggered drunkenly aboard the plane. During the flight I again ordered several drinks from the air hostess and began drinking from the Sambuca bottles. At one point newspapers were distributed and I was given a copy of the *Daily Mirror*. On the front page was a photograph of me and a headline 'He's alive'.

The article was full of the most amazing nonsense. It stated that I was living as a guest of the Mafia in Padua in a hideout known only to the Mafia. It went on to say that I was living undercover as a student, shielded and protected by Mafia gangsters. The article rehashed all the previous *Daily Mirror* reporting on me, including the same inaccuracies. On the inside pages were photographs of all my previous *Daily Mirror* front pages, photographs of Myfanwy and Rosie and a section of a photograph of those undergraduates who matriculated at Balliol in 1964, with my face ringed. Had they published the whole photograph it would have included Hamilton McMillan, my MI6 contact.

The aeroplane was full of people reading the 'Exclusive'. This, coupled with my drunken condition, produced in me a surreal mental state close to a complete crack-up. By the time the plane landed at Gatwick and passengers began to disembark I could hardly stand. My intention was to give myself up on arrival in England, but I could not bring myself to do it. I was stopped and questioned by both Immigration and Customs Officials, but cannot recall what they asked. All I can remember is giggling and laughing at

28/10/74.

Daily Mirror

TODAY IN YOUR EXCITING MIRROR

WHAT ALFIE'S BIRD SAYS ABOUT SEX..

PAGE THREE

EUROPE'S BIGGEST DAILY SALE

5p Monday, October 28, 1974 No. 22,011

Mystery man Howard Marks found by Mirror

HE'S ALIVE

MYSTERY man Howard Marks is alive . . . and living in Italy as a "guest" of the Mafia.

He was smuggled out of England before he was due to face a drugs trial six months ago.

Mirror Exclusive by EDWARD LAXTON in Padua, Italy

Link

Contact

MARKS—his silence was bought by the Mafia.

HOW TO STAY TRIM ON FIVE MEALS A DAY

PAGE 24

THE MEN WHO MAKE MODEL GIRLS CLICK

CENTRE PAGES

WATERHOUSE IN AMERICA

PAGE 10

WIN! WIN! WIN!

WITH YOUR RACING MIRROR

Scanlon rebels boost for Contract

HUGH SCANLON'S engineering union, the toughest and strongest critics of the Social Contract, are poised to give it a surprise boost.

Mirror Exclusive by ALAN LAW

SENIOR INDUSTRIAL CORRESPONDENT

Scrapped

Daily Mirror, 28 October 1974.

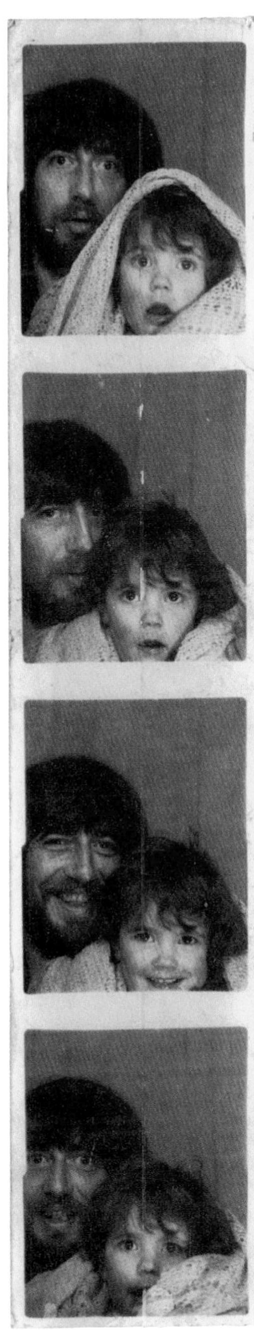

Howard enjoyed spending time with his family while on the run. This is Howard with his eldest daughter, born to him and Rosie Brindley.

them as I bumbled my way through their formalities. I followed the passengers through to Gatwick Railway Station and got on a train to Victoria. I was still drinking Sambuca when the train arrived at Victoria and some sort of homing instinct made me decide to go to Oxford.

I must have arrived in Oxford at about 9.00pm. I walked from Oxford Railway Station to St Aldates Police Station. When I got there, I was extremely confused. I could not get myself to believe that the events of the last six months, together with their coverage in the press, had really happened. I recall being under the impression that I was signing on for bail as I had done so many times in the past. I did not give myself up, nor did I attempt to sign on for bail, but I asked a police officer how I could get public transport to Northleigh, which was where Rosie Brindley, who had broken up with me for obvious reasons, was then living with our baby daughter Myfanwy, having bought a house with Julian Peto and his wife. The police officer told me it was too late to get a bus to Northleigh, but that I should try the taxi rank. I walked to the rank and came across a telephone box. I rang Rosie's number in Northleigh. There was no reply. I took a taxi to Leckford Road, which was the street in which Rosie and I had lived when I was abducted. At the end of the street was a pub called the Victoria Arms. The taxi stopped outside this pub and I went inside. A sudden silence fell upon the pub when I walked in. Inside were Julian and Richard Peto, who had just arrived back after driving from Genoa. This pub had been their local for a long time.

There were other people who I vaguely recognised. It was obvious, however, that a number of people recognised me. Julian and Richard simply exploded into helpless laughter. I asked where Rosie was and they told me that she and Myfanwy were at a party to which they themselves were going after the pub had finished serving. Rosie and Myfanwy had left the party by the time we arrived. I only recall sitting in the corner drinking punch and smoking hashish until Julian and his wife and children were ready to drive back to Northleigh. We left the party in the early hours of the morning. I was barely conscious and entirely unable to communicate. Rosie was shocked to see me and could tell that I was in an extremely delicate mental condition. She put me to bed immediately.

I later found out that Detective Chief Superintendent Fairweather had been to Northleigh a matter of hours before my arrival there to question Rosie. When I awoke I was no longer in Northleigh, but in bed in a flat off Walton Street, which was rented by Gale Mead, Richard Peto's girlfriend. At first I had no idea where I was and was feeling very ill indeed. I eventually worked out where I was and found a note from Julian saying that he would be home from work at 6.00pm and would explain everything. When he arrived, he told me that he and Rosie had carried me from her house to his car very early that morning and had driven me to Gale's flat. He explained that it would have been too dangerous and embarrassing to remain at Northleigh. He also told me that only the following day, Wednesday, 30 October, Judge Clarke would be making his final decision about my parents' bail sureties. The information had appeared in the article in Monday's *Daily Mirror*. I explained to Julian how I'd reached the decision to give myself up, not being confident of remaining in hiding from my enemies, and thinking that this would make it more likely that Judge Clarke would not rule that the sureties be forfeited. Julian made it clear to me that it was entirely my decision whether to give myself up or not, but he felt it would in no way influence the judge's ruling. This would be based on whether or not my disappearance was voluntary. For various reasons, including those which initially convinced me to remain in hiding and my very poor physical state at the time, I decided not to give myself up until after the court hearing.

Next day, Julian gave me news that the judge had decided that the sureties should not be forfeited. I felt happy and relieved for my parents. I was still feeling unwell and remained in bed the whole day. On 31 October, Julian brought me the newspapers, many of which contained reports of the previous day's proceedings at the Old Bailey. It stated that the police investigations as to my disappearance were at an end and it was not in the public interest to disclose details of my whereabouts. I found the reports rather puzzling. I resolved to carry on avoiding any confrontation with the authorities for the time being. I stayed at Gale's flat for a few days, trying to work out sensible plans for the future.

I had first met my future wife Judy in the autumn of 1971 at a dinner party given by an old friend of mine, Arthur Oppenheimer. When Rosie and I lived at Yarnton, Judy would often accompany Richard Lewis when he brought Rosie's daughter Emily up to us for the weekend. Apart from the above few occasions, I had not seen Judy at all until her visit to Gale's flat in Oxford with Rosie, Richard and Emily on 2 November 1974. During our meeting we discussed the problem of where I could stay. Judy at that time was living alone in her father's flat in Court Royal Mansions, Paston Place, Brighton. Judy suggested to me that I should move into her flat. I accepted. That evening we drove in Richard Lewis's car to Brighton. During my stay in Judy's flat we became very fond of each other and began to have an affair.

It became necessary to start using another name; I was nervous about being called 'Howard' in pubs, or in the company of strangers. The name 'Albert' began to be used. Firstly it was used largely as a joke, but gradually it began to stick in the abbreviated form of Albi. I decided to try to get a completely fresh identity and rent a place of my own with no direct connection with any of my known associates...

On or about Thursday, 17 April 1975 at about 4.00pm, I happened to look out of my window at the mosque, which was being built in Regent's Park, when I noticed a car draw up and park outside the block of flats. Out of the car tumbled four large gentlemen. They ran to the front entrance of the flats. I immediately formed the impression that they were 'heavies' who had come to get me. I slipped on my anorak and darted out of the flat and began running down the emergency stairs. I left behind all my money, false documents and possessions. The flat was on the ninth floor. When I reached the third floor I came out of the emergency stairwell and pressed the button for the automatic lift. I got into the lift and took it to the ground floor. When I emerged from the lift the four men were at the front entrance talking to the caretaker. I walked towards the front entrance which led on to the street. As I came to the doorway one of the men took out a flash camera and took a picture of me. I looked at him, feigning complete surprise and said, 'What the hell's going on?' One of the other men said, 'That's not him.' They let me through. I walked to the street and hailed a cab.

I then took a taxi to Judy's house in Gloucester Avenue. I arrived in a very nervous, frightened state, being by no means sure that whoever had discovered my whereabouts in Regent's Park had not also realised that I was frequently seeing Judy. Throughout the night, I sat up below the window ready to leave. The next day I decided to get out of London. Judy said that she would come with me and give up her job in London.

We caught a train to Liverpool. The choice of Liverpool was purely arbitrary. At the station we bought a copy of the *Daily Mirror*. Inside was a short article saying that I had returned to England and was living in a flat on the edge of Regent's Park. The article also summarised the *Daily Mirror*'s previous reports on my alleged involvement with the Mafia and my activities for MI6. Accompanying the article was a photograph of me taken when I was about 20 years old that luckily did not resemble my present appearance, which still featured a moustache and glasses. On arrival in Liverpool I stayed in a pub, while Judy went to look for suitable accommodation. After a couple of hours she found a room available for immediate occupation at a rent of only £6 per week. It was in a run-down area of Liverpool, near Shiel Park. The room was filthy, but I felt sure that I was safe and fell asleep as soon as we moved in. The next morning Judy bought a copy of Saturday's *Daily Mirror*. The entire front page was again devoted to me, with a large photograph which was clearly the one taken on leaving the block of flats two days previously. This was extremely disturbing. Luckily no one had yet seen me at the bedsit, so I shaved off my moustache, abandoned my spectacles, combed my hair back and plastered it with Brylcreem, which made me look completely different. I telephoned my parents, because I knew they would be worried.

We bought an old Bedford van for a couple of hundred pounds, basic camping equipment and set off for a campsite in North Wales. Before leaving, I opened up an answer service in Liverpool with a firm called Answering Limited in the name of John Phelan. This way I could receive messages and mail in that name and could give an address and telephone number to people without anyone knowing where I was. I would simply ring up every couple of days for messages.

19/4/75.

Daily Mirror

EUROPE'S BIGGEST DAILY SALE

5p Saturday, April 19, 1975 No. 22,154

INSIDE YOUR GREAT SPORTING MIRROR

WHIZZKID BUTCH, 18 IS CHELSEA'S SKIPPER
BACK PAGE

MIRROR PICTURE EXCLUSIVE ON Mr MYSTERY

THE FACE OF A FUGITIVE

DISGUISED: Mystery man Howard Marks, pictured while on the run in London last week. Picture: ERIC PIPER

By EDWARD LAXTON and TOM MERRIN

THIS is the new face of Howard Marks, the mystery man who has been on the run a year today.

Marks, disguised with a moustache and tinted glasses, was photographed last week in London, where he has been living in a luxury rented flat.

Neither the other residents nor the caretaker of the block in Park Road, Regent's Park, knew that the quiet man in Flat 92 was Marks. Yesterday senior Customs investigators raided the block and found the flat empty. Marks had left last Friday.

Now detectives from three forces have been alerted to step up the search for Marks, who is alleged to have worked for three separate bosses: the Mafia, the IRA and the British Secret Service.

Marks, a 29-year-old Oxford graduate, was arrested in Holland in November 1973.

He and five other people were accused of taking part in a multi-million pound drug smuggling plot.

Marks, who claimed that he had been pressed by the Secret Service into informing on the IRA, was allowed bail of £50,000.

But on the eve of his Old Bailey trial he vanished with a man who called at the flat in Lockford Road, Oxford, where he lived with 26-year-old Mrs. Rosemary Lewis and their two-year-old daughter Myfanwy.

Months later Marks turned up in Padua, Italy, living under cover as a student with a new name and a false passport.

Three men accused with Marks were jailed for four years at the Old Bailey and an American couple were deported.

But the judge later ruled after a secret hearing that Marks's father and a family friend should not forfeit their £40,000 share of his bail.

About two months ago Marks returned to Britain on a false passport. A friend said that he returned because he could not endure his existence abroad.

For the mysterious Howard Marks the price of freedom has been a life of fear as a fugitive.

NAP! NAP! NAP! THE MIRROR'S RACING EXPERTS STRIKE AGAIN BACK PAGE

PLUS MOORGATE THE FINAL VERDICT PAGES 2 and 11

PLUS SUPERGIRL YOUR LAST CHANCE TO ENTER PAGE 3

PLUS THE BEST WEEKEND TV GUIDE CENTRE PAGES

Daily Mirror, 19 April 1975.

The telephone number was given to my family and a number of my friends. Judy and I spent from the end of May to the end of September travelling around from one campsite to another. I purchased identity documents and began to live at 24 Marloes Road with Judy under the name of John Hayes. I began to grow a beard, but before doing so took photographs of myself in my clean-shaven Brylcreemed-hair appearance. I applied for a provisional licence in the name of John Hayes and eventually passed my test and obtained a full licence in that name. While living at Marloes Road, I began what was later to become an exhaustive study of the criminalisation of cannabis. It had always seemed to me completely idiotic that the use of a naturally growing plant (a use verified to be harmless by the simple fact that civilisations have used it for thousands of years without detrimental effects) could lead to people being locked up and having their lives ruined. In addition, the enforced prohibition yielded a profitable income for all kinds of criminal and terrorist organisations and a massive loss of revenue to the countries concerned.

In January 1976, Denys Irving told me that he would be able to offer me casual employment in the field of electronics, having found buyers for various devices which he had invented, mainly adaptations of synthesisers involving microchip circuitry. A great deal of this work was with Mike Ratledge, also a contemporary of mine at Oxford, who had since formed a successful pop group called The Soft Machine; Mike was voted by a *Melody Maker* poll as the best organist in the world. He had now left The Soft Machine, having been offered an independent contract by EMI, who were financing the building of a recording studio at his home. This required sophisticated electronics, which he commissioned Denys to work on. I, in turn, worked for Denys, figuring out the logic necessary to construct the circuit diagrams and finding out where to obtain the necessary microchips. Denys and I, independently of Mike Ratledge, also worked on electronic accessories to telephone equipment. We made pilot models of answer machines, remote telephone facilities, for example cordless extensions, and a relay machine. The relay machine was the most exciting of these inventions and one in which I had a vested interest, because one of its features was that I could give anyone a telephone number, the dialling of which would reach me wherever I was and the telephone number would not give any indication of my actual location.

My third and final source of income during this period arose through Penny Slinger. Penny was an artist who had studied under Max Ernst and was patronised by Sir Roland Penrose. Sometime before February 1976, Penny began living with a man named Nik Douglas, whom I met on a visit to Penny's flat in Gledhow Gardens. I found Nik a most interesting and talented man and we got on well together. His father had been one of the scientists responsible for the invention of the transistor, but had been killed during the Turkish invasion of Cyprus. Nik himself had an interesting curriculum vitae. He had been the spearhead of a movement which had the support of some Conservative MPs to make Lundy Island a home for Tibetans exiled by the Chinese invasion. The election of the Labour government in 1964 put a stop to this. Following this, he was road manager of The Cream for some time and then became a valuer for Sotheby's Oriental Department. He left for an extended stay of a number of years in the Himalayas to study Tibetan and Tantric practices. He acquired a priceless collection of oriental treasures, all of which were stored without any real security precautions in the flat at Gledhow Gardens. On his return from the Himalayas he wrote and had published two books on Tantric cultures and co-produced with Mick Jagger the film called *Tantra*. His collection of oriental art, together with the royalties he had received from the books published and an inheritance from his father, made him rich. After sitting up and talking to Nik for 36 hours non-stop, I confided in him who I was and asked if there was any possibility of being involved in his projects. He told me he would be delighted to have my assistance and would pay me for the work done.

At the beginning of April 1976 I was approached by an official of the Mexican government. Apart from the broad outlines of what was involved (working for a secret department formed to combat both terrorism and heroin smuggling), the only request made of me was that I get a false British passport which would stand up to the usual checks made at borders. I was told to expect further contact at the end of September 1976.

I had some notepaper printed up headed 'Insight Video' with the name John Hayes displayed on it. My next step was to go to Birmingham and book into a hotel. I then began searching for suitable office premises for Insight Video. While making enquiries, I maintained that the company's business was the retailing and hiring out of video machinery. I said that its head office was in Epsom and was thinking of branching out into the Midlands. I eventually found a firm in New Street, which rented offices by the day. I rented an office for about a month using the Epsom address as my reference. I then applied by post to the American Embassy for a visa for (→p60)

2 DESCRIPTION *SIGNALEMENT*

	Bearer Titulaire	Spouse Epouse
Occupation / Profession	Sales Representative	
Place of birth / Lieu de naissance	Norwich	
Date of birth / Date de naissance	27 Jun 44	/
Residence / Résidence	England	
Height / Taille	1.80 m	. m
Distinguishing marks / Signes particuliers		

CHILDREN *ENFANTS*

Name Nom	Date of birth Date de naissance	Sex Sexe
/		

Usual signature of bearer / Signature du titulaire

Usual signature of spouse / Signature de son épouse

3

Bearer / Titulaire

Spouse / Epouse

Photo

The bearer (and spouse, if included) should sign opposite on receipt

Howard's passport in the name of Mr Roy Green.

Old John does not feature greatly in *Mr Nice* because that was the way John would have wanted it. John lived in London, belonged to an acting agency for the ugly, drove an unlicensed London cab, picking people up and driving them around for free because he liked meeting people. He lived modestly, supporting his older brother who had special needs, his wife and son. John spent a lot of time in Nepal and his first work with Howard involved the exportation of Nepalese hash into Europe. He was not a dope smoker, but he loved the black market and reinvested his earnings from the Nepalese hashish exports in purchasing essential medical equipment for local communities in Nepal:

'Old John was a very tall, mature, masculine version of Mick Jagger. He was dressed like a Hell's Angel and adorned with necklaces, chains, beads, amulets and semi-precious stones. He was a walking bust. But Old John had never smoked a joint, and he bought and repaired stoves to make a living. His words were full of wisdom, but if one stopped concentrating on them for just one second, he seemed incoherent. Otherwise, his wisdom would seem to profoundly bypass all forms of convention and platitude. Old John's street sense was second to none; the streets of Fulham had given him that, as well as his accent. He was a keen soccer player and cricketer. His father had been educated at Oxford University. Old John had absolute integrity and honesty. No one could wish for a better, closer, or more trusted friend.

Jarvis rolled joints and made cups of tea. Old John smoked Tom Thumb cigars and drank whisky. We discussed the Welsh and English rugby teams. Wales had just slaughtered England 20–4 at Cardiff Arms Park. After an hour, I managed to bring up Nepal.

"You must have had an interesting time there, John."

"Interesting, yes, and they are superb people, the Nepalese, I promise you."

"Do you get many foreigners going there these days?"

"Well, the thing is there was this Englishman who told me he had nine talents. I told him I just had one: I could throw him out of the window. And he went and painted the outside of his house with religion, and then went to live inside the house. Madness."

I just about followed that one and took it to mean that Old John had a certain contempt for expatriate communities in the East. I had to get more to the point. "Did customs here give you a hard time when you came back?"

"Hard? No, not hard. I heard one of them say, 'Stop that cunt. I'm going to take him apart,' and he came up to me and said 'Excuse me, Sir,' and I said, 'Sir? No. Don't call me Sir. My name is Cunt. Please call me Cunt.' That dealt with him. Then the other one said, 'Can I see your passport?' and I said, 'It's not my passport, it's yours,' and gave it to him. He asked what I did in Nepal. I told him I was a barman. Vodka and lime. What would you like? He asked if I smoked any funny tobacco. I asked if he meant Kinabis, and he said it didn't matter. Then I caught a bus to Fulham."

I had to come straight to the point. "Can you send stuff out from Nepal by air, John?"

"Ooh! No. No. I can't do anything like that. No. No. No. Now, I know a man. He knows a man who might know."

"How much would it cost?"

"Well, money is the thing, and they always do things for a fair and honest price, I promise you."

"What's a fair price, John?"

"You will tell me, I'm quite sure."

"What will you want out of it, John?"

"If I help you do business, I'm sure you will give me a drink."

"A drink?"

"Yes. If a man does something for you, you give him a drink. Please, if everything goes well, give me a drink."

"Can you check that the quality will be all right?"

"I only smoke Tom Thumb, but I know a man who has a knife."

I took this as a yes. "Can you make it smell-proof?"

"Not if God made it smell."

"Do you know a man who can?"

"No. But if you do, let him come and do it, or give me instructions."

"How much can they send?"

"I should think it depends on when you want to do it by."

"Well, John, the Americans will want to do a ton as soon as possible."

"Now I was in America once, and the thing is that Americans will always want more, and there is no end to their madness. Lovely people, for sure, but you have to keep them in line. When my visa ran out, the immigration asked me why I wanted to extend it, and I said it was because I hadn't run out of money. He stamped it and said, 'Have a nice day.' So, if the Americans ask for a ton tomorrow, say you will do half a ton when Wales win the Triple Crown. That will deal with their madness, and everyone can get on with their lives. It saves all that tidding."

"Tidding?"

"Talking Imaginary Deals."' MN

both myself and Judy using passports I had acquired in the names of Mr and Mrs Tunnicliffe, supported with a reference from John Hayes. I purchased two return tickets from Birmingham to New York via London to facilitate the application. Within two weeks the passports arrived, each containing multiple indefinite visas.

During early November 1976, I was requested by the Mexican government official to arrive in Miami by the end of the month, where I would be met by my contact and co-worker. Judy and I took a British Airways flight from Birmingham to Brussels, stayed for one or two nights at the Holiday Inn there, took a train from Brussels to Frankfurt and a Lufthansa flight from Frankfurt to New York. We chose Birmingham from which to leave because my documents gave that place as my home address and place of work. We flew to Brussels because there was an audio-visual exhibition there and if questioned it fitted in with my ostensible occupation with Insight Video. I had also booked return flights from Brussels to Birmingham, and the flight from Frankfurt to New York, as precautions taken in the event of my true identity being realised by the authorities after I had landed in Brussels. The authorities would then be expecting me at either Brussels or Birmingham Airports rather than Frankfurt or New York. We stayed first at a hotel called The Executive and for the next few nights at the Holiday Inn, spending our time looking at the sights of New York, which I had never visited before.

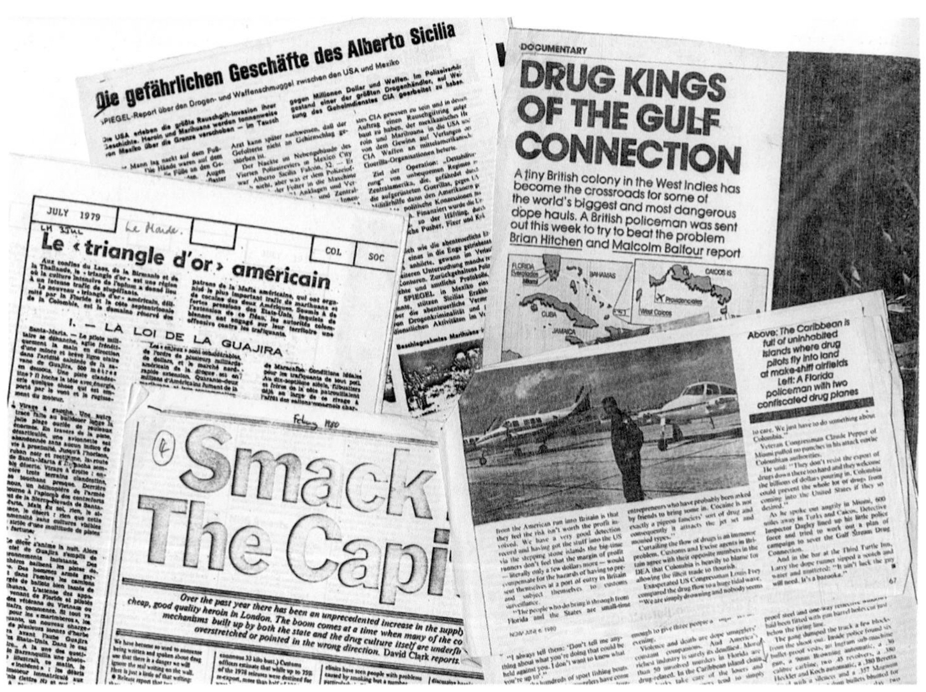

Die gefährlichen Geschäfte des Alberto Sicilia

DOCUMENTARY

DRUG KINGS OF THE GULF CONNECTION

A tiny British colony in the West Indies has become the crossroads for some of the world's biggest and most dangerous dope hauls. A British policeman was sent out this week to try to beat the problem Brian Hitchen and Malcolm Balfour report

Above: The Caribbean is full of uninhabited islands where drug pilots fly into land at make-shift airfields Left: A Florida policeman with two confiscated drug planes

JULY 1979 Le Monde

Le ‹triangle d'or› américain

I. — LA LOI DE LA GUAJIRA

Smack The Capi

Over the past year there has been an unprecedented increase in the supply of cheap, good quality heroin in London. The boom comes at a time when many of the co mechanisms built up by both the state and the drug culture itself are underfi overstretched or pointed in the wrong direction. David Clark reports.

This is a sample of the articles on Latin American smuggling routes that Howard read while on remand. By April 1981, he was well into his trial preparations, reading huge amounts on Mexico, a country which he had in fact never visited, but personal knowledge of which was the key plank in his defence. If Howard could persuade the court that he had worked for the Mexican Secret Service, he would be able to explain away large amounts of money. He would also be able to justify his interest in the Colombian importation. He wrote to his parents during his preparations:

'It's now seven in the morning on Easter Monday. I've been up for a while doing my exercises and will shortly have to start work. It's a fine morning and the birds are singing. Usually between my exercises and starting work I work on my case. The exercises I do in the morning are called Surya Namaskar. One is meant to do it at the bank of a river or a lake, facing east but at the moment I'm only practising!... You are right about being engrossed with my forthcoming trial. It's so difficult to think let alone concentrate on anything else and it's no good pretending that I'm not very nervous and worried about it. You will be glad to know that I'm still not smoking. It's now over five weeks. I still have the craving and don't feel any healthier but at least I've demonstrated my will power to myself as I know I'm in the hardest possible circumstances to make the attempt.'

Sometime after 20 November Judy remained in New York to search for an office with living accommodation, while I flew to Miami to keep my appointment with the Mexican official. My first task was to get an American driver's licence in the name of Tunnicliffe. This was done with the help of the official, who provided me with accommodation in Miami, the address of which was used for obtaining the licence. The licence was not a false one in the sense of being a forgery. I took my test, both written and practical, and provided my Tunnicliffe passport as documentary proof of identity. I was also given membership of the 'Mutiny', a well-known haunt to all kind of drugs smugglers, and membership of the Costa del Sol Tennis Club, a place frequented by individuals the Mexican government was interested in. I was told which days and evenings to turn up at these clubs and had also to take tennis lessons. I became quite proficient at tennis. The purpose of turning up was not to befriend anyone in particular, but simply to show my face. I had previously made it clear to my new employers that I was not prepared to work against people involved purely in the smuggling of marijuana. They respected my position and understood that it did not conflict with their specific aims.

The only other requirement made of me was to read as much as possible on the recent political history of Mexico, concentrating on the September 23rd League of terrorists. The September 23rd League is named after the date of an attack on military barracks at Ciudad Madero, Chihuahua, in 1965. The League had flourished particularly during 1975 when about 40 people, including a dozen policemen, were killed and many more injured by their activities. It had always been assumed that the League was on the extreme left in its ideology. This was indicated by its targets – industrial plants and law-enforcement officers; its financing methods – bank robberies; and its method of operating, ie explosive devices, accompanied by propaganda leaflets. This assumption first began to be questioned towards the end of 1975 when a number of people participating in a demonstration by the Worker Student Peasant Coalition of Oaxaca were shot and killed by members of the League. During the spring of 1976 the League was particularly active, killing over a dozen policemen and kidnapping the daughter of the Belgian Ambassador, who was released on payment of half a million dollars' ransom. Investigations into these events confirmed that the members of the League were right-wing terrorists.

At this time López Portillo was inaugurated as President and 'Operation Condor', the joint US/Mexico Anti-Heroin Drive, was implemented. 'Operation Condor' was designed to replace the abortive Mexican Opium Poppy Eradication Programme initiated in November 1975. After the termination of the 'French Connection' in 1972 and the virtual extinction of Turkey's opium production in 1973, Mexico became the United States' major supplier of heroin. Poppies had been brought to and planted in Mexico by immigrant Chinese labourers decades ago. All that the Eradication Programme managed to achieve was to move the poppy growers from the provinces in northern Mexico to those further south. 'Operation Condor' was headed by Carlos Aguilar Garza and the intention was to eradicate poppy fields by aerial spraying. At the end of 1976, however, under intense pressure from America, which included massive financial incentives, the Mexican authorities were persuaded to divert their attention from the spraying of poppy fields to the spraying of marijuana fields. The spray used was Paraquat, a British patented chemical known to cause pulmonary fibrosis. Outlandishly high prices were paid for this highly toxic chemical to be heavily sprayed on marijuana fields, while poppy fields were left untouched. This action was the subject of severe criticism in Mexico. Criticism of the policy reached climactic levels when it was suspected that there was CIA involvement with heroin and arms smuggling benefiting right-wing terrorist organisations in Mexico.

My work with the Mexican government continued until the beginning of August 1977. I will not elaborate any further on the details of this work until I have received confirmation from my superiors as to what it is prudent to disclose. On this visit I discovered that Judy was pregnant. She decided to return to Europe and stay with her brother Patrick and his wife at their Mill in the Dordogne, France, until my work in Mexico finished. Judy was very concerned that the baby should be born in England. Natasha, Judy's sister who was then still living in London, flew out to France bringing Judy's real passport to the Mill. Judy then flew from Paris to London, leaving her Tunnicliffe passport in the Mill, where it has remained ever since. French authorities searched the Mill at the request of British Customs in May 1980 and may well have taken it then. I followed Judy a couple of days later, using my Tunnicliffe passport.

During the time that I was working for the Mexican government, Nik Douglas had made quite a collection of newspaper articles about the recent exploits of James McCann. It appeared that during May 1977 he had been arrested by the Canadian authorities and visited by British Intelligence Agents in Vancouver. McCann maintained that he was not McCann, but someone called Kennedy and on the strength of this was released on bail, from which he promptly absconded. He then settled in the South of France, somewhere near Marseilles, where a kidnap attempt was made on him by the German authorities. Apparently the French police caught the German authorities attempting to kidnap him and arrested everyone. Eventually McCann was released and allowed to live in France, although the whole episode is still shrouded in mystery.

Shortly before Christmas 1977 I was alone in the flat with Judy and our baby, Amber, when the telephone rang. To my shock, James McCann was on the other end of the line. To this day I have absolutely no idea how he got hold of my number, but it was definitely him. He told me that unless I paid him £50,000 he was going to destroy my wife and child and blow up my parents' house in Kenfig Hill. Had it not been McCann I would have taken the call as the ravings of a lunatic, but McCann was quite capable of carrying out such threats and clearly felt that he had an old score to settle with me. I immediately told Judy. She panicked at the news. Her grandfather, a Catholic policeman in Belfast named Patrick Murphy, had been murdered by the IRA and she had always throughout our relationship been terrified of the threat that they held over me. Judy and I were again stuck without anywhere to live. Eventually we found a flat in January 1978 at 169 Queensgate, London SW7 and rented it in the name of Mr and Mrs Albert Lane. I continued working for Nik Douglas, but was very worried as to how long it would be before McCann tracked me down again.

At the beginning of February 1978, I was still living in Queensgate with Judy. I worked mostly at Carlisle Street and was leading a normal social life. I was attending parties, exhibitions, seeing old friends and keeping in touch with my family. This may have been foolhardy given the recent threats from McCann, but it was the way I wanted to live. I did, however, keep my Queensgate address and telephone number entirely private. Nik and Penny were very keen that Judy and I should join them in the United States so that we could live and work in New York. I was also keen on the idea, but was worried about which passport I could use to make the journey there. Although the Tunnicliffe passport had proved itself and still carried multiple indefinite visas for the United States, I could not really risk using it for fear of the name having become known by various terrorist organisations. In January 1978, the Mexican city hideout of the September 23rd League had been stormed under the personal leadership of the Mexican Chief of Police, Dorazo. There was always a two-way channel of information during such operations and my name could easily have featured. Also, some of my activities could well have been frowned upon by the CIA, who might then also have adduced that Howard Marks and Anthony Tunnicliffe were the same person. I decided that the best and safest solution was to get yet another fresh passport. I obtained one in the name of Donald Nice.

On New Year's Day, 1979, Judy and I attended a party given by John Nicolson. There I met an actor/director, called Tom Baker, and the pop singer PJ

Utility bills in the name of Donald Nice of World Wide Entertainments, headquartered on the corner of Carlisle Street and Dean Street in Soho, London.

1747

2

1 | TO BE COMPLETED BY ALL APPLICANTS (in block capitals) - See Note 1

State Mr., Mrs., Miss, Ms or title MR

Surname NICE

Christian names (or forenames) in full DONALD CHRISTOPHER

Maiden surname

Occupation SALES REP.

State whether married, single, widowed or divorced MARRIED

Town of birth DONCASTER

Date of birth 25-12-44

Country of birth ENGLAND

Country of residence ENGLAND

Age last birthday 33

Height 5 ft. 11 ins.

Present address 30 STEVENSON RD LARKMAN NORWICH

Height (see Note 1) 1·80 metres

Visible distinguishing marks

County NORFOLK Postcode/district

Has your name been changed otherwise than by marriage or adoption? (Please answer Yes or No NO). If so, state your previous name

Daytime telephone No.

2 | PARTICULARS OF WIFE/HUSBAND IF SHE/HE IS TO BE INCLUDED IN YOUR PASSPORT (in block capitals)—See Note 2

Surname

Occupation

Christian names (or forenames) in full

Town of birth

Date of birth

Maiden surname

Country of residence

Country of birth*

Height ft. ins.

Town and country of marriage

Height (see Note 1) metres

Date of marriage†

Visible distinguishing marks

* If ... family passport is a British subject or a citizen of the United Kingdom and Colonies by descent detail ... (See also Note 5.) Where the applicant has such status by descent he she should complete Section 5.
† If ... than once please give details of previous marriage(s) in Section 13 on page 4. See Note 2 of Notes

3 | ... REN UNDER 16 AND AT PRESENT IN THE UNITED KINGDOM TO BE INCLUDED ... block capitals)—See Note 3

Chri...	Surname	Town and country of birth	Date of birth	Relationship to applicant

If child(ren) born outside England, Scotland, Wales and Northern Ireland please state father's nationality and citizenship at date of child(ren)'s birth

4 | PARTICULARS OF NATURALISATION OR REGISTRATION—See Note 4

	Applicant	Wife/Husband	Children
Number of document			
Place of issue			
Date of issue			

5 | APPLICANT BORN OUTSIDE ENGLAND, SCOTLAND, WALES AND NORTHERN IRELAND—See Note 5

(A) **Full names of applicant's father***

His town and country of birth His date of birth

Father's nationality (and citizenship) at date of applicant's birth

If applicant's father a British subject or citizen of the United Kingdom and Colonies by naturalisation or registration

No. of his document Place of issue Date of issue

Full names of applicant's mother

Her town and country of birth Her date of birth

(B) **If applicant born in a foreign country and the birth was registered at a British Consulate**

Name of British Consulate Date of registration

* If applicant's father born outside England, Scotland, Wales and Northern Ireland, the town, country, and date of birth of applicant's paternal grandfather, or details of applicant's paternal grandfather's claim to British nationality should be stated in Section 13, on page 4.

In 1978, after 'Lebanese Sam' got busted with hashish destined for New York from Lebanon, Howard decided a new identity was in order. This is a photocopy of Howard's application for a passport in the name of Donald Nice, from the prosecution exhibits in Howard's 1981 trial at the Old Bailey.

2nd NAE

WORLD WIDE ENTERTAINMENTS INC

EUROPEAN HEAD OFFICE

OUR REF: DN/MI

YOUR REF:

18 CARLISLE STREET
LONDON W1V 5RJ

Tel: 01-437 4417

November 7 1979

Lochaber Estate Agents
38 High Street
Fort William

Dear Sirs,

During the winter period our company will be producing a semi documentary film located in the Western Isles and set in the latter half of the last century.

We intend to rent a large lochside property capable both of accomodating the staff (about 6 to 10 people) and of featuring in certain parts of the set.

We would wish to assume tenancy by about December 1st of this year and stay for a minimum of three months. Adequate funds are available for the right property.

If you have anything which you might consider suitable for our purposes, would you please let me know as soon as possible,

Yours faithfully,

Donald Nice.

MANAGING DIRECTOR: DONALD NICE

In November 1979 Donald Nice, of World Wide Entertainments, needed a property with access to lochs, ostensibly for filming purposes.

Proby. I was introduced to them as Albi and I got on with both extremely well. Tom Baker explained that he was in the middle of making a film entitled *Life After Elvis*, the theme being the extent to which Elvis Presley continued to 'live on' after his death. He had already filmed a great deal of footage in Memphis of the mourners at the Elvis Presley grave and had filmed Elvis Presley imitation acts in Las Vegas. He also had footage of Elvis Presley lookalikes including those who had undertaken plastic surgery. Baker was now intending to film similar phenomena in Europe including Elvis Presley fan club conventions and a PJ Proby concert. He had already scripted sequences featuring PJ Proby. Proby, an American, had been a close friend of Elvis Presley and was also responsible for singing the demonstration records from which Presley worked in the initial stages of his career. During the sixties Proby had a successful career in Great Britain, achieving several Number One hit records. He was a notoriously difficult artist for any manager to handle because of his acute alcohol problem and his compulsive nature. He had recently been dismissed from the stage show of *Elvis* at the Astoria Theatre. Baker told me that he was looking for a suitable recording and rehearsal studio. I told him that I had an interest in a recording studio which was frequented by session musicians of high quality. I offered the services of Archipelago. They both approved of the set-up. We all exchanged telephone numbers after tentative prices for the work had been discussed. The sum of all these different amounts was to be regarded as World Wide Entertainments' total investment in *Life After Elvis*.

Throughout this period I was heavily involved with the film. I co-ordinated locations and the concert, which was to be held at the Nashville Public House in West Kensington, attending and assisting at all rehearsals and recording sessions. One of the scripted sequences needed to be shot at a punk rockers' pub. A friend of mine, John Leaves, kept such a pub in Oxford, 'The Oranges and Lemons', and I made the arrangements with him. The PJ Proby concert at the Nashville on 29 January turned out to be a disaster. Although the supporting acts performed well, PJ Proby was too drunk to perform. The last half-hour of the concert was therefore a complete shambles. I even took the stage myself for a while and sang a couple of Elvis Presley songs and was followed by other members of the audience doing imitations of Elvis. The whole chaos was filmed and recorded on videotape and reduced to some sequences which we included in the final film. At one point John Nicolson came and took me off the stage because he thought that for me to give a public performance while I was on the run was both foolish and dangerous. Eventually, some weeks later, we were able to film Proby miming to the recorded songs at a film studio and superimposed this sequence to fit in with the Nashville concert. Mr Proby was grateful to me for my assistance and over the months we developed a strange friendship. He asked if I would manage him. I agreed, thinking that this would establish Donald Nice in the entertainment world. He gave me tapes of all his unreleased recordings and we began planning a further recording session. He told me that he had quite a following on the Continent, particularly in Germany and Holland, and that this should be further exploited. We set up a promotional campaign with the official PJ Proby fan club in Holland. Unfortunately my PJ Proby management career went no further because – as I will explain later – my identity was revealed to the world at large and I severed my connection with World Wide Entertainments.

At first we lived in Richmond, then at Queensgate. At both these places I used the name Albert Lane to give the impression that I was married to Judy. Our daughter Amber was born in October 1977 and I stayed in England until about April 1978. Throughout this period I worked for Nik Douglas and Penny Slinger. The work consisted of buying, selling, exhibiting and evaluating oriental antiques; selling and arranging exhibitions of Ms Slinger's paintings; creating, producing and publishing books. The enterprises we engaged in were highly successful. Due to my 'unofficial' existence, there is little written evidence of my involvement in the above projects. However, I do appear in the list of acknowledgements for *Encyclopaedia of Sexual Secrets* under the name of Albion Jennings. (I used Jennings as my surname when registering Amber's birth.) I met many people during the course of this work, including RD Laing and Lyall Watson. Ms Slinger was made Amber's godmother.

Sometime during May 1979, Tom Baker and I left England for Eire. We flew from Heathrow to Dublin. I used the name Nice. The purpose of the visit was to film an Irish group composed entirely of Elvis Presley impersonators. We were joined after a day or so by Judy and Amber. We stayed at the Shelbourne Hotel in Dublin. One day, I was approached in the bar by someone claiming to be an associate of James McCann who told me that McCann wanted to see me to discuss old times. He was friendly, spoke with an educated Dublin accent and said that there was nothing to worry about. I pretended to be accommodating and told him that I would be staying at the hotel for at least a week. I went into an extreme state of shock and immediately left the hotel with Judy and Amber. Judy and I left Dublin for an island in a car rented by Judy. While I was on this holiday I learnt after telephoning a friend that a London Weekend Television programme about me was being made. I decided that it would be better if Judy and I went abroad. We made immediate arrangements to fly from Dublin to Milan on the Donald Nice passport, staying with Patrick Lane in Lugano until the television programme had been shown.

The programme was cancelled at the last minute, even though it had been advertised in the *Daily Telegraph* the same morning. My relief was short-lived when I saw an article by Stephen Scott published in the *New Statesman*, essentially a summary of the proposed television programme containing the same inaccuracies, together with a further inaccurate statement to the effect that I had stayed at McCann's house at Greystones, near Dublin. The article went on to name the Security Services legal adviser who had confirmed my MI6 involvement as a Mr Bernard Shelton. An article about why the programme was not shown appeared in *Time Out*. The *New Statesman* article was a devastating blow to any hopes of continuing my existence as Donald Nice of World Wide Entertainments. I would have to take steps to obtain yet another false passport.

A few days after my arrival back in England, James McCann was arrested just outside Dublin in possession of a revolver and a lorry containing half a ton of Thai cannabis. There was a large item about it on the 6pm news. I thought that this was a mixed blessing. I was out of danger from him for the time being, but was worried about the consequences of any further publicity. For the next few weeks I remained indoors, anticipating that sensational news features would follow in the wake of the *New Statesman* article and McCann's arrest. However, a new wave of publicity was not sparked off and I began to relax. At the end of September a letter arrived for me from my previous employers in Mexico asking me to call them. They wanted me to undertake another delicate project. I was asked to attend a meeting in Mexico in November. I was assured that the Tunnicliffe passport

Howard, as Donald, was best man at the wedding of filmmaker Peter Whitehead (his films include several documentaries with the Rolling Stones and the documentary of 1960s London *Tonite Let's all Make Love in London*) to Dido Goldsmith, daughter of environmentalist Teddy Goldsmith. Bianca Jagger was Dido's maid of honour, much to Howard (Donald)'s delight. A keen egg collector, Peter was invited by Prince Khalid al-Faisal to assist in building the Al Faisal Centre, the world's largest falcon-breeding establishment.

Surveillance photograph, courtesy of Her Majesty's Customs & Excise. In 1979, Howard set about organising the biggest ever importation of cannabis (15 tons) into Britain, from Colombia, by boat. The load had to be transferred into smaller boats to navigate the sea lochs of the Inner Hebrides. This was a new venture for Howard, not only on account of the size, but also because of the source of the cannabis. Investigative journalists Sara Walden and Paul Eddy were subsequently to say of it:

'Combs, Howard's partner, blamed himself for Marks' arrest. The Colombian marijuana deal, which Combs had helped to organise, was probably doomed from the start because it brought into stark conflict the amateurism of the British dope distribution business with the much more demanding standard of the American suppliers. The marijuana had arrived on the west coast of Scotland at the end of December 1979. It was vastly more than the British distribution networks were used to dealing with and it saturated the market.' HMP

was 'safe' to use and that during my visit I would either be paid or loaned a substantial sum of money.

On Christmas Eve I invited a few friends for drinks including the film producer Peter Whitehead. He brought with him Dido Goldsmith, whom he had recently befriended, his daughter and a man introduced to me as Edward. From what I could gather, Edward lived in Pytchley and was in charge of looking after Whitehead's falcons, worth hundreds of thousands of pounds (Whitehead was in charge of the Saudi Arabian royal family's falcon breeding centre). A few days after Christmas, Whitehead announced his intention to marry Dido and asked me to be best man. I agreed. In late January, Whitehead and Ms Goldsmith became married, with myself as witness and best man. The wedding was held at Kensington Register Office and the reception at the Caviar Bar, Knightsbridge. It was a high-society affair. I used the name Donald Albertson. I had no identification in this name, it was chosen simply to resolve the difficulty of some people knowing me as Albie and others knowing me as Donald.

With hindsight, it is clear to me that the cannabis from Colombia was under way in December 1979, and that the yacht, the *Carob*, was on the high seas. I had no idea of this at the time. I spent a quiet December.

There is nothing in the prosecution evidence that jogs my memory as to what I was doing. On New Year's Eve, Judy, Amber and I stayed in the house. I believe that this is the day that Customs officers suspect that the 15 tons of cannabis imported on the *Carob* actually arrived at Kerrera.

On or about 1 February 1980, Judy, Amber and myself, using the name Albertson, took up residency in Hans Court, Knightsbridge. On 22 February, we held an engagement party. At first, this was to be hosted by Patrick at Orme Square to prevent too many people knowing where I lived, but it was eventually decided to give the party at Hans Court. Our families and friends attended. On 25 March, McCann was acquitted of his charges. This was an unpleasant surprise. Not only did he suspect me of attempting to assassinate him, but he had also accused me of being responsible for his arrest in August 1979. During the weekend of 28–30 March, there were various news reports on the radio and in the press that a large amount of herbal cannabis had been washed ashore in the vicinity of Oban. □

Surveillance photograph, courtesy of Her Majesty's Customs & Excise. Howard is leaning on the phone box with his back to the camera.

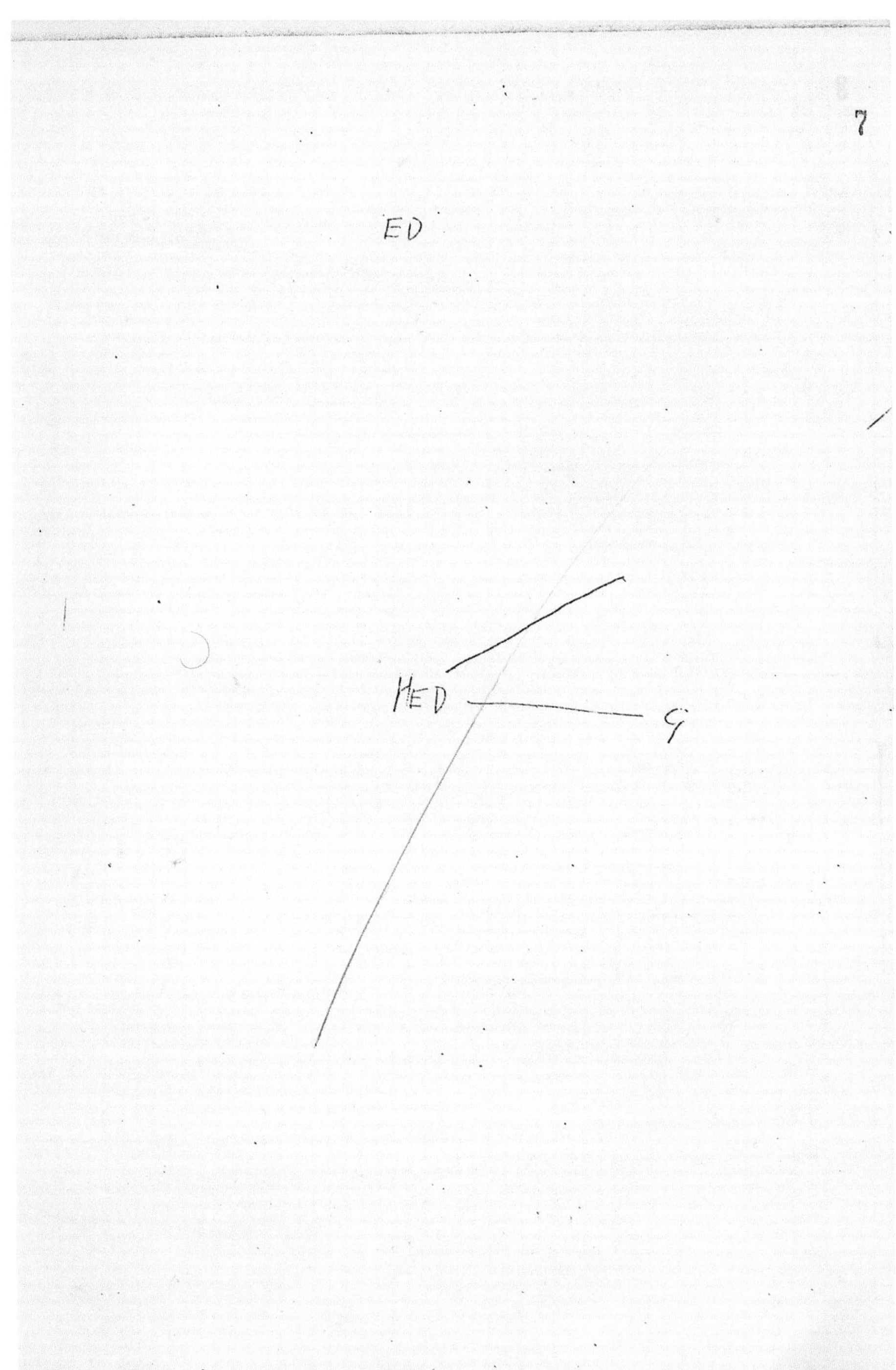

These diagrams are from the bundle of prosecution trial exhibits and were created during the course of Howard's police interview. The diagram on the left is by Customs Officer Baker, in which he illustrates how the evidence puts Howard at the centre of the importation. The second is Howard's first attempt at suggesting otherwise. It clearly dawned on Howard that this was not going to be easy to get out of.

(↓) Howard hired the same solicitor who had represented him before his disappearance in 1974, Bernie Simons. This is a note to Bernie from his legal clerk, David Walsh (DW). In it, David explains that Customs wanted to know if the defence required all of the seized cannabis retained for the trial, or if they could now destroy it, preserving just a sample for trial purposes, given the threat posed to the public by its continued presence on the British Isles. The incinerator used to destroy cannabis at that time was referred to in police circles as 'the Queen's Pipe'. David, on behalf of Howard's co-defendant, Nick Cole, said he had no objection to its destruction. He points out in his postscript that the amount in question was some 10 tons.

15/1

Note to Bms from DW

re MARKS/COLE.

Dear Bernie,

Customs SOLR, Mr HUGHES phoned today.

Says the confiscated dope is now a health hazard; the deadly drug has reacted with seawater producing noxious gas. (Can this be true?)

Anyway wants destroy most of it keeping samples. Do we object?
Sd. I didn't for Cole and wd. ask you. If you don't, can he have a letter ASAP so this threat to the national health can be eradicated?

DW.

P.S. They have 10 tons.....

(→) These cassette recordings of the International Cannabis Legalisation Conference in Amsterdam, February 1980, were seized from Howard's home following his arrest. Public support for its legalisation appeared to be gathering momentum around this time. In a letter to his parents on 30 October 1980 from Brixton Prison Howard writes 'This week the whole of the *Ecologist* is devoted to legalising marijuana with articles by eminent ecologists, economists and doctors – the most learned and erudite body of men to support this for some time. All this "Hempathy" is very welcome. (Sorry couldn't resist.)' While on remand in Brixton, Howard also became interested in prison reform, writing home in February 1981 'One thing that I have learnt over the last nine months is how utterly desperate is the need for penal reform in this country. Prison should surely be the last resort only for people whose behaviour defies our minds to find an alternative cause of action. Lack of funds for alternatives to prison is no argument as the vast waste of the already allocated funds for the prison department and even vaster waste of funds in other directions shows. One may not have any criminal tendency on entering into prison but it is virtually impossible to leave without them. One is completely immersed in a criminal environment and the most callous deviousness has to be employed to get the most basic necessities. How can this possibly reform anyone?'

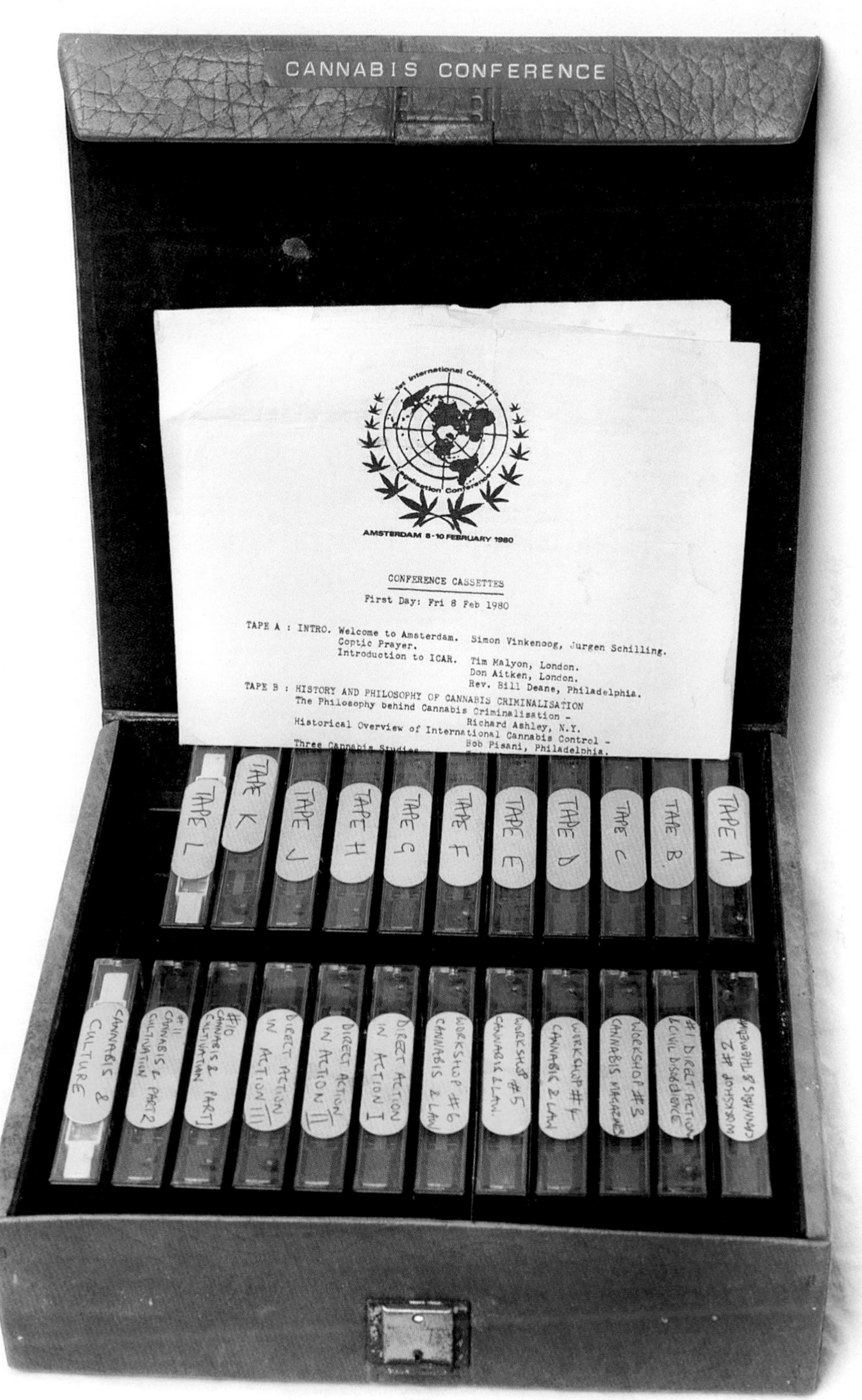
CANNABIS CONFERENCE
AMSTERDAM 8-10 FEBRUARY 1980
CONFERENCE CASSETTES
First Day: Fri 8 Feb 1980
TAPE A : INTRO. Welcome to Amsterdam. Simon Vinkenoog, Jurgen Schilling.
Coptic Prayer.
Introduction to ICAR. Tim Malyon, London.
Don Aitken, London.
Rev. Bill Deane, Philadelphia.
TAPE B : HISTORY AND PHILOSOPHY OF CANNABIS CRIMINALISATION
The Philosophy behind Cannabis Criminalisation -
Richard Ashley, N.Y.
Historical Overview of International Cannabis Control -
Bob Pisani, Philadelphia.
TAPE L
TAPE K
TAPE J
TAPE H
TAPE G
TAPE F
TAPE E
TAPE D
TAPE C
TAPE B
TAPE A
CANNABIS & CULTURE
DIRECT ACTION IN ACTION III
DIRECT ACTION IN ACTION II
DIRECT ACTION IN ACTION I
WORKSHOP #6 CANNABIS & LAW
WORKSHOP #4 CANNABIS & LAW

Judy was pregnant with their second daughter, Francesca, while Howard was on remand in Brixton. Regulations provided that in these circumstances, a remand prisoner could be allowed out to marry. Wedding arrangements were made and Howard was released for the ceremony alone, though the guards subsequently decided they could all go on to the reception party afterwards. On 30 July 1980, Howard wrote to his parents of the wedding:

'I'm so glad that Judy pursued with the arrangements for a proper reception otherwise I'd have had to come back straight away after the service. It was so kind of the officers to allow me to go to the reception. I'll never forget them for that. You looked so well and happy throughout the proceedings it was a joy to me. It's strange having my daughters as bridesmaids. Halfway through the service, I turned around and Amber caught my eye – she gave me a smile and what appeared to be a knowing wink. I expect Judy has told you that I am now a cleaner here in the prison. This makes the day pass much more quickly and also earns me some money. Besides keeping me fitter, it also makes me realise there is a strange sort of dignity in manual labour. "Idleness is the enemy of the soul." I hope that I'll be good enough to maintain the job. There's an art in everything – even mopping the floors.'

4

Regina v Dennis Howard Marks

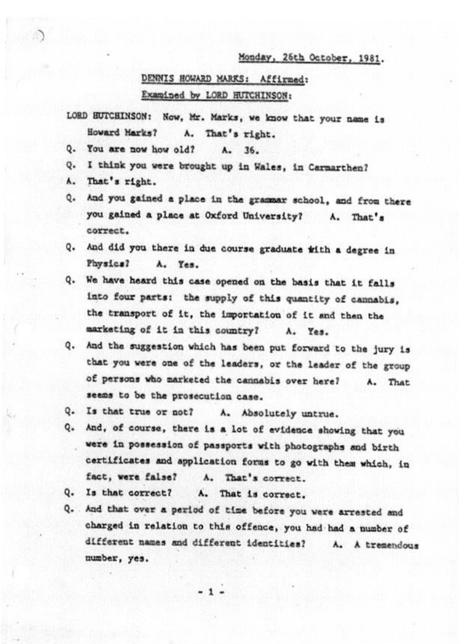

Monday, 26th October, 1981.

DENNIS HOWARD MARKS: Affirmed:
Examined by LORD HUTCHINSON:

LORD HUTCHINSON: Now, Mr. Marks, we know that your name is Howard Marks? A. That's right.
Q. You are now how old? A. 36.
Q. I think you were brought up in Wales, in Carmarthen?
A. That's right.
Q. And you gained a place in the grammar school, and from there you gained a place at Oxford University? A. That's correct.
Q. And did you there in due course graduate with a degree in Physics? A. Yes.
Q. We have heard this case opened on the basis that it falls into four parts: the supply of this quantity of cannabis, the transport of it, the importation of it and then the marketing of it in this country? A. Yes.
Q. And the suggestion which has been put forward to the jury is that you were one of the leaders, or the leader of the group of persons who marketed the cannabis over here? A. That seems to be the prosecution case.
Q. Is that true or not? A. Absolutely untrue.
Q. And, of course, there is a lot of evidence showing that you were in possession of passports with photographs and birth certificates and application forms to go with them which, in fact, were false? A. That's correct.
Q. Is that correct? A. That is correct.
Q. And that over a period of time before you were arrested and charged in relation to this offence, you had had a number of different names and different identities? A. A tremendous number, yes.

- 1 -

The text for this chapter comes from extracts of transcripts of Howard's two-month trial at the Old Bailey in the autumn of 1981. Howard was represented by Lord Jeremy Hutchinson of Lullington, and his then Junior, Stephen Solley. Hutchinson was a brilliant and famous QC, making his first contribution to history by successfully defending Penguin Books for publishing D.H. Lawrence's *Lady Chatterley's Lover*. His Honour Judge Peter Mason presided over the trial, which was heard by a jury. Before Howard took the stand, Hutchinson had already succeeded in demolishing much of the prosecution case. Officer Stephenson, for example, claimed that he had seen Howard meeting with the two Americans at the Dorchester Hotel. Jeremy subjected him to a scathing cross-examination:

'How did you know it was Mr Marks in Mr Nath's hotel room?'

'I viewed him through the keyhole.'

'Ah, so you recognised him by his knees, Mr Stephenson.'

LORD HUTCHINSON: Now, Mr Marks, we know that your name is Howard Marks?
A: That's right.
Q: You are now how old?
A: 36.
Q: I think you were brought up in Wales, in Carmarthen?
A: That's right.
Q: And you gained a place in the grammar school, and from there you gained a place at Oxford University?
A: That's correct.
Q: And did you there in due course graduate with a degree in Physics?
A: Yes.
Q: We have heard this case opened on the basis that it falls into four parts: the supply of this quantity of cannabis; the transport of it; the importation of it; and then the marketing of it in this country.
A: Yes.
Q: And the suggestion which has been put forward to the jury is that you were one of the leaders, or the leader of this group of persons who marketed the cannabis over here?
A: That seems to be the prosecution case.
Q: Is that true or not?
A: Absolutely untrue.
LORD HUTCHINSON: In 1971 did you, with three friends of yours, form a limited company in relation to premises in Oxford – a dress shop called AnnaBelinda?
A: That's correct, yes.
Q: Did that shop make quite a substantial success?
A: It was very successful, yes. It is still very successful.
Q: Is it still in existence?
A: Yes, but I don't have anything to do with it.
Q: It has become quite a well-known name in the fashion trade?
A: It has by now.
Q: And having started and you being involved with that, were you involved as a quite separate matter with dealing in stamps?
A: Yes. Yes, I had a philately business there, as well, although that wasn't anything like such a success.
Q: Now, during 1972 and 1973 did the idea of expanding

with other branches of that shop business into Europe arise?

A: Yes, it did. Initially we intended to branch out into this country, and then the idea of branching out to Europe became more appealing and we made many enquiries in that direction.

Q: As a result of that, did you go to Amsterdam at some time?

A: Yes. Yes.

Q: Now, while you were at the University, did you come into contact with people who smoked cannabis?

A: Oh, yes, a great number.

Q: And did you, yourself, smoke it?

A: A great deal.

JUDGE MASON: Can I just say – perhaps I need not – but if you consider the answer to any question may incriminate you, you are free not to answer it.

A: Thank you.

LORD HUTCHINSON: Did you have a friend who got into trouble during this period in relation to drugs in Germany?

A: Yes. Yes.

Q: Was he charged out there for possession of drugs?

A: He was charged with possession about March 1970, somewhere around there. About that sort of time.

Q: I am going to say this all the way through asking questions. If anybody wants to know the name, are you prepared to write it down?

A: On some of the occasions.

Q: There is no need to involve anybody who is not involved here. Did that person get into trouble again in early 1973 in Morocco?

A: Yes, he did. He was arrested by the Moroccan police. It might have been late 1972, it was that sort of period.

Q: Why I am asking that is, at some moment, as a result of his arrest out there, were you asked by him to contact somebody?

A: I was asked by his wife.

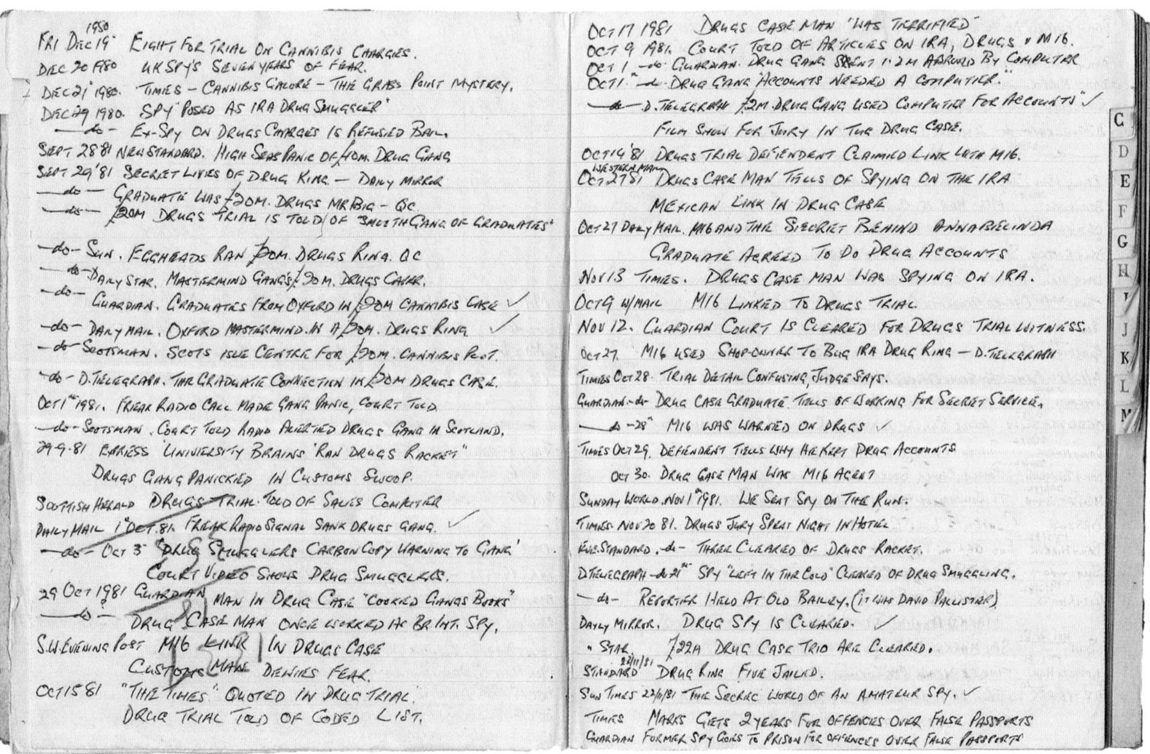
FRI DEC 19 1980 EIGHT FOR TRIAL ON CANNIBIS CHARGES.
DEC 20 1980 UK SPY'S SEVEN YEARS OF FEAR.
DEC 21 1980. TIMES – CANNIBIS GALORE – THE GRASS POINT MYSTERY.
DEC 29 1980. SPY "POSED AS IRA DRUG SMUGGLER"
— do – EX-SPY ON DRUGS CHARGES IS REFUSED BAIL.
SEPT 28 81 NEW STANDARD. HIGH SEAS PANIC OF £20M. DRUG GANG
SEPT 29 '81 SECRET LIVES OF DRUG KING – DAILY MIRROR
— do — GRADUATE WAS £20M. DRUGS MR BIG – QC
— do — £20M DRUGS TRIAL IS TOLD OF "SMOOTH GANG OF GRADUATES"
– do – SUN. EGGHEADS RAN £20M. DRUGS RING. QC
— do – DAILY STAR. MASTERMIND GANG'S £20M. DRUGS CAPER.
– do – GUARDIAN. GRADUATES FROM OXFORD IN £20M CANNIBIS CASE ✓
– do – DAILY MAIL. OXFORD MASTERMIND IN A £20M. DRUGS RING ✓
– do – SCOTSMAN. SCOTS ISLE CENTRE FOR £20M. CANNIBIS PLOT.
– do – D. TELEGRAPH. THE GRADUATE CONNECTION IN £20M DRUGS CASE.
OCT 1st 1981. FREAK RADIO CALL MADE GANG PANIC, COURT TOLD
– do – SCOTSMAN. COURT TOLD RADIO ALERTED DRUGS GANG IN SCOTLAND.
29·9·81 EXPRESS "UNIVERSITY BRAINS 'RAN DRUGS RACKET'"
DRUGS GANG PANICKED IN CUSTOMS SWOOP.
SCOTTISH HERALD DRUGS TRIAL TOLD OF SALES COMPUTER
DAILY MAIL 1st OCT. 81. FREAK RADIO SIGNAL SANK DRUGS GANG. ✓
– do – OCT 3rd "DRUG SMUGGLERS CARBON COPY WARNING TO GANG"
COURT VIDEO SHOWS DRUG SMUGGLERS.
29 OCT 1981 GUARDIAN MAN IN DRUG CASE "COOKED GANG'S BOOKS"
— do – DRUG CASE MAN ONCE WORKED AS BR. INT. SPY.
S.W. EVENING POST MI6 LINK IN DRUGS CASE
CUSTOMS MAN DENIES FEAR.
OCT 15 81 "THE TIMES" QUOTED IN DRUG TRIAL.
DRUG TRIAL TOLD OF CODED LIST.
OCT 17 1981 DRUGS CASE MAN "WAS TERRIFIED"
OCT 9 1981. COURT TOLD OF ARTICLES ON IRA, DRUGS & MI6.
OCT 1 – do GUARDIAN. DRUG GANG SPENT 1.2M ABROAD BY COMPUTER
OCT 1 " – do – "DRUG GANG ACCOUNTS NEEDED A COMPUTER."
— do — D. TELEGRAPH "£2M DRUG GANG USED COMPUTER FOR ACCOUNTS" ✓
FILM SHOW FOR JURY IN THE DRUG CASE.
OCT 14 '81 DRUGS TRIAL DEFENDANT CLAIMED LINK WITH MI6.
OCT 27 81 (WESTERN MAIL) DRUGS CASE MAN TELLS OF SPYING ON THE IRA
MEXICAN LINK IN DRUG CASE
OCT 27 DAILY MAIL. MI6 AND THE SECRET BEHIND ANNABELINDA
GRADUATE AGREED TO DO DRUG ACCOUNTS
NOV 13 TIMES. DRUGS CASE MAN WAS SPYING ON IRA.
OCT 9 W/MAIL MI6 LINKED TO DRUGS TRIAL.
NOV 12. GUARDIAN COURT IS CLEARED FOR DRUGS TRIAL WITNESS.
OCT 27. MI6 USED SHOP-OWNER TO BUG IRA DRUG RING – D. TELEGRAPH
TIMES OCT 28. TRIAL DETAIL CONFUSING, JUDGE SAYS.
GUARDIAN – do – DRUG CASE GRADUATE TELLS OF WORKING FOR SECRET SERVICE.
— do – 28th MI6 WAS WARNED ON DRUGS ✓
TIMES OCT 29. DEFENDANT TELLS WHY HE KEPT DRUG ACCOUNTS.
OCT 30. DRUG CASE MAN WAS MI6 AGENT
SUNDAY WORLD. NOV 1st 1981. WE SENT SPY ON THE RUN.
TIMES. NOV 20 81. DRUGS JURY SPENT NIGHT IN HOTEL
EVE. STANDARD. – do – THREE CLEARED OF DRUGS RACKET.
D. TELEGRAPH – do 21st SPY "LEFT IN THE COLD" CLEARED OF DRUG SMUGGLING.
– do – REPORTER HELD AT OLD BAILEY. (IT WAS DAVID PALLISTER)
DAILY MIRROR. DRUG SPY IS CLEARED. ✓
" STAR. £22M DRUG CASE TRIO ARE CLEARED.
STANDARD 23/11/81 DRUG RING FIVE JAILED.
SUN TIMES 22/11/81 THE SECRET WORLD OF AN AMATEUR SPY. ✓
TIMES MARKS GETS 2 YEARS FOR OFFENCES OVER FALSE PASSPORTS
GUARDIAN FORMER SPY GOES TO PRISON FOR OFFENCES OVER FALSE PASSPORTS

Howard's arrest and trial were mainstream news. This is an extract from the notebook of Howard's father, who kept a record of all media reports.

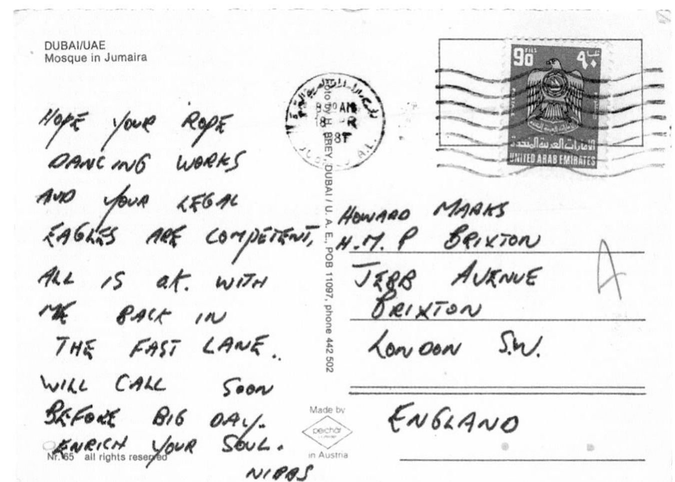
DUBAI/UAE
Mosque in Jumaira

HOPE YOUR ROPE DANCING WORKS AND YOUR LEGAL EAGLES ARE COMPETENT, ALL IS O.K. WITH ME BACK IN THE FAST LANE. WILL CALL SOON BEFORE BIG DAY. ENRICH YOUR SOUL.
NIBBS

HOWARD MARKS
H.M.P BRIXTON
JEBB AVENUE
BRIXTON
LONDON S.W.
ENGLAND

Postcard from 'Nibbs', i.e. James McCann, to Howard in Brixton.

Q: Where was that?
A: In Amsterdam.
Q: To which you were going to?
A: I had already been, and was planning further business.
Q: Did you contact this person?
A: Yes, I did. I met him at the American Hotel in Amsterdam.
Q: Under the name of?
A: My name, Howard Marks. His name was James O'Neill.
Q: And what was the purpose of your being asked to see him?
A: To explain to him what had happened to my friend who had got into trouble in Morocco.
Q: Had you met O'Neill before?
A: No, this was my first meeting with him.
Q: Later on, did you discover who he really was?
A: I think I discovered at that meeting. He told me his real name was James McCann.
Q: Did you later see any article about him?
A: Yes, I saw a number of articles, one in *Playboy* in 1973, February 1973, and some other magazines, underground magazines, in this country.
Q: Who was he?
A: He was in those days a leading IRA Provisional Activist, he organised bombings and so on. That is in those days.
Q: Did he make a notorious escape from somewhere?
A: Yes. I believe he was the first person to escape from Crumlin Road, Belfast, since the War. His escape had a lot of publicity.
Q: And had you any idea up to that time that this person you knew, who had got into trouble with drugs, was in any way connected with this particular man?
A: No, I had no idea about that.
Q: Well now, did you have a friend at the University, who became a great friend of yours, called McMillan?
A: Yes. His surname was McMillan.
Q: Where did he work after he left the University?
A: After he left the University he worked for the Foreign Office.
Q: And did you see him around this time, after you had met McCann in Amsterdam?
A: Yes. Yes, about a month or so after I met McCann, I think.
Q: Did you talk with him about your friend and the person you met?
A: Not at that first meeting with him. In general, I was what we talked about.
Q: Yes?
A: At that first meeting he told me he worked for MI6, which was the security branch of the Foreign Office, and would I be interested in helping them out in any way through my AnnaBelinda dress business.
Q: Just pause there. How would the AnnaBelinda dress business assist the Intelligence Services?
A: That was my question to him. What he wanted to do was have us open up in Europe for staff from their own Intelligence and that would be their cover.
JUDGE MASON: AnnaBelinda would be the cover?
A: That's right. AnnaBelinda would be the cover abroad.
LORD HUTCHINSON: After this discussion, and after giving the thing consideration, did you agree?
A: Yes, I did, yes.
Q: Coming back to your agreement that you would

assist, and give such information, or assist in whatever way it might be, as far as McCann was concerned – we will just deal with that aspect of the matter. Did you mention to him, or he mention to you, the situation about McCann and information?
A: I volunteered him the information that I had met McCann and told McMillan about my meeting with McCann. In particular I told him that McCann was using arms-smuggling routes to smuggle drugs and thereby finance further arms smuggling through drugs smuggling.
Q: Was he interested in this?
A: Oh, yes, very.
Q: Did you, in fact, meet his superiors?
A: I met two of his superiors on separate occasions and volunteered the same information as I had given to McMillan to one of the superiors.
A: After I had given them this information, they wanted me to get more information, either through the drug-smuggling route or arms-smuggling route, and just supply them with as much information as possible.
JUDGE MASON: Just a moment. Infiltrate the arms organisation?
A: Yes, to give them as much information on the drugs smuggling.
Q: The drug smuggling would give you a lead on the arms smuggling?
A: That's right.
LORD HUTCHINSON: Now, I want to ask you just shortly about this question of drug smuggling within your knowledge from this time on. Does this drug smuggling on a large scale have an international aspect?
A: Obviously, by definition.
Q: Is it mixed up with politics?
A: Very much so.
JUDGE MASON: This is the drug smuggling, Lord Hutchinson?
LORD HUTCHINSON: This is the drug smuggling. I am talking about it in an international way. I am not talking about politics in England.
A: No. I meant there are international links with terrorist groups which relate to the arms industry.
LORD HUTCHINSON: Now, in 1973, or thereabouts, did you go to Ireland at any time?
A: Yes, I did, yes.
Q: And the purpose was?
A: To get information from McCann to carry on the infiltration.
Q: What was your cover there?
A: Again, AnnaBelinda to a certain extent, and – plus philately I used. On the occasions I met McCann, I used both of them.
Q: Did you meet him then?
A: Yes, I did.
Q: And as a result of these meetings, did you discover anything about what the operation was that was current at the time?
A: A particular operation, you mean?
Q: Yes?
A: Yes, they were smuggling arms from Rotterdam to (inaudible), which is a border port of Southern Ireland.
Q: Now, you were in Amsterdam in 1973?
A: Yes.
Q: And you were arrested in Amsterdam?
A: Yes, I was.
Q: Was that in relation to the possession of some cannabis?
A: That's right, yes, a very small amount, which was in my pocket.
Q: Having been so arrested, did somebody come over to see you from England?
A: Yes, two British Customs Officers came over.
Q: And both interviewed you in Amsterdam when you were in custody?
A: Yes.
Q: And was that in relation to the matter which you were later charged with being concerned in?
A: Yes, it was.
Q: That matter we will come to in a moment, but you have never been tried for it?
A: No, no.
Q: We will come to it in a moment. So that is still in the air, as it were?
A: Yes.
Q: So I shall not ask you very much about the situation as regards that matter, other than to ask you how was it that you came to be involved, either innocently or not, in relation to that matter?
A: Through the same person who was in trouble in Morocco, whose wife had asked me to meet O'Neill.
Q: And can we leave it that if that matter had been tried out, you were intending to plead not guilty?
A: That's correct.
Q: And the allegation was?
A: The exportation of cannabis from Holland to the United States.
Q: From Holland to the United States?
A: Yes, but the charge was in this country.
Q: Because certain things were done in this country?
A: That's right, yes.
Q Did you agree to come back to this country, or were you...?
A: I came back voluntarily.

INGENIERIA, S. A.

FABRICANTE DE EQUIPOS CONTRA INCENDIO
VENTA-SERVICIO-MANTENIMIENTO

PROLO CALLE 8 No. 4-BIS. FRACC. INDT. ALCE BLANCO
NAUCALPAN DE [illegible], EDO. MEX. TELS. 373-28-66 CON TRES LINEAS 560-10-90

" 2 "

algún lugar de Inglaterra, ignorando las razones. Cabe aclarar que el Sr. Tunnicliffe ha tenido tratos comerciales con nosotros antes, realizando operaciones por mayor cuantía que la que nos ocupa ahora, sin haber tenido nunca el más mínimo problema con él, por lo que consideramos al Sr. Tunnicliffe una persona honesta y seria en sus tratos comerciales y de negocios, extrañándonos el porqué de este problema.

Nuestro interés es saber si por medio de esa Representación Diplomática, es posible:

a) Recobrar nuestro dinero en el menor tiempo posible.

b) Informarnos sobre el paradero y el lugar donde se encuentra detenido el Sr. Tunnicliffe.

c) Los trámites que debemos seguir, para la recuperación del dinero aquí en México ó en Inglaterra.

En espera de la valiosa ayuda y orientación de Usted, para la solución de nuestro problema y en espera de su amable respuesta, quedamos de Ud.

ATENTAMENTE
ALPHA INGENIERIA, S.A.

HECTOR DEL RIO TORRES
Gerente General.

HDRT/aph'

This paperwork appears to have been submitted to the court in support of Howard's defence, that he was working on behalf of the Mexican Secret Services, and to show that the money in Howard's possession was held on their behalf. The letter, written in Spanish and signed by Hector Del Rio Torres (in his capacity as the 'President of the Board of Directors for a group of companies') was sent in July 1981 to the British Embassy, enquiring after a Mr Anthony Tunnicliffe, from whom they claim they are keen to recover money. The Company Ingenieria S.A. is described in the letterhead as a producer of fire-proof equipment.

Q: So once again he extracted himself from this?
A: Yes.
Q: And settled in France?
A: In Southern France, and in the meantime, I went to Mexico to work there under the auspices of the government.
Q: You went to Mexico?
A: I went to Miami and then went to Vancouver and then went to Mexico and stayed there for seven or eight months.
Q: I want to ask you just this, as far as McCann and Mexico were concerned, you touched on it earlier today. Were and are there certain departments of the American government involved in drugs?
A: The CIA used narcotics missions as covers for their operatives. The DEA was formed in 1972.
Q: The DEA we have heard about?
A: The DEA is an amalgamation of ODALE, which is the Office for Drug Abuse Law Enforcement, and ONNI, which is the Office of National Narcotics Intelligence. They were headed by (inaudible) who were indicted for Watergate and they thought they had (inaudible) that.
Q: They have links with the British Customs?
A: Yes, they use them quite a lot.
Q: And then you came back to this country?
A: Via Europe, but eventually I came back here, yes.
Q: In May of 1979 did you go to Ireland?
A: Yes, I went to Dublin.
Q: The reason being?
A: To film a group which consisted entirely of Elvis Presley impersonators.

...

JUDGE MASON: Can I just ask your client one thing, Lord Hutchinson? (To the witness) Mr Marks, the jury and I have watched you in the dock during the course of this case.
A: Yes.
Q: And watched you during the course of your evidence.
A: Yes.
Q: And you have been constantly smiling. Now, can you say why?
A: Good heavens, I am afraid I can't. I don't think I am smiling more than I normally do. I normally smile a lot. That is all I can say, my Lord, with respect.
JUDGE MASON: Thank you.
LORD HUTCHINSON: I am not quite sure. Do you consider this is a serious matter?
A: Yes, of course.
Q: Is there anything unnatural about the fact that you do, in fact, smile most of the time?
A: I do smile most of the time.
Q: Does that mean that you could not care less about what happens in this case?
A: No, it doesn't mean that at all.
Q: Is it a very serious matter for you?
A: Yes, very serious indeed.

...

Q: Now, I want you just to look at the article. (Handed) The date of that article is the...?
A: July 13th, 1979.
Q: 13th July, 1979, and you saw it about how long after that, do you remember?
A: A few days. Within a few days.
Q: My Lord, if the jury could have a copy of this, it would make it easier to follow. My Lord, I want to make it perfectly clear that the reason for the witness looking at this article is to tell the jury what the effect of it was upon him, and what is written in this article cannot be evidence of what is in it as being correct because this is an article in the newspaper, and it is not going to be cross-examined. In the Law, the only importance of the article is the effect it had upon Mr Marks. (To the witness) Now, at the top on the left there is a picture of Hamilton McMillan and Howard Marks as undergraduates, and it says: 'The Recruiter and the Secret Agent'. Is that the Mr McMillan you were referring to yesterday?
A: Yes, it was.
Q: Yes. In the middle there is a photograph of you, and you are referred to as: 'A drug smuggling hippy'.
A: Yes.
Q: And: 'MI6 assigned target Provisional IRA arms smuggler James McCann'. Is that McCann?
A: That is McCann, yes.
Q: And then it shows the photographs which were taken of you in Amsterdam by the police?
A: Yes.
Q: In the bottom right-hand corner?
A: Yes.
Q: I am not going to read all this article, but at the bottom of the first paragraph on the left, it says: 'New evidence proves that they are closely linked to the activities of MI6, Britain's Secret Intelligence Service'. That is your disappearance?
A: Yes.
Q: And then there is a bit about you and the boutique and so on, and then it says: 'McCann, a well-known IRA activist, had escaped from the Crumlin Road prison in 1971 and Marks' arrival in the milieu had not escaped the notice of British and foreign authorities. In 1972 according to Marks he was approached by his former Balliol friend (→p92)

INTELLIGENCE

The secret war for Ireland

The war in Northern Ireland, seen from Whitehall's operations rooms, is wholly different from its public image. The two articles following illuminate different aspects of the secret war with the IRA. STEPHEN SCOTT explains how MI6 recruited a drugs smuggler to monitor IRA arms deals. Scott's investigation was to have been transmitted on London Weekend Television's London Programme last week, but was cancelled at the last minute.

DUNCAN CAMPBELL discusses the secret army intelligence report which states plainly that talk of 'getting on top of the gunmen' is a pipedream.

Howard Marks disappears

Hamilton McMillan and Howard Marks as freshmen Balliol undergraduates; the recruiter and the secret agent.

HOWARD MARKS, a 33-year-old Oxford graduate, is still coming and going freely from Britain five years after he disappeared from his home and avoided standing trial on charges which would probably have left him still in prison. The circumstances of his sudden disappearance have never been fully explained. But new evidence proves that they are closely linked to the activities of MI6, Britain's Secret Intelligence Service.

In 1972, through a former undergraduate colleague, he was recruited by enticement or blackmail into their service to spy on IRA arms dealing. He was pushed closer into arms and drugs dealing in Europe and America.

Howard Marks graduated in physics from Oxford University in 1967. Five years later, after a chequered further education, he was back in Oxford running a boutique, dabbling in property speculation and stamp dealing with little success. He became closely involved with large scale drugs smuggling through another Oxford friend, Gordon Plinston, also now wanted in several countries. In the drugs business, Marks and Plinston came to know well a Provisional IRA arms dealer then based in Amsterdam, James McCann.

McCann, a well known IRA activist, had escaped from Crumlin Road prison in 1971. Mark's arrival in the *milieu* had not escaped the notice of British and foreign authorities. In 1972, according to Marks, he was approached by his former Balliol friend called 'Mac'. Mac told Marks that he was a member of MI6, and that unless he co-operated, he would be turned over to the customs. Marks agreed to co-operate.

It is, of course, notoriously difficult to separate fact from fiction in stories of the secret agencies and their contacts. In the case of Howard Marks, however, his involvement is confirmed by fresh information: the police report investigating his disappearance in April 1974, which has been seen by the programme's reporters. Marks had been entirely indiscreet – indeed braggardly – about his intelligence connection, and it quickly came to the attention of the policemen investigating his absconding from bail. The police superintendent in charge of the enquiry was summoned to the offices of the Security Service to be told by the Service's legal adviser, Bernard Shelton, that Marks had been in 1973, 'an agent for MI6'. He added:

> A former Balliol college fellow undergraduate of Marks, who is now an MI6 officer, contacted Marks with a view to using his company 'Annabelinda', which also had a shop in Amsterdam as a cover for his activities. He later realised that Marks was engaged in certain activities and requested him to obtain information concerning the Provisional IRA.

'Mac' – the Balliol undergraduate who recruited Marks – is Norman Hamilton McMillan, who joined the Foreign Office in 1968. He now works – quite openly – as a First Secretary in the Rome embassy. Marks, McMillan remembered, was a mildly right of centre hearty, scarcely discreet about his own associations. Balliol comtemporaries, including a NEW STATESMAN reporter, knew well that he had joined MI6. An Oxford solicitor who knew Marks told police the same story:

Howard Marks as the drug smuggling hippie and his MI6 assigned target. Provisional IRA arms smuggler James McCann.

'some time before, it had been rumoured and gossiped about that a former Balliol student who is now an MI6 officer was recruiting for agents.'

The version of the recruitment story given to Superintendent Fairweather, investigating Marks's disappearance, was that Marks had only been an agent 'at one time, for a short period'. It was said that 'in September 1973, however, his superiors instructed the (MI6) officer to sever contact with Marks'. But this version of the story – which may be all the MI6 was prepared to tell the independently run Security Service – seems to be far less than the truth. MI6's involvement with Marks ran longer and deeper than a former chum's 1973 whim to use his Annabelinda boutique as cover for MI6 work.

MARKS AND HIS RECRUITER Hamilton McMillan had been close as students. But when McMillan went back to look up his old friend in 1972, it wasn't exactly friendly. According to Marks, MI6 knew all about his drug smuggling from the start and simply blackmailed him into working for them. The work was certainly dangerous. The police report tends to confirm this earlier association: Marks's common law wife, Rosie Brindley, who was living with him when he disappeared, told police how 'Mac' visited Marks late in 1972 and made the recruitment pitch. Her account – judged 'truthful' by the police – was that his assignment was to report on the Irish arms dealer McCann. He also told his mother, 'a person of the highest character', that MI6 had assigned him to gather information about James McCann.

To answer these enquiries he was inevitably pushed further into the drugs underworld. Marks got to know McCann increasingly well. He stayed at his home at Greystones near Dublin. When he and his girl friend Rosie holidayed in Ibiza in early 1973, McCann flew out to join them. But by the end of 1973, things were going seriously wrong.

In September, the US end of the major drugs conspiracy was busted. The ring, said to involve Plinston and Marks as the major European partners, had arranged to smuggle vast quantities of cannabis to the US from Europe concealed inside musical and electronic equipment. By chance, part of the drugs shipment was discovered in New York, and the investigation quickly closed in.

In October 1973, McCann's girlfriend was arrested in Hamburg and questioned in depth about his activities. McCann began to suspect that Marks was an informant. Soon after this, McCann was unsuccessfully ambushed in his hotel by a number of well armed men – he claims it was an attempt by British Intelligence to assassinate him, set up by Howard Marks. Before McCann took revenge however, Marks himself had been arrested in Amsterdam, the unfortunate victim of a chance raid on a drugs dealing friend while he was present.

Marks was held while charges were investigated, but apparently was not implicated in the charges against his friend and would eventually have been released. But news of his arrest reached British customs, however, over the Interpol network, and two customs officers flew to Amsterdam. Curiously, although

Mark's police file photographs, taken by Dutch police after his arrest in Amsterdam in 1973.

40

A *New Statesman* article about Howard's recruitment to Britain's Secret Services was published in 1979. The only evidence of Howard having worked for the Secret Services consisted of newspaper and magazine articles attesting to this fact. When Lord Hutchinson sought to introduce these into the jury bundle of evidence, he argued that this was not to suggest that the contents of the articles were true (hearsay evidence, whereby assertions of fact are made by persons who are not themselves giving oral evidence to the court, is not admissible as proof of its contents) but to explain Howard's state of mind at the time, on reading the articles and, in particular, why he felt the need to change identity after doing so. The prosecution objected on the grounds that the articles were hearsay evidence: 'All my learned friend obviously hopes to get from it is a certain amount of substantiation perhaps, via the back door, for some of the contentions his client has been putting in the witness box.' The prosecution argued that in order to prove that Mr Nice's true identity had been outed, Hutchinson could instead simply show the jury the published photos 'mounted quite separately, on a piece of paper' instead of providing them with the full article. Judge Mason was persuaded otherwise, the context was important: 'You say: "The picture." It might have been a picture in a Brylcreem advertisement.' All the articles made it into the jury bundle.

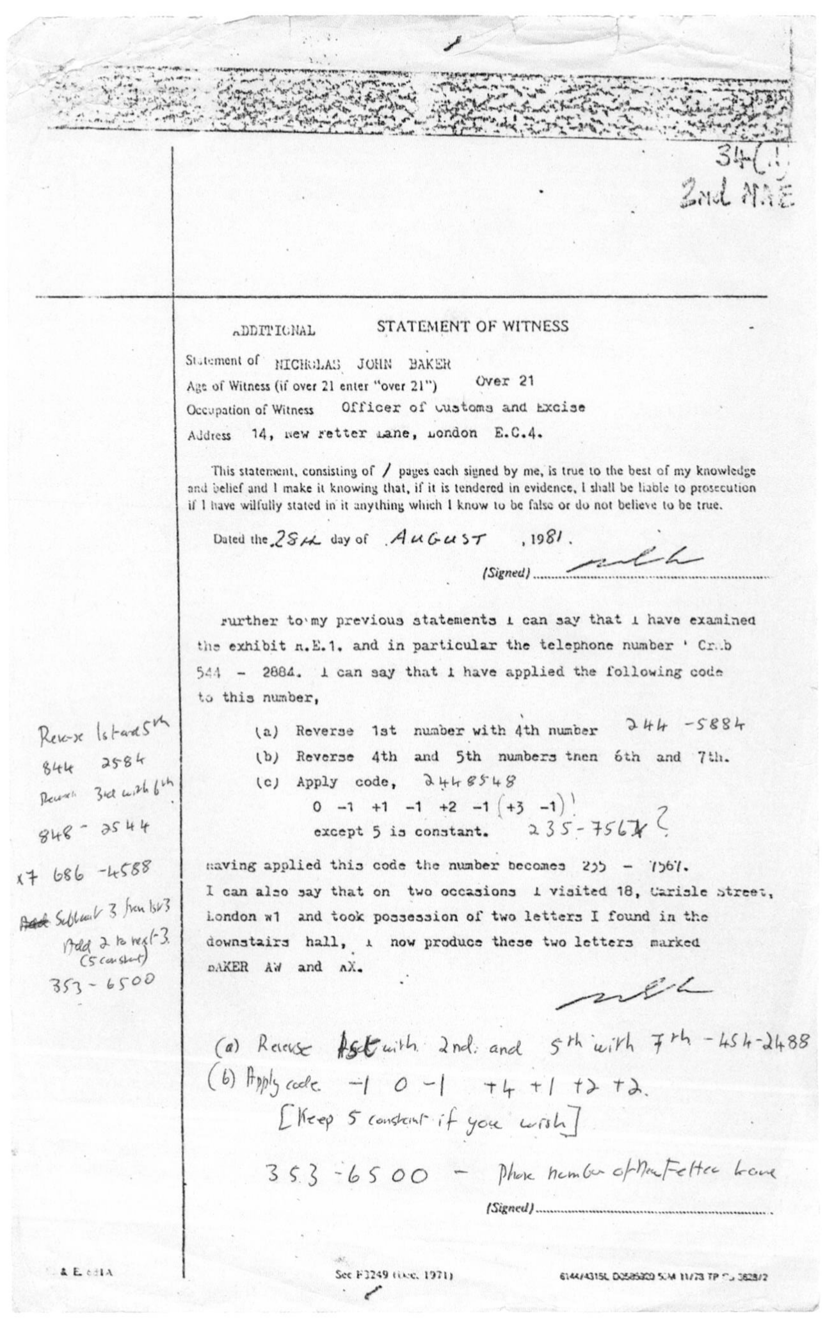

34(.)
2nd MAE

ADDITIONAL STATEMENT OF WITNESS

Statement of NICHOLAS JOHN BAKER

Age of Witness (if over 21 enter "over 21") Over 21

Occupation of Witness Officer of Customs and Excise

Address 14, New Fetter Lane, London E.C.4.

This statement, consisting of / pages each signed by me, is true to the best of my knowledge and belief and I make it knowing that, if it is tendered in evidence, I shall be liable to prosecution if I have wilfully stated in it anything which I know to be false or do not believe to be true.

Dated the 28th day of AUGUST, 1981.

(Signed)

Further to my previous statements I can say that I have examined the exhibit N.E.1. and in particular the telephone number ' Cr..b 544 - 2884. I can say that I have applied the following code to this number,

(a) Reverse 1st number with 4th number 244 -5884

(b) Reverse 4th and 5th numbers then 6th and 7th.

(c) Apply code, 2448548

0 -1 +1 -1 +2 -1 (+3 -1)!

except 5 is constant. 235-7567?

Having applied this code the number becomes 235 - 7567.

I can also say that on two occasions I visited 18, Carlisle Street, London W1 and took possession of two letters I found in the downstairs hall, I now produce these two letters marked BAKER AW and AX.

Reverse 1st and 5th
844 2584
Reverse 3rd with 6th
848 - 2544
x7 686 -4588
Subtract 3 from 1st 3
Add 2 to rest -3.
(5 constant)
353 - 6500

(a) Reverse ~~1st~~ with 2nd and 5th with 7th - 454-2488

(b) Apply code -1 0 -1 +4 +1 +2 +2.

[Keep 5 constant if you wish]

353 -6500 - Phone number of New Fetter Lane

(Signed)

Sec F3249 (Rev. 1971)

(↗→) In this witness statement (annotated in ink by Howard) HM Customs & Excise officer Nick Baker explains numbers found in Howard's handwriting, employing what Baker claimed to have been Howard's coding system. Howard's lengthy handwritten note explains the logical flaws in Baker's code, demonstrating it would not have been a code he used because it wasn't coherent.

Howard worked on his defence throughout his time on remand, writing regularly to his parents. In July 1980 he wrote that he was relieved to have returned to his academic frame of mind and was enjoying reading books while working on his defence. He noted that:

'Mr Harré [Horace Romano Harré, Howard's favourite tutor in the Philosophy of Science at Oxford University] once told me that what I had to realize, with a mind like mine, was the fact that academia was much better than the real world

Baker's Code   2nd NAE 34(H)

Baker is maintaining that 544 2884 is a coded version of 235 7567 and sets the decoding system in three stages (a) (b) (c). There are at least two other numbers which when subjected to Baker's decoding system also give 235 7567.

Starting with	(i) 544 2884	(ii) 645 2684	(iii) 344 2847.
Apply step (a)	(i) 244 5884	(ii) 245 6684	(iii) 244 3847.
" " (b)	(i) 244 8548	(ii) 245 6648	(iii) 244 8374
" " (c)	(i) 235 7567	(ii) 235 7567	(iii) 235 7567.
	0-1+1-1 5+2-1	0-1 +1-1+2	

Baker, understandably, does not hint at what sort of code when applied to 235 7567 would give 544 2884. There cannot be one which corresponds to the decoding system which he refers to as this would leave us with an arbitrary choice of at least three numbers – an absurd situation.

I am sure Baker cannot realize that his code could also give the same result for completely different numbers as starting points and this question should be put to him.

The mathematically naive, among whom I would include Baker might think that the coding system is simply the reverse of the decoding system. i.e. Step (c) reversed followed by step (b) followed by step (a). In Baker's example this would be

(a′) Apply code
0 +1 −1 +1 −2 +1 −3 +1.
except 5 is constant.
(b′) Reverse 4th and 5th and 6th and 7th numbers
(c′) Reverse 1st with 4th

If we attempt this on 235 7567 we get
(a′) 245 6575
(b′) 245 5657.
(c′) 545 2657
which is <u>not</u> 544 2884.

In fact it is impossible to arrive at a coding system which corresponds to any decoding system which has steps in it like '5 is constant' coupled with adding or subtracting numbers. The reason is that one would never know on coming across a 5 whether it was the result of keeping it constant or the result of an addition or subtraction.

because one could always turn to new problems without causing upheavals by their solution…

There was an interesting article in today's *Sunday Times* about the new theory of evolution. I don't like to boast (well, I do actually, as you know), but back in 1969 I was convinced that Lamarckism (the inheritance of acquired characteristics) was far more viable than Darwin's survival of the fittest through mutations, which was the subject of the article…

Tragically enough, the person who introduced me to Ayer, Gareth Evans, the young genius of the seventies, died late last summer of cancer. Of the many extracts which Ayer quotes in his book is the following couplet of William Blake's "He who would do good to another must do it in minute particulars. General good is the plea of the scoundrel, hypocrite and flatterer." I don't know why but I feel that message is very important.'

called Mac.' Therefore, there is reference there to your contact with the Intelligence being McMillan?

A: Yes.

Q: And being in relation to James McCann of the IRA?

A: Yes.

Q: And then it says that it is notoriously difficult to separate fact from fiction in these stories of secret agents and contacts, and then it says that your involvement is confirmed by fresh information, and it refers to a police report investigating your disappearance in April 1974 and being seen by these reporters of the programme. That is the television programme?

A: Yes.

Q: And it says you were indiscreet about your connection with the Intelligence. And it cites the police superintendent in charge of the enquiry meeting Mr Bernard Shelton of the MI6. And refers to your contact with an MI6 officer. And again refers to Hamilton McMillan as being in the Foreign Office. Under the photograph it refers to Superintendent Fairweather, who investigated your failure to turn up. To your having been an agent at one time for a short period, that superiors instructed MI6 officers to sever contact. That this version of the story may be all that MI6 were prepared to tell, which is far less than the truth, and so on. Then there is a reference: 'MI6 involvement with Marks ran longer and deeper than a former chum's 1973 whim to use his AnnaBelinda boutique as cover for MI6 work.' So there is a reference to the AnnaBelinda boutique, and it goes into your contact again, and then on the right-hand column: 'In October 1973 McCann's girlfriend was arrested in Hamburg and questioned in depth about his activities. McCann began to suspect Marks was an informant. Soon after this McCann was unsuccessfully ambushed in his hotel by a number of well-armed men', and so on. 'He claims it was an attempt by British Intelligence to assassinate him set up by Howard Marks.' Well, you read that, did you?

A: Yes, that's nonsense.

Q: True or false?

A: Absolutely false.

Q: But you read that this was what McCann was saying?

A: Yes, yes.

Q: Was that part of what you were just saying to the jury?

A: It made me fearful of what McCann would do.

Q: And being released on bail, and then it says the trial was going to be bad news for Marks – that's you – and MI6, and so on, and then it makes reference to what you were saying yesterday about Kenneth Littlejohn and Kenneth Lennon?

A: Yes.

Q: I am not going to read all about the case. My learned friend can refer to anything I miss out. Then at the bottom of the middle paragraph it deals with your non-appearance at the Old Bailey, and it was decided that the sureties should not lose their money?

A: Yes.

Q: And again at the bottom of that column it says the Intelligence Service seems to have been involved in handling the case against Marks, and it says that one of the Customs Officers had an Intelligence connection?

A: I don't know if that is so, or not.

Q: Now, you come back to London, and between your return to London and the 11th November, did you see Natasha?

A: Yes, on at least two occasions. She told me that. Howard, the New Yorker, was feeling out Stewart Prentiss with a view to importing cannabis to Scotland, and she also mentioned a figure of 30 tons of Colombian.

Q: In what way did she impart that information to you?

A: Confidentially.

Q: Yes. Did she give any reason why she was telling you this?

A: No, she didn't.

Q: What was her attitude to this, as far as you could understand?

A: Well, she wasn't worried about it – indifferent. Indifferent really, but aware it was happening.

Q: Now, what effect did that have on you – how did you react to that in your own mind?

A: The figure of 30 tons of Colombian was obviously very significant to me. This was precisely the figure that I had been told by Clark, McCann's reluctant employee, months previously as the amount of cannabis which was going to be sent to McCann by his extremist terrorist associates in Latin America.

Q: Now, having gained that information, did you do anything about it afterwards?

A: As I was going to Mexico anyway, I obviously thought it would be relevant information for them, and before I went I informed Antonio of what I had heard, who suggested obviously that I bring it up with my superiors in Mexico.

Q: And what would be the importance of this information as far as you were concerned?

A: They were associates of McCann, plus I have to backtrack a bit to 1977.

Q: Yes?

A: When McCann was arrested in Vancouver, I continued my work in Mexico, which was research into the activities of arms smugglers and heroin smugglers in Mexico. Many of these involved CIA operators, past and present, some working under the guise of the DEA, all of whom, or a large majority of whom, were associates of McCann.

Q: Was there – and this may become relevant later – any particular individual, by name, who you were interested in?

A: Yes, there was.

Q: Can you say that name?

A: Yes. Mario Cantu.

Q: Spelt: C.A.N.T.U.?

A: T.U., yes.

Q: And this person Cantu – what was allegedly his role?

A: He was allegedly a CIA agent sent to destabilise the Mexican regime.

Q: You use the word 'destabilise'. What does that mean?

A: It is a euphemism for replacing democratically elected governments by military dictatorships.

JUDGE MASON: I hope the jury are following all this, because I am a little lost. I am sure they are.

LORD HUTCHINSON: I hope so too, my Lord. May I make it quite simple, if I can. (To the witness)

The prosecution brought one sack of the confiscated cannabis into the courtroom for the jury to see. Judge Mason reportedly prodded it before asking how it was ingested. Photograph courtesy Her Majesty's Customs & Excise.

Having been told this information about the possibility of 30 tons of Colombian cannabis coming to Scotland, you connected that with what you had been told by this man, Clark, when you were in Ireland?
A: Correct.
Q: That 30 tons of Colombian cannabis was coming to the west coast of Ireland?
A: Yes.
Q: And that you connected with McCann and the IRA?
A: Yes.
Q: When you heard about this, you thought that might be the same lot?
A: Yes, I was sure of it in my own mind.
Q: In your own mind. So you reported that matter to your contact?
A: Yes.
Q: Well, now, you had got a good deal of information about what had happened.
A: Yes, I had got a good deal, but nowhere near enough. My next step was to see Stewart Prentiss and find out more information, if possible, about Alex, and also to warn him about Alex's malevolent intentions.
JUDGE MASON: Why didn't you run a mile when you heard these people were suspicious about you?
A: Because I had to find out information – about Alex in particular.
Q: Why?
A: Because I had been instructed to do so.
LORD HUTCHINSON: Let us explore that situation. It has been suggested it would have been better if you had run a mile. Let us deal with that. You now knew what you have told the jury you had

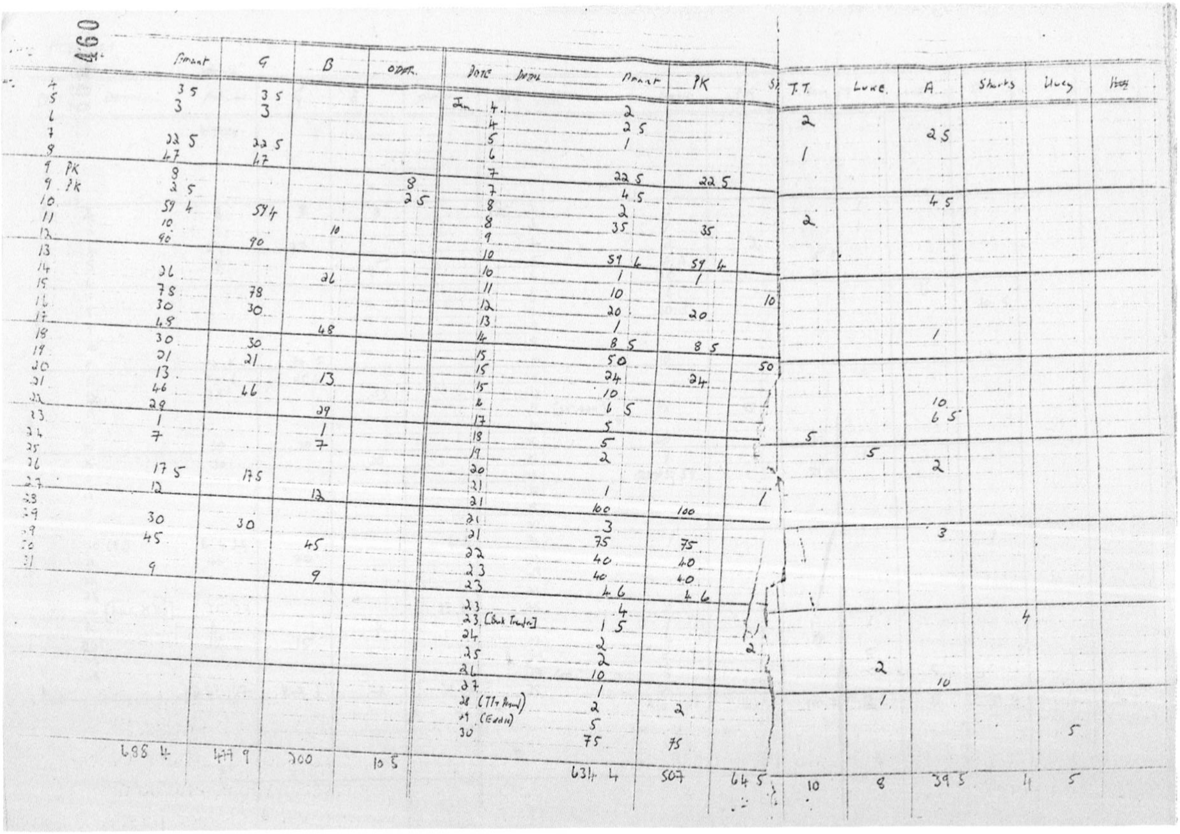

Howard was examined at length about the accounts in his handwriting. He explained that Patrick Lane had asked him to cook some accounts for the purpose of placating the American contingent because they suspected they were being ripped off. He used a 'calculating machine' to work out the accounts. When inconsistencies were found in Howard's explanations, he pointed out that it was precisely because of such discrepancies that his assistance had been required. These accounts were merely an early draft.

been told?
A: Yes.
Q: You have told them why you were interested in the American end of this business?
A: Yes, the Colombian end in particular.
Q: That was what you were interested in – the source of this supply?
A: The identification of the people responsible, in particular.
Q: Yes. You met this man Alex?
A: Yes.
Q: And here you were with the opportunity of meeting this man, Lacey?
A: Yes. I didn't know it was Lacey at the time – to meet someone else.
Q: To meet this other man?
A: Yes.
Q: And the basis of that was that they suspected you might be the person who had given information about them?
A: Yes. Something had obviously gone wrong from their point of view with this cannabis importation, and there was a suspicion, amongst other suspicions, that I might have been in some way responsible, because of my past and because of McCann's revelations in the newspapers.
Q: Yes. So what the learned Judge was saying was: 'Why didn't you scarper at that moment?'
A: Because at long last I had the necessary information almost at hand which I had been for months and months trying to find out. It would be absolutely the wrong time to scarper. Virtually any other time would have made more sense. This time was absolutely wrong.
Q: Did you...?
JUDGE MASON: Just a moment, please. Because vital information was about to be to hand?
A: Yes. When one takes on such a project one realises there will be dangerous moments in it.
LORD HUTCHINSON: You see, I want you to not skip over it because the learned Judge has shaken his head and expressed disbelief in what you are saying. Therefore, I want you to deal with it, and deal with it slowly and in detail. Why didn't you run away at that moment?
A: Because vital information was at hand concerning the project I had been financed for and instructed to do months previously.
Q: Did you think you could deal with this gentleman who was coming over?
A: From what Patrick told me – Patrick said that he was an extremely understanding, good man. If Patrick had said: 'When this gentleman comes over you had better hide,' then I wouldn't have thought twice about hiding, but Patrick gave no indication whatsoever that this chap would be of that nature.
Q: How did he compare him with Alex?
A: Well, he didn't actually make that comparison, but, I mean, I inferred that he was a non-aggressive, non-malevolent person. I think Patrick...
JUDGE MASON: Non-aggressive, non?
A: Non-malevolent person. Patrick described him as simply a free-trader. That was the expression used, I think.
LORD HUTCHINSON: And did you, in fact, meet that person?
A: Yes, I did.
Q: In what circumstances?
A: I first of all went to see Prentiss. Do you want a description of that first?
Q: Yes.
A: I went to see Prentiss and told him about my meeting with Alex, that Alex was extremely hostile towards Prentiss and suspected him of various things and I also told him that Alex seemed to know my enemies – that was the way I put it.
Q: Yes?
A: I asked him if he could help me with any information about Alex. He told me that he couldn't really.
Q: And again, cutting it short, having talked to him, did Prentiss eventually agree that it would be a good thing for him to meet Lacey?
A: Yes, he was completely in favour of the idea, actually.
Q: And what arrangement was made?
A: Stewart simply said I could give Randy his phone number.
Q: His phone number?
A: Yes.
Q: And did you do that?
A: Yes, I did, later on that day.
Q: And later on that evening did you hear again from Lacey?
A: Yes, he telephoned me and said that things had cleared up now with Stewart Prentiss. He was with Patrick Lane and said that there was so much – so many discrepancies and so much confusion regarding who had been paid what, how much cannabis was left, all sorts of things like that, and said that he and Patrick had been talking and would I be prepared to do the accounts up to that date for the whole operation, as a kind of arbitrator, more than anything else.
Q: It sounds dangerous to me.
JUDGE MASON: Just a moment. Can I at some

stage please have the shorthand transcript of that answer?
LORD HUTCHINSON: Would your Lordship like a transcript of anything else?
JUDGE MASON: No, just that single answer, thank you.
LORD HUTCHINSON: Was this said on the telephone?
A: Yes, it was.
Q: And why was it that he wanted you to do this: was there an argument, was there a dispute, or what?
A: There were a great many disputes between a great many of the personnel, which is why it needed an arbitrator. I simply...
JUDGE MASON: Just a minute, not too fast.
LORD HUTCHINSON: What did you understand the disputes were about?
A: About how much cannabis had been jettisoned, about how much money associates of Prentiss had received, and about how much money other personnel had received.
JUDGE MASON: Stop. How much cannabis had been jettisoned?
A: How much cannabis was left, how much cannabis had been sold, how much money various personnel had received.
LORD HUTCHINSON: And you are saying this in a very calm voice?
A: Yes.
Q: What was the situation, as you gathered it?
A: As far as I was concerned, I seized upon the opportunity to find out more about Alex.
Q: Yes – I am going to ask you whether you agreed, and why, in a moment.
A: Sorry.
Q: What was the background to this dispute – what was happening amongst all these people, as you understood it from Lacey?
A: Yes. That cannabis had been jettisoned. There was a dispute about: (a) whether it had, in fact, been jettisoned, or not; and: (b) how much had been jettisoned, and there were also disputes about how much money various personnel had received.
Q: You were using the phrase from Alex: 'ripped off'?
A: Yes, yes. I mean Alex, as I mentioned yesterday, had accused Prentiss of having ripped off cannabis.
Q: Why were you asked to do this, as you understood it?
A: I imagine that Patrick would have suggested in strong terms to Lacey I was a trustful person, and I had also, I think, given that impression to Lacey during my meeting with him.
Q: What about your ability?
A: I did have a training in mathematics, and I used to do the accounts for AnnaBelinda and various shops connected – which AnnaBelinda controlled. Patrick knew this.
Q: Yes...
JUDGE MASON: Just a moment.
LORD HUTCHINSON: Why couldn't Patrick do this, as he had apparently been looking after the money side of the matter?
A: He would have been responsible for most of the payments made and, therefore, would not be in an unbiased position when making a true and accurate record.
Q: At what stage after this – we are on the 8th May at the moment – did Patrick Lane leave the country?
A: A few days later.
Q: A few days later?
A: Yes. He gave me a lot of information...
Q: Yes. We will come to that in a moment. We know that he left the country. We know that every one of the Americans left the country, or were not arrested by the Customs, and on this day, the 8th May, this proposition was being put to you?
A: Yes, on the evening of the 8th May.
Q: Now, what did you think – what did you decide to do about it?
A: I seized upon this as an opportunity to do two things. One was to prevent the malevolent contentions of Alex and prevent them from bearing fruit insofar as they were directed against Stewart Prentiss, because, after all, my sister-in-law worked for him.
Q: What, Natasha?
A: Yes.
JUDGE MASON: Preventing the what – benevolent?
LORD HUTCHINSON: Malevolent.
JUDGE MASON: Preventing Alex's malevolent...?
A: Hostile.
LORD HUTCHINSON: Malevolent feelings, because of all this ripping off suggestion and all that?
A: Yes.
JUDGE MASON: Preventing Alex's malevolence from bearing fruit?
A: Yes.
LORD HUTCHINSON: In other words, it would avoid them getting into trouble with the Americans because of this?
A: Yes.
LORD HUTCHINSON: The persons who were paying you and for whom you would be working were representatives of?
A: The Mexican government.
Q: The Mexican government?

A: Yes.
Q: And you said there was an international tie-up about this supply of drugs?
A: Yes, obviously the Secret Services of various countries are also in touch with each other.
Q: Yes. If you are exporting drugs from Colombia to America, and exporting drugs from Colombia to Ireland and maybe exporting drugs from Colombia to England, is the origin of all this a crucial matter?
A: Yes.
JUDGE MASON: So you were going there as a representative of the Mexican government?
A: Yes, sir.
Q: To find out what?
A: To find out – well, it was a project which I don't want to go into, coupled with giving them the information which I had learned from Natasha.
LORD HUTCHINSON: And when his Lordship says the Mexican government, is it the Mexican government?
A: Yes, it is the Mexican government.
JUDGE MASON: Who was going to pay you?
A: The Mexican government.
LORD HUTCHINSON: Which part of it?
A: It is a secret department set up solely for the purpose of combatting terrorism and drug smuggling.
JUDGE MASON: A secret department set up to combat terrorism and drug smuggling?
A: Yes.
LORD HUTCHINSON: You had said yesterday when there was a little discussion before the end, that you saw this press report from the Irish newspaper about McCann's acquittal?
A: That's right, yes.
Q: And that you were extremely frightened?
A: Yes.
Q: When did you see it?
A: The day after it came out.
Q: The day it came out is 30th March?
A: Yes.
Q: Of 1980?
A: Yes. I first learnt of McCann's acquittal on the 26th or 27th March, through another article which is not present.
Q: Now, just pass those up to the jury. (Shown to jury)
LORD HUTCHINSON: Mr Marks, we are not interested in what Mr McCann said about some top politician being embarrassed, but if you look at the second paragraph, which starts: 'McCann was released from Dublin's Central Criminal Court'.
A: Yes.
Q: Have you got that?
A: Yes.
Q: 'Interviewed yesterday, McCann claimed that British Intelligence have been attempting to "set him up".'
A: Yes.
Q: Then, missing out the next three paragraphs: 'When I first claimed MI6 had set up a drug-smuggling ring in order to get close to me with a view to assassinating me, many might have believed it was daydreams. But London Weekend Television and the *New Statesman* spent months investigating and discovered that every word was true.'

Then over the page. Again we need not read the first three or four paragraphs. The last but one says: 'McCann's sensational allegations followed his release from Dublin's Central Criminal Court last Tuesday.'

Then, the last paragraph: 'McCann, who has also been dubbed: "The Green Pimpernel" for his bizarre exploits, told *Sunday World* he believed he was "set up" by the British Secret Service on the drugs charges. McCann maintained that at the time of his arrest he was on the trail of British spy Howard Marks who three years ago was exposed by the respected left-wing magazine *New Statesman* as being an MI6 operative. McCann, who was alleged in British press stories to have been involved in gun running in Holland five years ago, said: "It was during my time in Holland that Marks tried to infiltrate my activities under the guise of being a drugs dealer. I believed him at first but the more stories that were leaked about me to the English press the more suspicious I became of him. Marks eventually attempted to have me shot by a British undercover hit squad. Luckily I escaped, but Marks ended up being arrested on a big drugs charge."'

And then he said his next encounter with the man who tried to have him killed was early last year when he discovered that Marks was staying in Dublin's Gresham Hotel.

'He had been staying in the hotel under the name of Nice. An actual Mr Nice,' said McCann, 'But by the time I reached the hotel he had checked out.' He said that after a few days he tracked Marks down at a house in Dublin which he claimed the British spy had been renting. 'He was staying there with some other men and it was then that I discovered that they were engaged in a drugs-smuggling operation.' McCann refused to say what happened between then and August 25th when he was discovered on the Naas dual carriageway with a lorry containing 892lb of cannabis.' □

The Times, 21 November 1981, reporting that Howard and all his co-defendants who pleaded not guilty had been acquitted. Following his acquittal of the Colombian importation, Howard was sentenced to two years for the false passport charges to which he had pleaded guilty. A plea bargain was subsequently negotiated in relation to the Transatlantic Sounds importation charges and on 16 February 1982 at the Old Bailey Howard was sentenced to three years for these. The Recorder of London noted his relative youth at the time of the offences, that it had been his first criminal offence and that he had pleaded guilty to it. As Howard had already served time on remand in Brixton, he only had to spend another three months in prison, which he did in HM Prison Wandsworth.

Lord Hutchinson said of Howard's acquittal for the Colombian importation: 'If ever there was a case for the legalisation of cannabis, this is it.' Howard, as he later recounted in his sell-out one-man show in the 2000s, eventually took his acquittal as a 'message from "God" to keep on smuggling'. If this was indeed God's plan, however, then the Devil set out to foil it.

THE TIMES SATURDAY NOVEMBER 21 1981

The four tons of cannabis taken from Alan Arthur Grey's bungalow at Glengarry, Invernessshire.

Oxford graduate cleared of £20m drugs link

By Stewart Tendler, Crime Reporter

Howard Marks, the Oxford graduate charged with being the British mainstay of a £20m cannabis smuggling ring, was acquitted yesterday at the Central Criminal Court of involvement with the drug organization.

In his defence Mr Marks, aged 36, told the court during an eight-week trial that he had worked for MI6 to infiltrate an IRA arms and drug smuggling business, and later for Mexican agents against South American terrorists financed by drugs.

Yesterday the jury, which had been deliberating since Thursday morning, also acquitted a Briton and an American of charges connected with the smuggling ring which brought 15 tons of cannabis from Colombia to Britain. But they found Mr Marks guilty of two offences involving false passports.

Mr Marks may also face proceedings alleging that he absconded from bail in 1974 while awaiting trial on a separate drug charge. Judge Mason, QC, was told yesterday that the Director of Public Prosecutions is considering the earlier charge.

While the jury was out the court began to hear pleas in mitigation by five men who had earlier pleaded guilty to charges connected with the cannabis in Britain. After the verdicts on Mr Marks, Morgan Stewart Prentiss, aged 41, the American, of no settled address, and Hedley Morgan, aged 34, of Potters Bar, Hertfordshire, the judge was asked to make an application preventing details of some of the mitigation pleas for the five from being reported by journalists.

Lord Hutchinson of Lullington, QC, for Mr Marks, of Hans Crescent, Chelsea, London, said nothing should be reported from the pleas of mitigation which might be prejudicial to Mr Marks if the 1974 case came to trial. The judge refused to grant the application.

Mr John Rogers, QC, outlining the case against the five, had earlier told the court that James Goldsack, aged 32, an Oxford graduate from London, had acted as accountant for the cannabis in Britain, was stock-taker, and had driven one load down from Scotland to a warehouse at Laindon, Essex.

Martin George Langford, an artist, aged 36, of no settled address, took messages at a flat in London and collected 180lb of cannabis from a storehouse at Pytchley, Northamptonshire.

Mr Rogers said Alan Arthur Grey, a farmer, aged 47 of Glengarry, Inverness-shire, took no part in the import of the cannabis to a place on the coast of West Scotland, but he stored four tons at his bungalow.

Mr Rogers said Robert Keningale, aged 35, a carpenter of no fixed address, was the storeman for cannabis kept at Pytchley. Customs men found one and a half tons of the drug there.

The fifth man was Nicholas Cole, aged 35, a barrister, of Daniel Farm, Laindon. Mr Cole ran a furniture business and stored more cannabis. Customs men found 2.75 tons stored at the farm.

Mr Richard Du Cann, QC, defending Mr Goldsack, said his client had been a drug addict. He had had no direct contact with his colleagues in the ring because that was the way Mr Marks ran the organization.

During the course of Mr Marks's trial Mr Marks told the court that he had been recruited in 1972 by MI6 to spy on Mr James McCann, a leading Provisional IRA activist who used the finances from drug smuggling to finance arms purchases.

He traced Mr McCann three times but Mr McCann managed to get away. He also worked for Mexican agents who were trying to uncover a terrorist group financed by drugs. The Mexicans were trying to identify those exporting Colombian cannabis to finance arms.

Mr Marks said he was introduced to the Mexicans by Mr and infiltrated a cannabis smuggling ring to get information for them.

□ Sir Michael Havers, the Attorney General, is to consider allegations that a journalist may have committed contempt of court in talking to a juror after Mr Marks had been aquitted.

The possible contempt, by David Pallister, of *The Guardian*, was reported to Judge Mason. Mr Pallister was placed in custody, but was released after Mr Geoffrey Shaw, appearing for the reporter, told the court that the question of contempt might be disputed. He said the Contempt Act, 1981, did not prohibit conversation with jurors.

Agreeing to send the matter to the Attorney General, the judge said that by placing Mr Pallister in custody he had "demonstrated to everyone how serious this court would regard the matter".

5

Operation Eclectic

(↓) On 6 May 1982, the same month as this cover story appeared in *Rebecca* (a Welsh news magazine that ran a print edition between 1973 and 1982), Howard was released from HMP Wandsworth. Howard was now a household name, but this would not pay the bills.

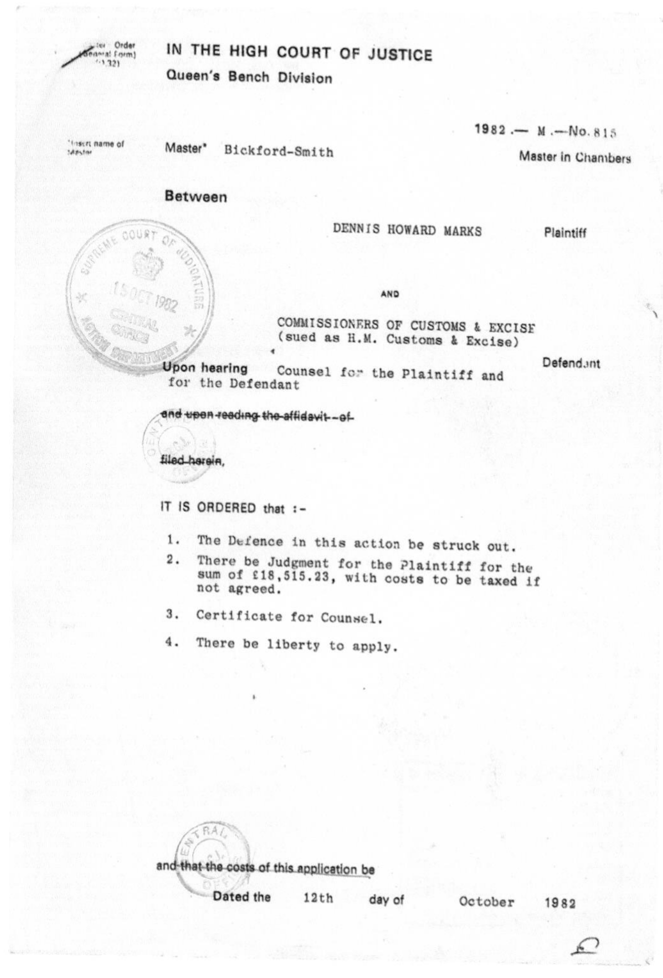

IN THE HIGH COURT OF JUSTICE
Queen's Bench Division

1982.— M.—No. 815

Master* Bickford-Smith — Master in Chambers

Between

DENNIS HOWARD MARKS — Plaintiff

AND

COMMISSIONERS OF CUSTOMS & EXCISE (sued as H.M. Customs & Excise) — Defendant

Upon hearing Counsel for the Plaintiff and for the Defendant

~~and upon reading the affidavit of~~

~~filed herein,~~

IT IS ORDERED that :-

1. The Defence in this action be struck out.
2. There be Judgment for the Plaintiff for the sum of £18,515.23, with costs to be taxed if not agreed.
3. Certificate for Counsel.
4. There be liberty to apply.

~~and that the costs of this application be~~

Dated the 12th day of October 1982

(↗) Howard decided to sue Customs & Excise for the return of the twenty odd thousand pounds seized following his arrest. The case was heard in the High Court. Customs & Excise argued that Howard's only source of income was cannabis; his acquittal at the Old Bailey was irrelevant. Master Bickford Smith struck out the Defence of Her Majesty's Customs & Excise; a conviction was required for money to be forfeited: 'It is not open to the police to go into any old tart's flat and clear out all the china and money they can find on the assumption that these are the proceeds of immoral earnings… [new laws have been introduced since; today money can, and very often is, confiscated from suspects even in the absence of a criminal conviction]. Mr Marks might be the biggest smug druggler [*sic*] in the world, but money is money, and we have to stop somewhere. He has been acquitted. The money is his. But before I finish, I want to say a few words about kif. Last summer, my wife and I went to Morocco, to the Casbah and the Rif. We were driving through the kif plantations when we came across a man sitting in the road blocking our course. My wife told him in no uncertain terms to move. She threatened him with our gun. Do you know he just stayed there! He wouldn't budge. He was stoned. That's how strong that stuff is. Well, good luck, Mr Marks. The money is yours.'

WEST END
SECRETARIAL SERVICES

Howard Marks
Consultant

18 Carlisle Street
London
W1V 5RJ

Telephone : 01 434 4272
Telex : 263056 MONTAP G

(↑↗) In partnership with Old John, Howard set up Drinkbridge Ltd for wine importation, on John's advice to 'forget all the other kinds of madness for now'. Howard also established West End Secretarial Services. Both businesses operated from premises on the corner of Carlisle Street and Dean Street in Soho, formerly operated by World Wide Entertainments.

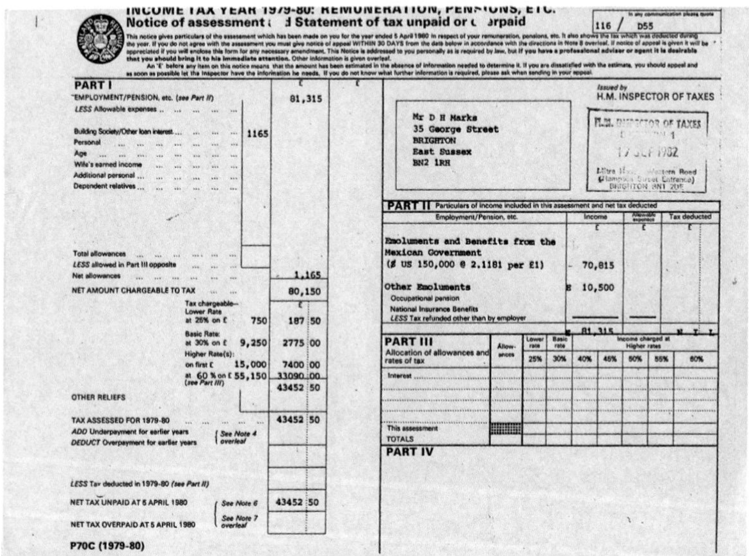

INCOME TAX YEAR 1979-80: REMUNERATION, PENSIONS, ETC.
Notice of assessment and Statement of tax unpaid or overpaid

116 / D55

Issued by H.M. INSPECTOR OF TAXES

Mr D H Marks
35 George Street
BRIGHTON
East Sussex
BN2 1RH

PART I

		£
EMPLOYMENT/PENSION, etc. (see Part II)		81,315
LESS Allowable expenses		
Building Society/Other loan interest	1165	
Personal		
Age		
Wife's earned income		
Additional personal		
Dependent relatives		
Total allowances		
LESS allowed in Part III opposite		
Net allowances		1,165
NET AMOUNT CHARGEABLE TO TAX		80,150
Tax chargeable— Lower Rate at 25% on £	750	187 50
Basic Rate: at 30% on £	9,250	2775 00
Higher Rate(s): on first £	15,000	7400 00
at 60 % on £	55,150	33090 00
		43452 50
OTHER RELIEFS		
TAX ASSESSED FOR 1979-80		43452 50
ADD Underpayment for earlier years / DEDUCT Overpayment for earlier years (See Note 4 overleaf)		
LESS Tax deducted in 1979-80 (see Part II)		
NET TAX UNPAID AT 5 APRIL 1980 (See Note 6)		43452 50
NET TAX OVERPAID AT 5 APRIL 1980 (See Note 7 overleaf)		

PART II Particulars of income included in this assessment and net tax deducted

Employment/Pension, etc.	Income £	Allowable expenses £	Tax deducted £
Emoluments and Benefits from the Mexican Government ($ US 150,000 @ 2.1181 per £1)	70,815		
Other Emoluments	10,500		
	81,315		NIL

PART III Allocation of allowances and rates of tax

PART IV

P70C (1979-80)

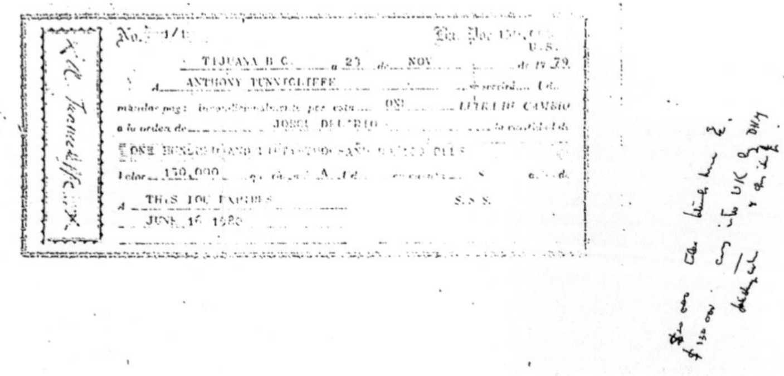

(←↑) When the Inland Revenue got in touch, asking Howard to pay tax on his ill-gotten gains, Howard tried his luck again. In the Income Tax Assessment he submitted in response, he claims he received only emoluments and benefits from the Mexican government, to the tune of $150,000. Winding up Inland Revenue turned out not to be as much fun as Howard had hoped. This was one government department he would not get the better of.

(→) It wasn't long before James McCann got in touch:

'At my Old Bailey trial, I had publicly accused him of being the world's biggest narco-terrorist and arms smuggler. He owed me for that bit of PR. The phone rang.

"Get out of the room, take the lift downstairs, and walk slowly out through the hotel's main doors," whispered a soft Dublin brogue. "Your man will be outside."

I did as instructed. Jim was parked outside in a big Mercedes, bigger than mine. I got into the passenger seat, and he drove off. He burst out laughing and handed me a very strong joint. I burst out laughing and smoked it.

"I've got everything under control, kid, from the fucking Khyber Pass camel jockeys to the decadent fascists that run this poxy pisshole," he boasted, for some reason pointing to the Louvre. "I can get what I want, where I want, when I want. I'm back in the fast lane."

"That's great, Jim. You know I still owe people for those Thai sticks you lost in a lorry load of bananas outside Dublin."

"I owe you nothing, you Welsh scumbag. You owe me your freedom and your life."' MN

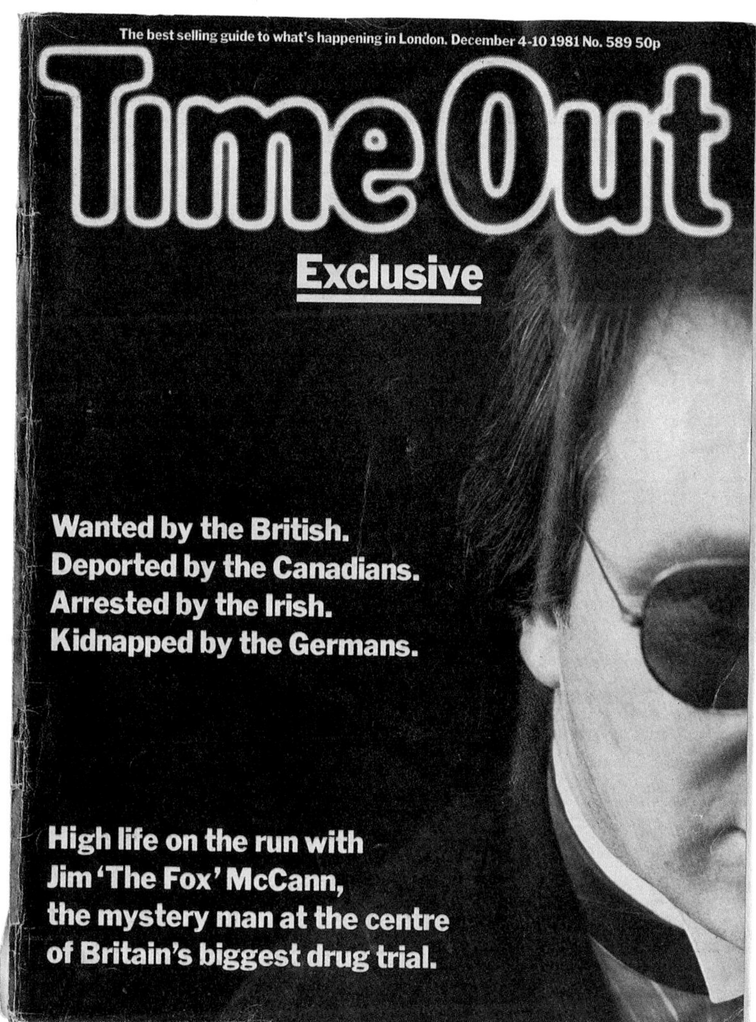

The best selling guide to what's happening in London. December 4-10 1981 No. 589 50p

Time Out

Exclusive

Wanted by the British.
Deported by the Canadians.
Arrested by the Irish.
Kidnapped by the Germans.

High life on the run with Jim 'The Fox' McCann, the mystery man at the centre of Britain's biggest drug trial.

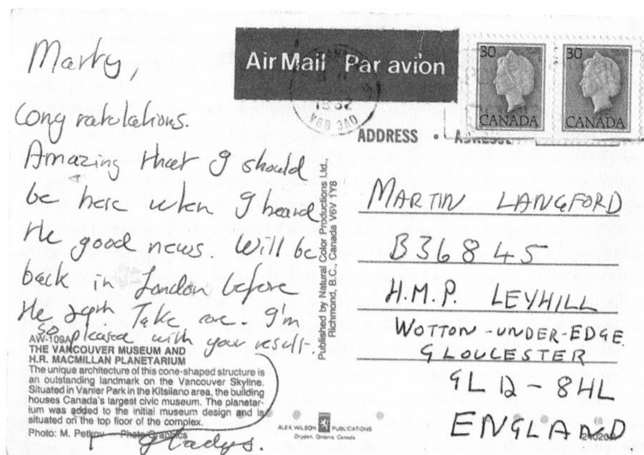

Air Mail Par avion

CANADA 30 CANADA 30

Marty,
Congratulations.
Amazing that I should be here when I heard the good news. Will be back in London before the 30th. Take care. I'm so pleased with your result.
Gladys.

ADDRESS

MARTIN LANGFORD
B36845
H.M.P. LEYHILL
WOTTON-UNDER-EDGE
GLOUCESTER
GL12-8HL
ENGLAND

AW-109A
THE VANCOUVER MUSEUM AND
H.R. MACMILLAN PLANETARIUM
The unique architecture of this cone-shaped structure is an outstanding landmark on the Vancouver Skyline. Situated in Vanier Park in the Kitsilano area, the building houses Canada's largest civic museum. The planetarium was added to the initial museum design and is situated on the top floor of the complex.
Photo: M. Petkov — Photo Graphics

Published by Natural Color Productions Ltd. Richmond, B.C., Canada V6V 1Y8

(←) In 1976, while travelling under the name of Mr Tunnicliffe, Howard had come across Marty Langford (also on the run after Howard's disappearance) by pure chance, in Vancouver's planetarium. Meeting up with Ernie Combs in Vancouver in 1982, Howard sent this card to congratulate Marty for his imminent release on licence from his four-year prison sentence for the 1980 charges (Marty had pleaded guilty). Ernie was still a fugitive from justice. As a result of thyroid cancer he had been unwell and was becoming increasingly dependent on prescription painkillers. Ernie's trusted advisers had lost all his savings and he felt he was going to have to make a few more deals.

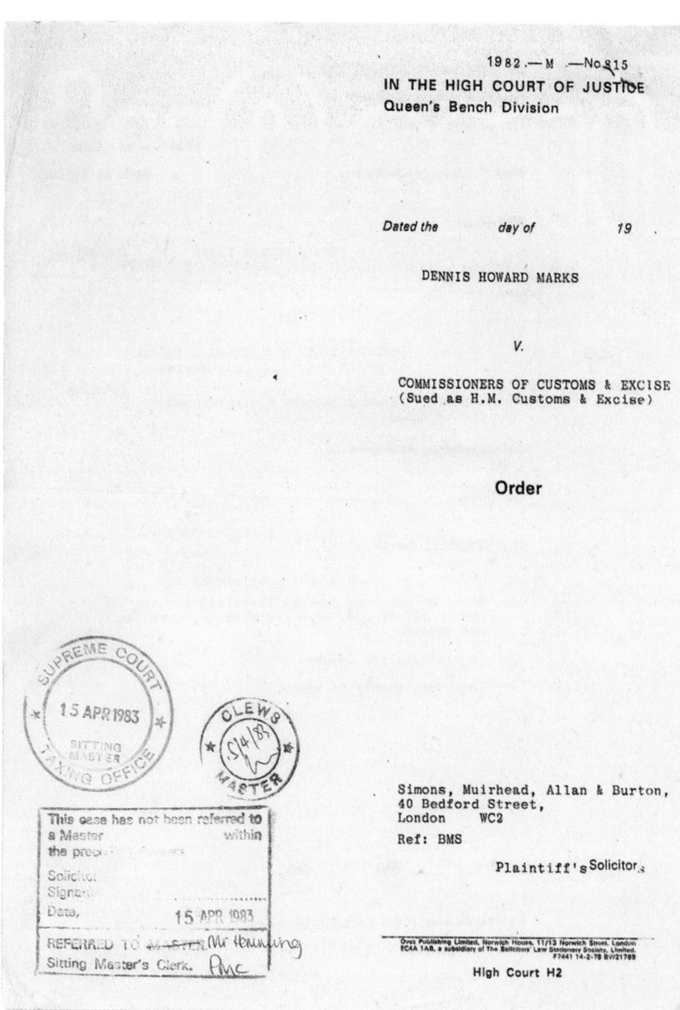

1982.—M .—No.815

IN THE HIGH COURT OF JUSTICE

Queen's Bench Division

Dated the day of 19

DENNIS HOWARD MARKS

v.

COMMISSIONERS OF CUSTOMS & EXCISE
(Sued as H.M. Customs & Excise)

Order

SUPREME COURT
15 APR 1983
SITTING MASTER
TAXING OFFICE

CLEWS
5/4/83
MASTER

This case has not been referred to a Master within the prec...
Solicitor
Signat...
Date, 15 APR 1983
REFERRED TO ~~MASTER~~ Mr Henning
Sitting Master's Clerk.

Simons, Muirhead, Allan & Burton,
40 Bedford Street,
London WC2
Ref: BMS

Plaintiff's Solicitors

Oyez Publishing Limited, Norwich House, 11/13 Norwich Street, London EC4A 1AB, a subsidiary of The Solicitors' Law Stationery Society, Limited.
F7441 14-2-78 BW21769

High Court H2

(←) Her Majesty's Customs & Excise lodged an appeal against Master Bickford Smith's decision on forfeiture, but they didn't have a leg to stand on. A compromise was reached between Howard and Customs; Her Majesty's Customs & Excise would relinquish the £20,000 if it went to the Inland Revenue, where it would be put towards Howard's debt to them. This was a tidy solution, but the Inland Revenue had decided they wanted a lot more than £20,000 from Howard.

(←↑) *High Times: The Shocking Life and Times of Howard Marks* by David Leigh was published in 1984. The book, clearly written with Howard's collaboration (half of its proceeds were apportioned to him) amounted to a clear admission by Howard of guilt to the charges for which he had been acquitted at the Old Bailey. The book was not a huge success except amongst law-enforcement officers, who purchased it in droves and read it with fury. The first sentence of the last paragraph in the book reads 'Howard, last public representative of the Spirit of the Sixties, had finally won.'

Members of the UK law enforcement later explained that 'irritation' did not express their feelings on Howard's acquittal. Better words would be 'astonishment', 'disbelief', 'incredulity'. They recounted how a man on the Isle of Kerrera had been found with bales of cannabis in his house. Bales had been wheeled up his garden path and 'six months later you could see the cannabis plants which had sprouted from the seed which had spilled...' (documented in the photograph above, courtesy of Her Majesty's Customs & Excise).

Peter Nelson of Her Majesty's Customs & Excise gave his copy of *High Times* to DEA agent Craig Lovato. Nelson told Lovato that Howard 'enjoys having a number of deals in operation at the same time. Gets a kick out of it. Needs to fill in his time and mental space, otherwise he gets bored'. The copy of the cover pictured is from the discovery material generated by the DEA's investigation into Howard. DEA agents read the book and believed every word of it, several becoming obsessed with catching Howard as a result. Shortly after Howard and Judy's arrest by the US's Drug Enforcement Agency in 1988, Jack Hooks of the DEA said, 'Marks said in the book that he was too smart for us. We are very pleased to make him eat his words.' This interpretation of the book is an odd one; most of the scams described in the book sound more like the fortuitous machinations of Cheech and Chong than the sophisticated handiwork of a cocky genius. Perhaps it was the success of this comic ease that irritated certain individuals in the DEA most.

(↘) Howard continued to seek the money required to settle his debt with the Inland Revenue. In this letter from both Howard Marks and Donald Nice, dated June 1984, the Commerce Bank in Frankfurt is authorised to open the safety deposit box Howard had opened in the name of Donald Nice, and hand its contents over to representatives from the Inland Revenue. A reply from the bank to the Inland Revenue in August 1984 explained that its contents had long since been seized by the Frankfurt Inferior Court and handed over to the Frankfurt Customs investigation authorities.

18 Carlisle Street
London
W1V 5RJ

June 29, 1984

The Manager
Commerce Bank
Frankfurt
Germany

Dear Sir

Further to our previous correspondence I hereby authorise you to cut open my safe deposit box and to give all the contents to representatives of the Inland Revenue after deducting any costs to yourselves.

Yours faithfully

D.H.Marks a.k.a Donald Nice

(←) With the Inland Revenue on his back, Howard decided it was time to move abroad. In January 1984, Howard and Judy took their daughters out of school to travel round the Far East and Europe, settling on Palma de Mallorca as their final destination, where the girls would start school in September 1985, after a second round-the-world family trip.

Ernie's double-agent friends claimed they could get hashish from Pakistan to the US via the American President Line at Karachi. Neither Howard's friend in Pakistan, Mr Malik, nor Old John, were keen on working with North Americans – the amounts involved were always big, the parties often bizarrely embedded in government shenanigans – but they were always willing to help Howard. Howard told Ernie he'd get the hash together and collected a suitcase containing several million dollars in cash for its purchase in Hong Kong. Howard was convinced he was being followed by the DEA. The suitcase turned out to be an encumbrance as strikes broke out across the city and riots erupted. Howard hid in the premises of Sam's, Hong Kong's best tailor. Days later in Pakistan, Mr Malik informed Howard that there was a DEA Agent named Harlon Bowe and a British Customs Representative called Michael John Stephenson stationed in Karachi. Stephenson was the Customs Agent who claimed to recognise Howard through the keyhole of his hotel room at Howard's Old Bailey trial.

Howard was unable to deliver the hashish personally to the American President Line as planned, and someone else went in his place. The scam later went awry and the hash 'disappeared'. Ernie's double-agent friends claimed Howard or Mr Malik had ripped Ernie off but there was sufficient love and trust between Mr Malik and Howard and Howard and Ernie not to suspect each other. They set out to make back the money lost with other scams.

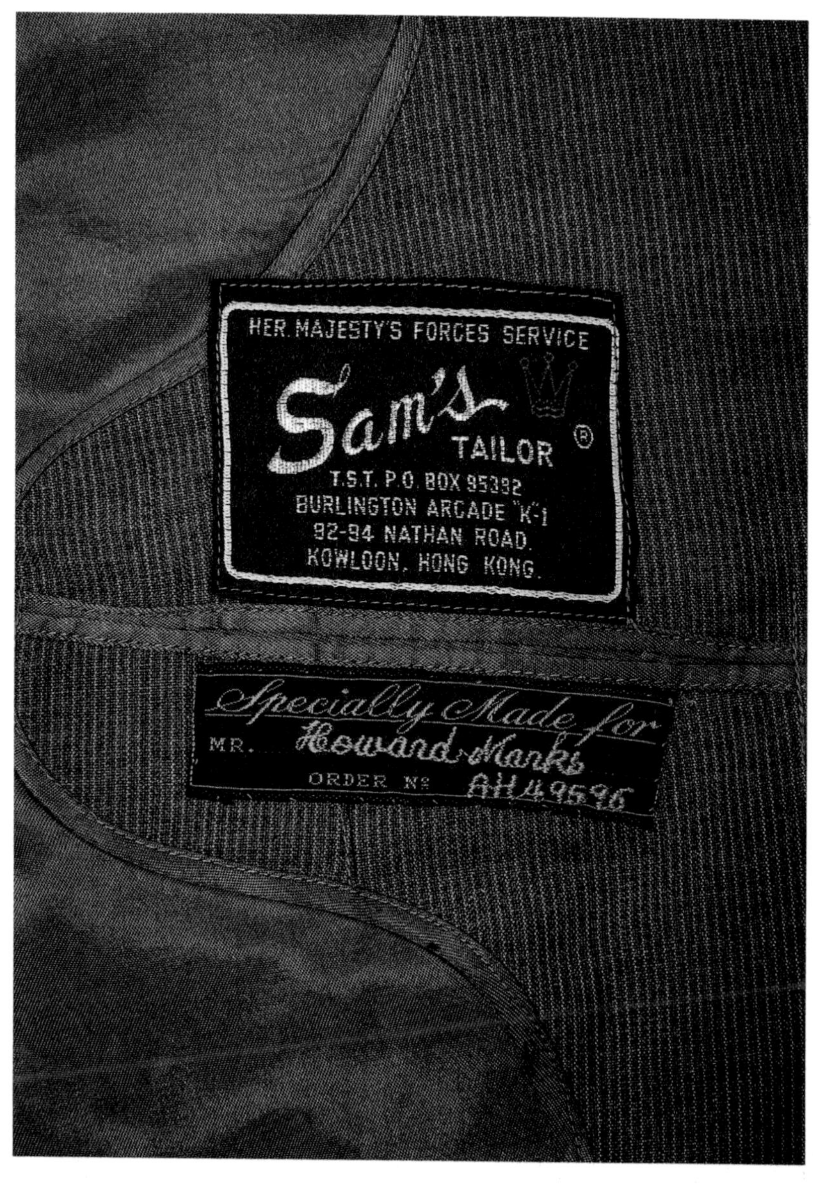

(↓) 'Howard was once again smuggling from Pakistan and Thailand to the United States and Europe. He travelled extensively on his own passport, including dozens of separate visits to Pakistan, the Philippines, Thailand, Morocco and Hong Kong as well as to China, Japan, India, Korea, Kenya, Taiwan and virtually every European country. He avoided travelling to the United States of America.

Howard became very fond of Pakistan and made a life-long friend in Mr Malik. Howard and Mr Malik set up several legitimate and increasingly successful businesses in Pakistan. In late 1985, when Howard turned up at the American Club and Harlon Bowe was there, Bowe appears to have felt Howard had gone there with the express intention of provoking him. It's more likely that Howard went because it was one of the very few establishments serving liquor in Pakistan. Harlon Bowe sent over a waiter to Howard's table asking him to leave the American Club. Howard refused: "Ask Mr Bowe if I can buy him a drink."

Within days, the story went around the world that Howard Marks was a counter-surveillance expert. As other surveillance teams awaited his arrival at airports throughout Asia, they received urgent messages from the DEA advising "extreme caution". For years after, the reputation followed Howard wherever he went and, to a degree, it protected him. More than once the watchers stayed so far behind, they lost him.' HMP

D. H. Marks
Manager

Hammond House,
117 Piccadilly,
London, W1V 9FJ

Tel: 01-629 2484
Telex: 291015 PORTAG G

D.H. Marks

Hammond House,
117 Piccadilly,
London W1V 9FJ.

Tel: 01-629 2484
Fax: 01-491 2367
Telex: 291015 PORTAG G.

(→) This document provides a chronology of law-enforcement surveillance of Howard and friends between 1973 and 1985. Harlon Bowe had come to believe that Combs and Marks and their associates were too well organised and too ingenious to be caught. In 1985, Ernie was finally busted for the 1973 scam. He was bailed, but it caused logistical complications and was unsettling. It looked like the agents on Ernie's payroll were no longer as reliable as they had once appeared.

Federal Participation in the Joint Venture [1]

The government claims that its involvement in the present case did not commence until January 1986. This assertion is comprehensively refuted by the following information, all of which is actually provided by the government.

Sep 1973 DEA agent BOWE is appointed to head a joint DEA/British Customs investigation following a seizure of hashish at Las Vegas airport, Nevada. [Lovato affidavit]

Mar 1976 MARKS, COMBS, and BROWN are indicted in Nevada as a result of the above DEA/British Customs investigation.

1978 Lovato is appointed DEA agent in Las Vegas, Nevada. [Lovato affidavit]

1982 DEA instruct government witness Lickert to testify against MARKS at a trial in the United Kingdom. [Lickert 480]

May 1984 DEA agent BOWE and British Customs observe MARKS arriving in Karachi, Pakistan. [Bowe 636]

Dec 1984 DEA agent LEONG submits report of hashish seizure in Alameda, California. [Ex 272]
DEA agent WHITESIDE participates in investigation of Alameda seizure. [Whiteside 536]

Mar 1985 COMBS arrested in Nevada. Forfeiture proceedings initiated by DEA.

May 1985 DEA agents BOWE and WHITESIDE, together with Dutch police observe MARKS and LANE in Karachi, Pakistan. [Bowe 636]

Jul 1985 Spanish police participate in investigation. [Letter from Spanish police 23/07/86] with DEA.

Aug 1985 British Customs observe MARKS and SPARROWHAWK in London. [Cairney]

Oct 1985 British Customs observe MARKS, DENBIGH, WILLS and ALLEN in London. [Dewar]

Nov 1985 DEA agent BOWE together with British Customs and Dutch police observe MARKS, LO, WILLS, ALLEN and LANE in Karachi, Pakistan. [Bowe]
Dutch police intercept telephones of HOBBS therby allegedly obtaining information regarding the involvement of MARKS, COMBS and MALIK in a proposed shipment of ten tons of hashish to the United States. [Wezain affidavit]
DEA agent DUGAN observes MARKS, WILLS and ALLEN in Bangkok, Thailand. [Lovato affidavit]
DEA agent SCALZO observes MARKS, SPARROWHAWK and WILLS in Manila, Phillipines. [Scalzo 1828]
DEA agent LOVATO informs DEA agent DESM about DEA investigation on MARKS. [DEA 6]
DEA request Singapore police to locate WILLS. [Tai Hunt 1476]

MARKS, COMBS, BROWN, LANE, SPARROWHAWK, DENBIGH, LO, WILLS, ALLEN, HOBBS and MALIK are codefendants in the instant case.

D H Marks
Director

HONG KONG INTERNATIONAL TRAVEL CENTRE

22-23 Denman Street,
Piccadilly Circus, London, W1V 7RJ
01-734 9476 Sales
01-434 9067 Reservation
Telex: 8955534 HKITC

Specialists in Australia and the Far East.

HONG KONG INTERNATIONAL TRAVEL CENTRE

22-23, Denman Street,
Piccadilly Circus, London, W.1.V, 7RJ
01-734 5511/437 0963
Telex: 8955534 HKITC

Specialists in Australia and the Far East.

Proprietors: Liew & Liew Ltd.

September 3 198[illegible]

PRESS RELEASE

AN OPENING WITH AN EASTERN PROMISE

HONG KONG INTERNATIONAL TRAVEL CENTRE opened its new offices in Denman Street, London W1, last night, to the sound of popping champagne corks and a huge sigh of relief from its owner, Orca Liew. "After 13 years of various back rooms," she beamed "it'll be wonderful to have a view at last."

The view, precisely, is a huge fully glass-fronted Piccadilly office, with a Chinese rock garden and waterfall, imported enamel screens, and computers clocking up more and more new customers. There was indeed, something to smile about.

The celebration was officiated by HIS EXCELLENCY HU DING-YI, The Ambassador for the People's Republic of China and MADAME XIE HENG, the Ambassador's wife. THE HON PETER BROOKE MP introduced His Excellency and relayed a message from RICHARD LUCE MP, Minister of State, Foreign and Commonwealth Office. Other guests included THE RT HON LORD BETHELL MEP, senior members of foreign embassies to the Court of St. James and Hong Kong Government officials. About 100 people from the travel industry itself were present - all curious to see this new addition to the ranks of the independent high street travel agencies.

HONG KONG INTERNATIONAL have joined forces with DEBENHAMS Stores for the occasion, and launched a competition through MS LONDON magazine for readers to win a trip for two to China. The competition, which hardly tests the intellect - make words

more...

Howard decided to invest in the travel agency Hong Kong International and became its co-director, a promising legitimate venture at last. He travelled to China on its behalf and it became the first foreign agency allowed to sell domestic flights within China. The Chinese Ambassador to Great Britain officially opened Hong Kong International Travel Centre's new offices in Piccadilly and Howard later opened a branch in Bangkok. Philip Sparrowhawk, Howard's contact for Thai sticks, introduced Howard to Lord Antony Moynihan. Moynihan was a bent British aristocrat and fugitive from justice in the Philippines, friendly with the President of the Philippines, the kleptocrat Ferdinand Marcos. Moynihan could get whatever he wanted through the airport but wasn't, according to Philip, to be trusted. Howard was lunched and dined by Moynihan on several occasions. Howard's objective was to further the interests of Hong Kong International there, something Moynihan told Howard he could help him with.

D.H. Marks

Consultant

HONG KONG INTERNATIONAL TRAVEL CENTRE (BANGKOK Ltd.)

41 Sukhumvit Soi 19
Bangkok, Thailand
Phone (662) 253-3495
Telex 84783 SARCO TH

Specialists in Europe and the Far East.

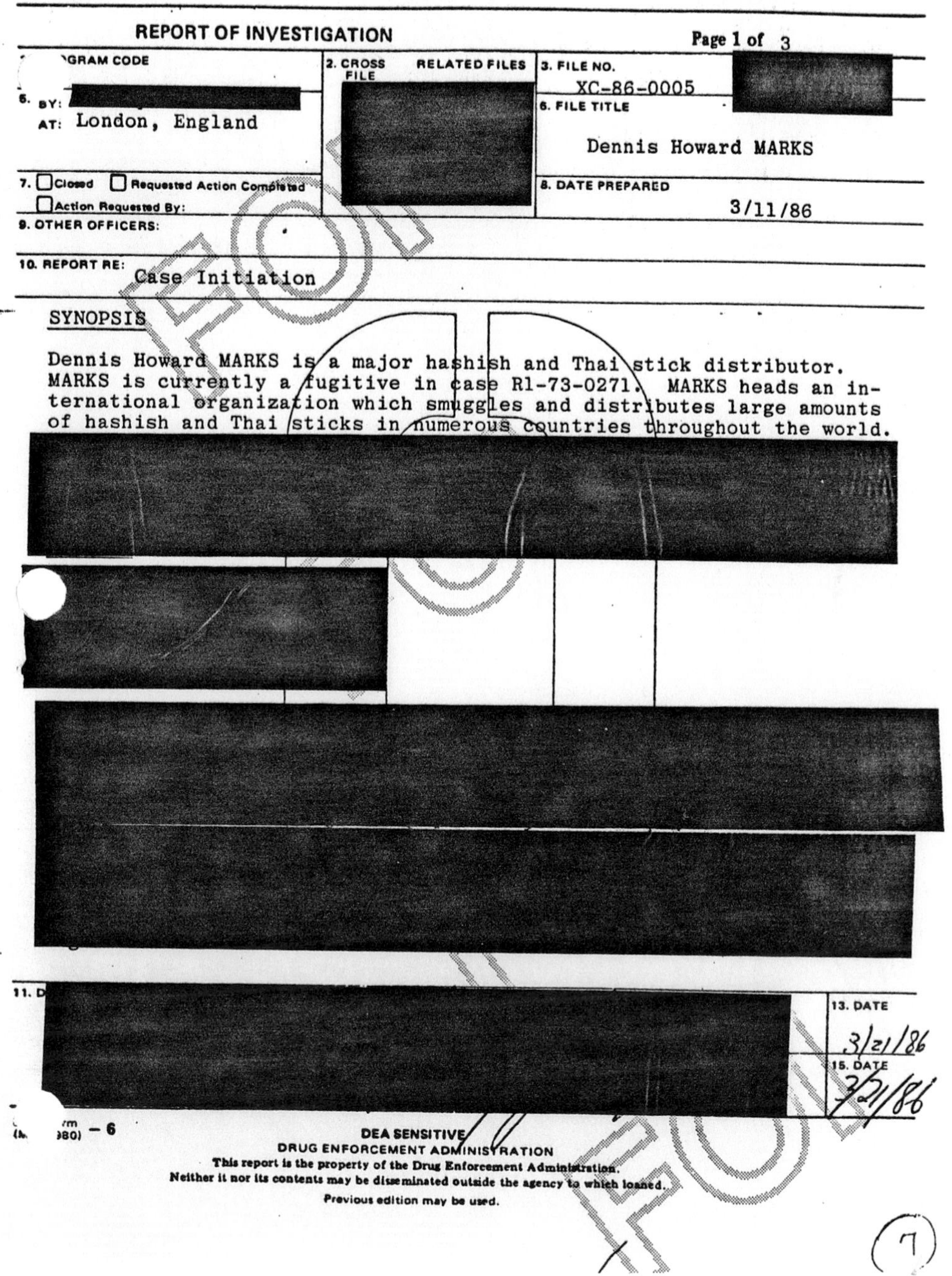

REPORT OF INVESTIGATION

Page 1 of 3

GRAM CODE

2. CROSS FILE RELATED FILES

3. FILE NO. XC-86-0005

5. BY:

AT: London, England

6. FILE TITLE Dennis Howard MARKS

7. Closed Requested Action Completed Action Requested By:

8. DATE PREPARED 3/11/86

9. OTHER OFFICERS:

10. REPORT RE: Case Initiation

SYNOPSIS

Dennis Howard MARKS is a major hashish and Thai stick distributor. MARKS is currently a fugitive in case R1-73-0271. MARKS heads an international organization which smuggles and distributes large amounts of hashish and Thai sticks in numerous countries throughout the world.

11. D

13. DATE 3/21/86

15. DATE 3/21/86

rm (... 980) – 6

DEA SENSITIVE
DRUG ENFORCEMENT ADMINISTRATION
This report is the property of the Drug Enforcement Administration.
Neither it nor its contents may be disseminated outside the agency to which loaned.
Previous edition may be used.

(7)

The redacted DEA Report of Investigation, dated 3 November 1986. It identifies Howard as the head of an international organisation that distributes hashish and Thai sticks in numerous countries around the world.

This graphical representation of the 'Marks Cartel' was prepared by the DEA for enforcement officers working on the investigation into Howard. The investigation was codenamed 'Operation Eclectic'.

Carlo Morselli was awarded a doctorate in criminology for his thesis on Howard's career:

'Marks was argued to be the principal member of an international cannabis smuggling ring, referred to as the "Marks Cartel", that DEA officials claimed was responsible for 15% of the cannabis entering the US throughout the seventies and eighties... Marks was indeed a cannabis trade participant for two decades. This capacity to persist on a consistent basis in the trade, however, was not achieved at the helm of any international smuggling cartel. Marks wasn't even a member of a cartel; nor was he a member of "organised crime" in its orthodox conceptualization. Marks was neither part of a monopolist nor oligopolist attempt to control the cannabis trade at any level or in any region. He was indeed a liberal-minded, free-willed, and independent illegal entrepreneur, but a closer analysis of the inner workings of his cannabis smuggling activities brings us to see that there was a structure to this apparent disorganization. The structure came in the form of his personal working network that, in its own waxing and waning, embedded his career in the international cannabis trade. Marks' positional privilege came as a result of a cumulative process of seizing and accessing one entrepreneurial opportunity after another until he himself became the entrepreneurial opportunity to be seized by others. His favourable reputation established with those players with whom he was in business, particularly Ernie Combs, added to the circumstances which led to his fitting between links in the trade... Violence is often argued to be the obvious mechanism regulating competition in illegal trades. Marks' career provides evidence that it is possible to persist and actually succeed in illegal enterprise without having to rely on instrumental violence. Structuring one's personal working network to include trade members who are not directly connected to each other but who may have interests in dealing with one another represents a cooperative way of being competitive.' SMN

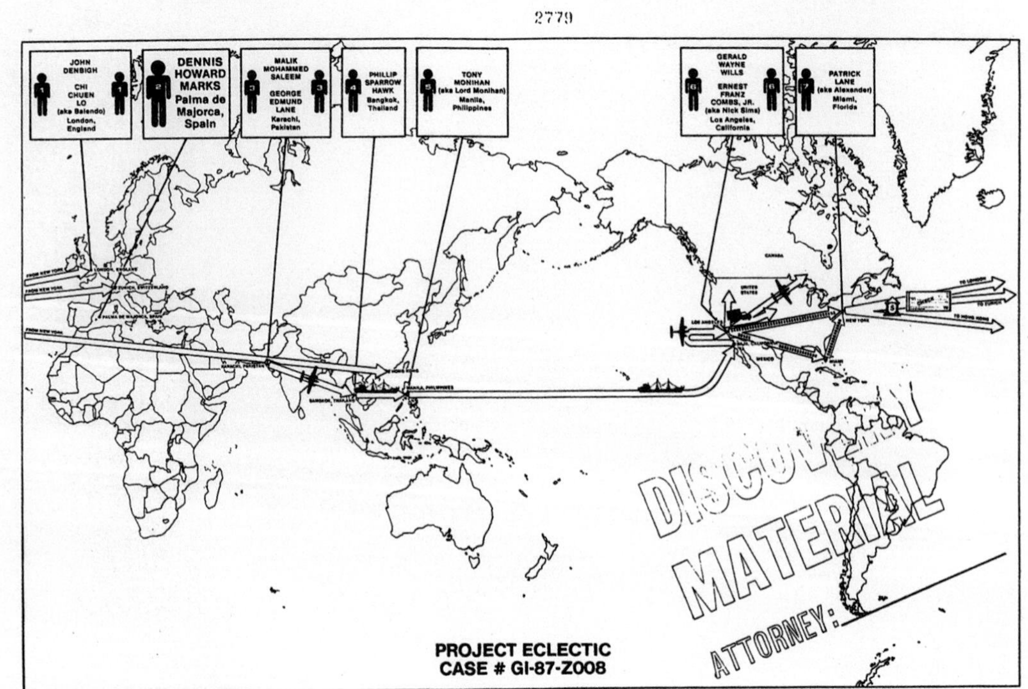

Her Majesty's Customs & Excise identified 'Peter' or 'Mr Simms' as a Californian who 'considers himself, with Marks, as one of the pioneers of marijuana smuggling' and a major player in Howard's network. They informed the DEA, who quickly worked out that the Californian in question was none other than Ernie Combs, the man who had been on the run for the Transatlantic Sounds shipments between 1973 and 1985.

But why was Combs telephoning Howard to say 'good job, I'm really proud of you' in March 1986? And where was Combs now? Once again, he'd disappeared.

1843

A B Si Translation Services, Inc.

2002 Brickell Ave.
Miami, FL 33131
(305) 854-9575

(JD) Yeah, I'll be seeing the other fellow said.

(HM) Well, I was hoping to be able to tell you now, but Im still waiting for a call from Him, okay?

(JD) O.K. but I'm here, I'm here,I'm here to twelve o'clock or one o'clock.

(HM) Yes, right.

(JD) You ███ to tell me.

(HM) Yes, I will, now in case there's some delay with the assistant chef, yeah?

(JD) Yeah.

(HM) Do you want me to, either send the septic tank or the dog handler?

(JD) (UI) the office is closed at the moment, yeah?

(HM) Yes.

(JD) It's ███, I have to ah, in case the foreman came in, yeah?

(HM) Yeah.

(JD) I was to tell you just to (UI) I'm here in the wilderness at the moment. ███) again. (UI) there's nothing we can do, with the engineer, when his turn comes, maybe from the other place, yeah?

68

(↑↗) The DEA found Howard's telephone conversations difficult to follow. Agents assumed, perhaps because this was 'organised crime', that codenames were systematic and used consistently. In fact, Howard and his friends' 'codes' were more often than not the improvised and humour-driven nicknames that arise amongst friends cognisant and fond of each other's foibles, and were far from consistent in their application. This made the DEA's job hard; Mr Nice, for example, was thought to be code for Gerry Wills.

Lovato knew that to succeed in incarcerating Howard he would need a good attorney. At the beginning

1844

A B Si Translation Services, Inc.
2002 Brickell Ave.
Miami, FL 33131
(305) 854-9575

(JD) Yeah, yeah, O.K.

(HM) And I'll bring you right up to date with every thing I know.

(JD) All right, but if you can get in touch with (UI) as much as you can, don't sound concerned you know, just keep in touch, that's all you can do.

(HM) Yeah, O.K.

(JD) I mean you phoned her, she went to phone him, and I was at his hotel, yeah. as I told you (UI)so then when she does phone back, they're all upset because she phoned back, it's all kind of ah...

(HM) Silly.

(JD) I still got to finish the porch which is more important.

(HM) Well, [redacted] the entrance, yeah.

(JD) Well, that's [redacted], it was, that measurement was one point six, something,it wasn't one point nine, I [redacted] you, it was one point six.

(HM) Ah, that's Bruce , you mean?

(JD) No, no, ah, Touch.

(HM) One point six, that's right, yeah, right, O.K.

70

of 1987, Lovato sought to persuade up and coming hotshot attorney Bobby O'Neill to take on the case by showing him the evidence he had so far. O'Neill had been unimpressed; there was nothing he could take to a jury – it was clear Howard was conspiring to do something illegal, but in the absence of any cannabis or any money, all Lovato was offering the government was his own 'expert' opinion on what reels and reels of phone taps meant. O'Neill was interested, but he needed Lovato to get him more persuasive evidence. The DEA set their eyes on Lord Antony Moynihan as a likely informant.

A facsimile from Mr Malik to DH Marks, offering a potential supply schedule and containing information on the latest prices for various products.

Mr Malik and Howard hoped to shift their entrepreneurial flair into legal businesses, but both remained deeply attached to what Mr Malik referred to as the Mother Business. Howard had fun in Pakistan, albeit of a sometimes unnerving nature:

'I dressed up in my Afridi costume and drove Eddie's car to the airport. Gerry and Ron were arriving from London. They had flown via Amsterdam. I hung about in a crowd of Pakistanis waiting for their friends and families to arrive. [Harlon] Bowe and [Michael] Stephenson, each wearing dark glasses, drove up in the same white car I'd seen previously and ran into the airport. They quickly returned, got into another car, a dark blue one, and drove off.

Gerry and Ron came through customs and immigration. They laughed at my outfit as we climbed into Eddie's car. I gave each of us a ready-rolled joint of our freshly made hashish. Blue fumes filled the car. I drove off in the direction of the city centre.

It wasn't long before the dark blue car appeared in the rear mirror. As a pedestrian I have no difficulty losing a tail. As a driver I do, particularly when I'm stoned. I couldn't think where to go. Bowe and Stephenson did not know I was driving this car. They were following Gerry and Ron, not me. There was no pressing reason to think they knew we were fellow scammers. I shouldn't go anywhere where I was known. But I only knew how to get to places where I was known. God, I was stoned.

I mustn't let Bowe and Stephenson get any information they don't already know. That's the key. I drove Eddie's car to the Aga Khan hospital and parked in the car park. Ron turned down the radio.

"Whaw, this is some hash you got us buddy. What do you think of it, Ron? You gotta sell it."

"I'm stoned all right, guys, but I'd like to smoke some without tobacco, and without that fucking music. Man, is this place primitive. It's like Mexico. Howard, why are we parked in this hospital? You got an appointment or a sudden medical problem? Don't tell me this is where the dope's stashed."

"Hey, that's real cool," said Gerry, "stashing it in a hospital. I told you, Ron, this Howard is something else. Do you have another joint, buddy? This one's kinda had it. Man, this is good gear."

"The DEA were waiting for you at the airport here."

"So fucking what," said Ron. "Those bastards wait for us everywhere. They were always on our backs in Mexico. They don't know what we're doing here. They don't even know where we are right this minute."

"Yeah, it would be a drag if they knew where our stash was," commented Gerry.

"They followed us here from the airport. They're probably parked outside waiting for us to leave. The stash is nowhere near here."

"Then why the fuck are we here?" asked Ron. "Let's drive off, lose the tail, and go to the stash."

"This car belongs to someone who works at this hospital. That's why we're here."

"Oh you're returning his car," deduced Gerry.

"No, he's away for the week."

"Then why the fuck are we here?" asked Ron, again. "Gerry, turn that fucking music off."

"Hey, man, some of it's really far out. They can get it on. What's the night life scene like here, Howard? As good as Hong Kong? I thought Amsterdam was kinda neat with them hookers in the windows and cafés selling joints. I bet there's loads of them here."

"Gerry, there's nothing here: no bars, no hookers, no night-spots, nowhere you can smoke hash in public. Everything is illegal."

"You're kidding. I thought this was where it all happened."' MN

Xcid 20.5.87

No copy

SALEEM INVESTMENTS PAK (PVT) LTD.

1ST FLOOR, SAIFEE HOUSE, DR. ZIAUDDIN AHMED ROAD, P.O. BOX 10214, KARACHI, PAKISTAN
PHONES: 219171 - 74, GRAMS: SONSUM TELEX: 24608 SOSUM PK

MAY 19, 1987.

Dear Mr. D.H. Marks,

With reference to your telex of 16th May, 1987 and our reply of 18th May, 1987, we enclose herewith photocopy of Tender for supply of Tripple Super Phosphate (TSP) to Bangladesh.

We have very little time therefore if we have to complete all formalities before the tender closing date 8th June, 1987, then we must rush and get all prices and ship freight from the port of supply to Chittagong or Mongla port.

We can offer our supply schedule but the four shipments must leave before 25-7-1987, 29.8.1987, 20.9.1987 and 5-101987.

We would like our represntative Mr. Afzal Mobin to visit Spain or ask the supplier/manufacturer representative with sufficient authority to visit us to finalise the tender documents and bid bond which is 1% of the value of goods. We request you to do your best to get some manufacturer to commit TSP for Bangladesh.

The fertilizer tender business is re-occuring in Pakistan and Bangladesh. They contineously need the following. We give the latest accepted price also.

1. Triple Super Phosphate.

2. Urea - $.93.90 per M.T. C&F Karachi.

3. Diammonium Phosphate DAP Granular Fertilizer $.146.00 per M.T. C&F Karachi.

Kinly telex us future line of action immediately.

Best regards.

Yours faithfully,

M. Saleem Malik

(M. SALEEM MALIK)
CHAIRMAN.

INDUSTRIAL & COMMERCIAL CONSULTANTS, DEVELOPERS & FINANCIERS.

(↓) In April 1986, when Ernie Combs phoned Howard, the call was traced to his hotel room in Los Angeles. The DEA's plan was to arrest Ernie and let him go, in the hope he would lead them to a bigger haul with Howard. The amount of hashish and Demerol they found in his room left them no choice but to lock him up. Howard was informed that evidence in proceedings against Ernie suggested Howard's home phone in Mallorca was being tapped. Reports were reaching Howard, largely from Ernie's chameleon-like double agents, that the DEA was getting ready to bust Howard big time. They wanted protection money.

In February 1986, President Marcos was ousted by the People Power Revolution and Moynihan's world crumbled. In 1987 articles started to appear in newspapers in the Philippines, alleging Moynihan was involved in drug dealing and highlighting the UK allegations of fraud and people trafficking that had led to his fugitive status. When informed that his name had been placed on a stop list and that he was not allowed to leave the country pending investigation, Moynihan sought the help of his golfing partner in Manila, drug liaison officer for the Australian Federal Police, John Robinson. Within days Robinson got back in touch, suggesting Moynihan meet with the DEA. Agent Art Scalzo told Moynihan the DEA had enough evidence to have him extradited to the United States on drugs charges and to lock him up for decades. His only way out was to get evidence on Howard. Scalzo told Moynihan to think things over and that he'd be back in touch but Scalzo 'didn't leave it to chance. He called him at places he knew he would be – because Armed Forces Narcotics Command (NARCOM) were tapping his phone. How you doing, Tony? Making a decision Tony?' HMP

Eventually Moynihan agreed to collaborate, but only on the condition that all fraud charges awaiting him in the UK be dropped so that he could return there. Howard and Judy's son, Patrick, was born in London in 1986 (pictured).

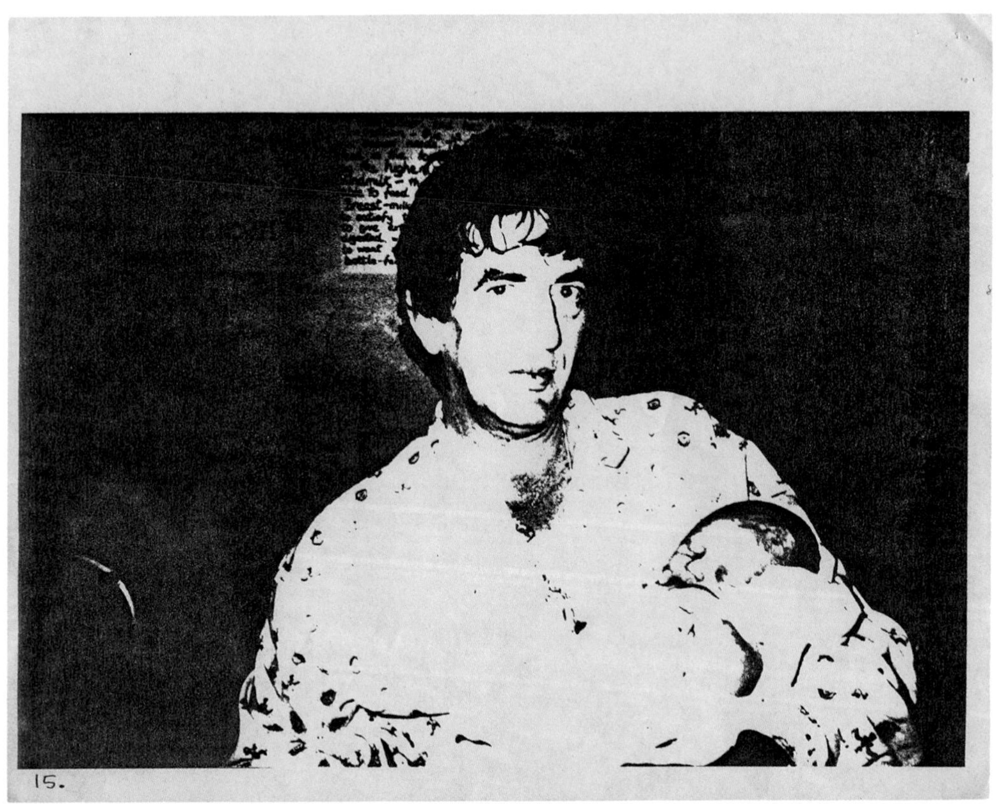

(→) Police surveillance photographs of Howard and Philip Sparrowhawk, alleged member of the 'Marks Cartel', having a drink in Bangkok. There was no suggestion that Howard was aware that these photographs were being taken, or that he was deliberately impersonating Elvis in any of them. It is, however, the case that in late 1987, Lovato correctly surmised a load of cannabis was about to arrive in Vancouver when he saw Old John, Gerald Wills, Philip Sparrowhawk and Ronald Allen walk into a make-your-own-video establishment there, and pretend to be the Rolling Stones, miming to 'Let's Spend the Night Together' with Old John apparently giving a very fair impression of Mick Jagger.

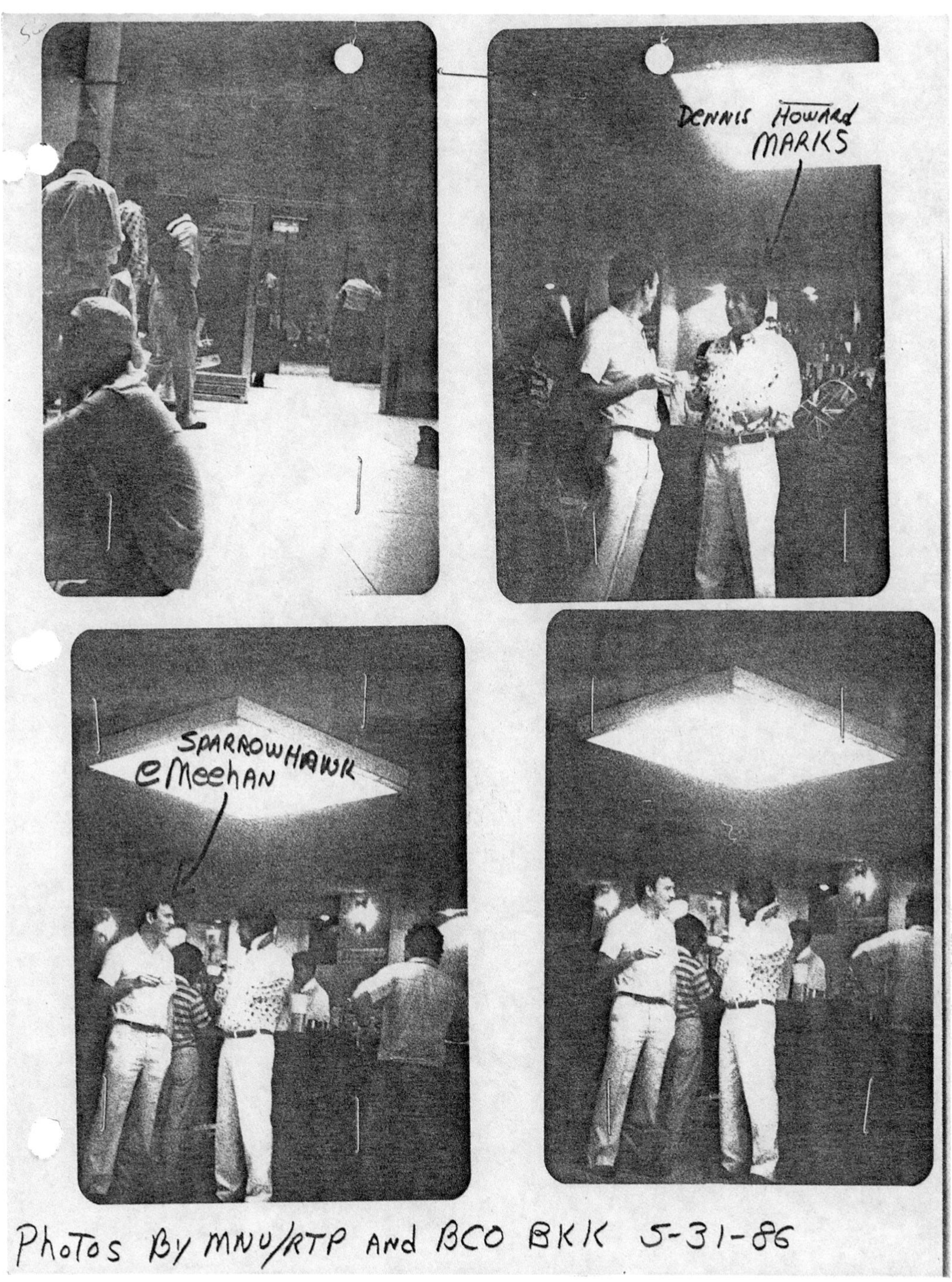
DENNIS HOWARD
MARKS
SPARROWHAWK
@Meehan
PHOTOS BY MNU/RTP AND BCO BKK 5-31-86

As well as believing he was head of an organised cartel, those seeking Howard's capture appear to have become paranoid about the power of his intelligence and to have convinced themselves Howard was playing games with them. In April 1988, the lawyer Michael Katz visited the office of the Attorney General, leaving a message that he wished to speak with the attorney Bobby O'Neill on behalf of his client, Howard Marks. O'Neill asked those who had attended to him what the man had looked like:

'Given a vague description – "English, tallish, longish hair"– O'Neill immediately jumped to the wrong conclusion. He called Lovato at the DEA and said, "I think Howard's just been in my office, pretending to be a lawyer." They both raced to the airport from their separate offices and searched the departure terminals, looking for Howard Marks. The fact that they did not find him only confirmed their suspicions that Marks was playing games with them.'[HMP]

On 13 July 1988 the Attorney General succeeded in persuading a grand jury to issue a bill of Indictment against 22 persons, including their supposed ringleader Howard Marks. It read:

'From on or about an unknown date, at least as early as April 1970, and continuously thereafter, up to and including December 22, 1987, an Enterprise existed within the meaning of Title 18, United States Code, Section 1961 (4), that is, it was a group of individuals and entities, foreign and domestic, associated in fact for the purpose of importing and distributing marijuana and hashish, laundering the proceeds and profits, and investing monies derived from marijuana and hashish importation and distribution through the use of foreign and domestic corporations, financial institutions, and business entities utilised to conceal the true owners of the acquired assets and the true source of the finances for the acquisition of these assets.'

The indictment was sealed by the court and security measures taken to ensure it remained secret until those charged, scattered across the globe and constantly on the move, could be arrested simultaneously.

(↓) Howard was busy establishing himself as a trade and travel consultant in Taiwan. Ernie was in prison, Old John had been arrested in the Canadian bust. Judy had put the Mallorca house on sale, the family was going to move back to the UK, Howard was going to dedicate himself full-time to his travel agency and develop business links between Taiwan and Europe. On 22 July, after visiting a dog temple in Taiwan and having offered a prayer to be allowed to be with his children, Howard flew home (believing this to have been the meaning of the message given to him at the temple, legal and double-agent advice being even more ambiguous). His arrival in Palma was missed by waiting DEA agents because he had been met by the Chief Inspector of Police who liked to save Howard from the hassle of passport control by taking him through a side door.

HOWARD MARKS
Travel and Trade Consultant

8th floor Shin Kong World Commercial Building
287 Section 3, Nanking East Rd. Taipei, Taiwan R.O.C.
TEL: (02) 7129368 FAX: (02) 7130812
TLX:16533 CENTRECO

(↗) In 1988 George Pasenelli, the intelligence analyst working alongside Craig Lovato (having been assigned to the Marijuana Unit of Operational Intelligence in 1986), posted Lovato silver handcuffs with Pasenelli's name engraved on them. On 24 July, Lovato watched Howard's family home in La Vileta, Palma de Mallorca. He played out in his mind how the next 24 hours would unfold:

'The iron gates leading to the courtyard, controlled by an electronic lock, looked much more formidable than they really were. Lovato imagined the Spanish police battering them down with sledgehammers, while Howard calmly erased the databases on which, Lovato was convinced, he kept the details of his organization.' HMP

-- Page #1. of statement made by Amber Mary Marks --

STATEMENT by Amber Mary MARKS, elder daughter of Dennis Howard MARKS and Judith Margaret MARKS, born in London, England, on the 29th. day of October 1977. This statement refers to events ocurring on the morning of Monday the 25th. day of July 1988, at the domicile of her parents in PALMA DE MALLORCA, BALEARIC PROVINCE, SPAIN, in the CALLE FUEGO 3, district of LA VILETA:---.

Francesca's scream woke me up and I thought she'd hurt herself badly. I got out of bed and went into the hall where I saw two men. One of them was fat, and I later heard him say his name was CRAIG LOVATO. Across the hallway was Mummy, pale and shaking. As I was naked I ran back into my bedroom to get my dressing-gown. I went into Mummy's arms and asked her what was happening, She said she didn't know but had heard Francesca scream. She went to the top of the stairs and called Francesca who then came up with a third man. Together we went to the bedroom. The men followed.-----------------------------------.
Mummy asked what was happening but no-one answered. I asked in Spanish and Lovato answered me but I didn't understand what he said. Patrick my baby brother, woke up and I went to get him and I heard Mummy ask this man if he could speak in English. He said: "We're arresting your husband who's downstairs being questioned in the sitting-room." Mummy said: "You're American aren't you?". He said: "That's right Ma'am, I'm Craig Lovato from the D.E.A.." Mummy said: "Are you going to take me?" and he said it would just be for a few hours of questioning. Mummy told him she wasn't going to leave us and cuddled us. She asked where my Daddy was, and Lovato said he was downstairs. The two men with Lovato went out and another three came in, including a Spanish man who said he was an Inspector, and I thought I recognised from the night before, when we went to a Restaurant. They looked Mummy up and down. She didn't have the belt to her dressing-gown. She said: "Can I get dressed?" and Lovato said he'd have to search the wardrobe first. He said he was looking for rifles. After searching the wardrobe he said she could get dressed in the bathroom. Then she asked if she could use some creams. He said, no in case there was something in them.-----------------------.

-- Page #2. of statement made by Amber Mary Marks.--

---.
He told us we'd all go downstairs, and when we were in the hall Mummy suggested I get dressed. Lovato said I could. When I got downstairs I saw Marie there. I sat down. Mummy was white. Men were all over, upstairs, outside, and in the sittingroom. I asked if I could see Daddy, but Lovato said he'd already gone. Mummy asked for a bucket, so I got her one, and an icepack. The 'phone rang and I was going to answer it, but Lovato said: "No!" and picked it up. "Ah, Marsha!" he said. "Come over, I've just arrested your sister, Judith Margaret Marks, and her husband, Howard Marks." I cuddled Mummy who was being sick.---.
Ten minutes later the doorbell rang and I thought it was Masha, so I went out, but Lovato brought me back in. It was some male secretaries with note-books. They came in and talked and started writing things down. Another man walked by who looked English. Mummy asked him who he was and he answered he couldn't tell her, but after a while he said he was from Scotland Yard.-----------------------------------.
Masha arrived and hugged us. Marie and Lovato were chatting and Mummy was being sick again. Lovato turned to Mummy and said he was going to extradite her and Daddy to America. Men were making lists of all our things. I saw one of my bracelets, and mine and my sister's walky-talkies. Lovato asked for the keys of the car and I fetched Mummy's handbag. He took the keys and gave her the purse back and said she'd need it where she was going. I asked him to please bring her back to say goodbye if they were extraditing her. He said "Maybe.", then told Mummy to go with him. She kissed us goodbye and left. She was still sick, so he put his arm around her. He said she'd be back that afternoon if she was innocent.-----------.

I, the undersigned, Amber Mary MARKS, hereby declare this statement to be in my own words, and to be my own recollection of the events recorded above.--.
Signed in Palma de Mallorca the ....th. of June 1989.

Signature witnessed by (Testigo a la firma)

J Marks

(←↑) At the request of Howard and Judy's legal teams, their daughters wrote accounts of the events that took place on 25 July 1988, when Amber, author of the above, and their eldest, was aged ten.

While Lovato explained to the children that he intended to lock both parents up in the United States of America for the rest of their lives, he received an urgent phone call from the headquarters of the Spanish police. They were unable to remove the Pasenelli engraved handcuffs from Howard's wrists without the key in Lovato's possession.

Some of the haul of drugs and guns police found in a cave in Spain

MY WIFE IS INNOCENT, SAYS Mr BIG

Howard Marks

EX MI6 man Howard Marks, branded the world's biggest drugs godfather, made a desperate plea from his Majorca prison cell yesterday.

Near tears, he begged Spanish police: "Please let my wife go. Judy is innocent."

His emotional "hands off" message came in an interview behind bars in Palma Prison on the holiday island.

Judy Marks

SHAKEN

Marks, dishevelled and shaken after three days in jail, hit out angrily at the tactics of Miami Drugs Squad officers who swooped on the couple this week after a year-long undercover operation involving half a dozen police forces across the world, including Scotland Yard.

Leaning on the bars of his cell, he said: "I would like to protest very strongly about my wife's imprisonment. They are committing the biggest crime of all by taking my wife away from her children."

By FRANK THORNE

Marks was speaking for the first time since his dramatic arrest by Spanish police and officers from the American Drugs Enforcement Agency on Monday.

The ex-MI6 man went on to describe the horror of the arrests at gunpoint, watched by their three young children.

"It was cruel. It was terrible," he said.

The children are now being cared for by Marks' sister-in-law. They have three children, two daughters aged ten and seven, and an 18-month-old boy, Patrick.

In an emotional voice, and red-eyed through lack of sleep, Marks vowed to fight his extradition to America where he will face at least 14 charges involving the importation of cannabis and hashish, money laundering and passport offences.

According to the Miami Drugs Squad, Oxford graduate Marks is the evil genius behind an international drugs empire that has made billions.

WRONG

Yesterday, clearly depressed, Marks protested: "I don't know why they arrested my wife. I think it's to put pressure on me."

About the allegations, Marks replied: "They are only in America – and they are wrong."

Marks, who planned to return to London with his family soon to have the girls educated at a posh private school, chain-smoked through the interview.

His hair was unkempt and despite occasional laughter, his depression at being locked up was obvious.

He claimed the US courts had named him as a worldwide drugs godfather only because of the audacious book he wrote boasting that he would never be caught.

It was written after he was cleared from a sensational £20 million drugs trial at the Old Bailey seven years ago, when he said he had been working for MI6, using drug deals to infiltrate the IRA.

Yesterday he was allowed to see his British-based American lawyer, Michael Katz.

Mr Katz said later: "Mr Marks denies all the charges. He has done nothing, and he has nothing to fear."

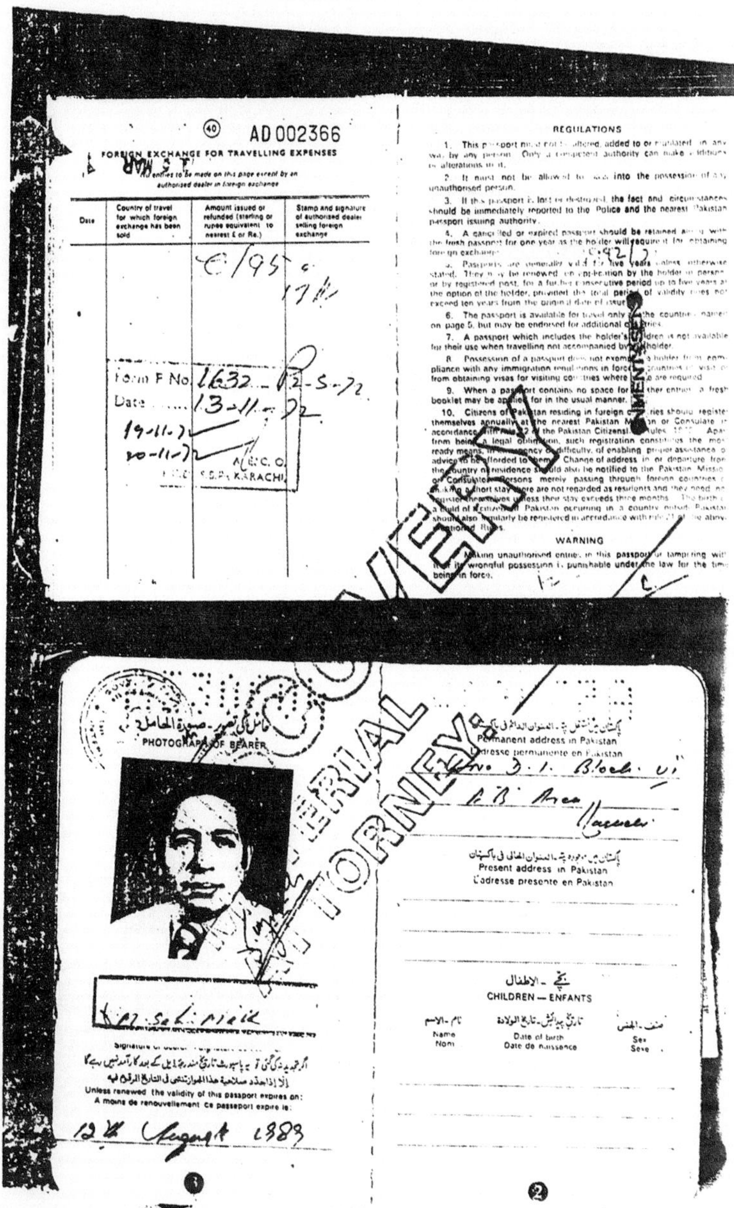

40 AD 002366

FOREIGN EXCHANGE FOR TRAVELLING EXPENSES

No entries to be made on this page except by an authorised dealer in foreign exchange

Date	Country of travel for which foreign exchange has been sold	Amount issued or refunded (sterling or rupee equivalent to nearest £ or Re.)	Stamp and signature of authorised dealer selling foreign exchange
		£/95	

Form F No. 1632 - 12-5-72

Date 13-11-72

19-11-72

20-11-72

S.B.P., KARACHI

REGULATIONS

1. This passport must not be altered, added to or mutilated in any way by any person. Only a competent authority can make additions or alterations in it.

2. It must not be allowed to pass into the possession of any unauthorised person.

3. If this passport is lost or destroyed, the fact and circumstances should be immediately reported to the Police and the nearest Pakistan passport issuing authority.

4. A cancelled or expired passport should be retained along with the fresh passport for one year as the holder will require it for obtaining foreign exchange.

5. Passports are generally valid for five years unless otherwise stated. They may be renewed on application by the holder in person or by registered post, for a further consecutive period up to five years at the option of the holder, provided the total period of validity does not exceed ten years from the original date of issue.

6. The passport is available for travel only to the countries named on page 5, but may be endorsed for additional countries.

7. A passport which includes the holder's children is not available for their use when travelling not accompanied by the holder.

8. Possession of a passport does not exempt the holder from compliance with any immigration regulations in force in countries of visit or from obtaining visas for visiting countries where visas are required.

9. When a passport contains no space for further entries, a fresh booklet may be applied for in the usual manner.

10. Citizens of Pakistan residing in foreign countries should register themselves annually at the nearest Pakistan Mission or Consulate in accordance with rule 22 of the Pakistan Citizenship Rules, [illegible]. Apart from being a legal obligation, such registration constitutes the most ready means, in emergency or difficulty, of enabling proper assistance or advice to be afforded to them. Change of address in or departure from the country of residence should also be notified to the Pakistan Mission or Consulate. Persons merely passing through foreign countries or making a short stay there are not regarded as residents and they need not register themselves unless their stay exceeds three months. The birth of a child of a citizen of Pakistan occurring in a country outside Pakistan should also regularly be registered in accordance with rule 21 of the above mentioned Rules.

WARNING

Making unauthorised entries in this passport or tampering with it or its wrongful possession is punishable under the law for the time being in force.

فوٹو حامل - صورة الحامل

PHOTOGRAPH OF BEARER

Signature of bearer

Unless renewed the validity of this passport expires on:

A moins de renouvellement ce passeport expire le:

12th August 1983

1

پاکستان میں مستقل پتہ - العنوان الدائم في باكستان

Permanent address in Pakistan

L'adresse permanente en Pakistan

House 3.1. Block VI

P.E.C.H.S. Area

Karachi

پاکستان میں موجودہ پتہ - العنوان الحالي في باكستان

Present address in Pakistan

L'adresse presente en Pakistan

بچے - الاطفال

CHILDREN — ENFANTS

نام - الاسم Name Nom	تاریخ پیدائش - تاريخ الولادة Date of birth Date de naissance	صنف - الجنس Sex Sexe

2

(←↗) In an interview with *Dazed* in 2016, DEA Agent Craig Lovato admitted that his reason for arresting Judy was to put pressure on Howard. He asserted that she '*was* guilty of some kind of crime so we used her as a pawn'.

Now that Howard had been arrested, the go-ahead was given for arrests around the world, including Old John in Vancouver, Philip Sparrowhawk in Bangkok, Patrick Lane in Florida and Ernie Combs and his wife in Los Angeles. Combs was arrested despite having been granted immunity in 1987 for providing testimony on his double-agent associates. Mr Malik was also arrested, the first extradition of a Pakistani national to the United States of America on drugs charges, in what some saw as evidence of Pakistan's new Prime Minister Benazir Bhutto's resolve to improve relations with North America. The simultaneous arrests around the world provoked a media frenzy in which Howard was described as 'the evil genius behind the world's biggest marijuana and hashish racket'. Dramatic headlines were accompanied by photographs of vast stashes of cannabis in underground hideaways (despite there being no connection between these seizures and Howard or any of his associates).

The Mail on Sunday, July 31st, 1988

Marks in top-security jail 'to foil $1m escape'

Mail on Sunday Reporter

DRUGS baron suspect Howard Marks was locked in Spain's terrorist prison last night because of a $1 million-dollar escape plot.

Oxford graduate Marks and William Reaves, his alleged top aide in the world's biggest hashish ring, were taken secretly from the holiday island of Majorca under heavy armed guard.

A judge at Spain's National Court in Madrid ordered the switch after being told that American Reaves had $1 million to bribe his way to freedom from the island's Palma jail.

The men, arrested six days ago, were taken to grim Alcala-Meco prison, east of Madrid, their guards under orders to shoot if they tried to escape.

SWITCH: Howard Marks

Palma's jail governor, Joaquin Mejuto, said he had been tipped off about the plot.

He said: 'I was informed that Reaves intended to arrange his escape in whatever way possible — legal or illegal. I knew he had tried to bribe my guards.

'I talked to Reaves and his lawyer and told him that he and Marks would only leave the jail through the main gates, or over my dead body.'

The governor described as 'extraordinary' the measures taken against the two men.

'They were watched around the clock by a special group of guards and stripped of all clothes and possessions.'

Marks's wife, Judith, is being kept in the Palma jail with Geoffrey Kenion, 46, a Palma restaurant owner from Rickmansworth, Herts. She has been allowed to have a radio and photographs of her three young children.

The governor said of her husband: 'You can tell he was Oxford-educated. He acts like a gentleman, intelligent, well mannered — a lot of class. She is also well-mannered.'

It is the first time that the Alcala-Meco has been used to hold prisoners on remand for alleged drug offences.

The jail is in open flat country, 'where from a helicopter you can spot a rabbit running', according to police. It is used to hold the country's top terrorist prisoners.

Marks, 42, and Reaves, 46, will appear before a judge in Madrid on Tuesday at the start of legal moves for extradition to the United States to face charges in Miami.

(←) The effect of the US government's erroneous portrayal of him as a high-security risk resulted in Howard being held, pending extradition, under the strictest conditions available in Spain. 'Intelligence' on a planned escape by Howard's co-defendant, pilot Roger Reaves (wrongly described as William Reaves and as one of Howard's employees in this article), resulted in both being moved to Alcalá-Meco prison in Madrid, built to house political prisoners. Both were stripped and placed in cages under 24-hour guard. It didn't take long for the Spanish authorities to appreciate that such conditions were unnecessary. Howard would, however, remain housed in Alcalá-Meco until his eventual extradition.

CAFETERIA

ALDONZA

MAYOR, 44
TELEF. 888 10 05
ALCALA DE HENARES

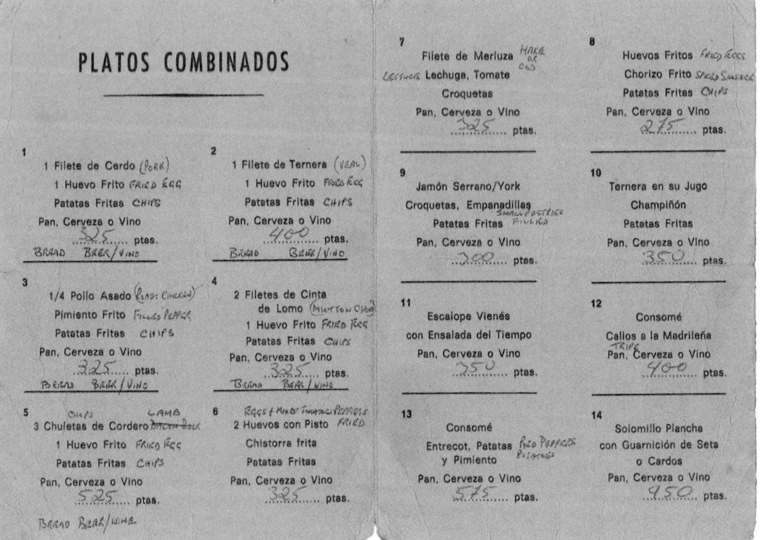

PLATOS COMBINADOS

1
1 Filete de Cerdo
1 Huevo Frito
Patatas Fritas
Pan, Cerveza o Vino
325 ptas.

2
1 Filete de Ternera
1 Huevo Frito
Patatas Fritas
Pan, Cerveza o Vino
400 ptas.

3
1/4 Pollo Asado
Pimiento Frito
Patatas Fritas
Pan, Cerveza o Vino
325 ptas.

4
2 Filetes de Cinta de Lomo
1 Huevo Frito
Patatas Fritas
Pan, Cerveza o Vino
325 ptas.

5
3 Chuletas de Cordero
1 Huevo Frito
Patatas Fritas
Pan, Cerveza o Vino
525 ptas.

6
2 Huevos con Pisto
Chistorra frita
Patatas Fritas
Pan, Cerveza o Vino
325 ptas.

7
Filete de Merluza
Lechuga, Tomate
Croquetas
Pan, Cerveza o Vino
325 ptas.

8
Huevos Fritos
Chorizo Frito
Patatas Fritas
Pan, Cerveza o Vino
275 ptas.

9
Jamón Serrano/York
Croquetas, Empanadillas
Patatas Fritas
Pan, Cerveza o Vino
300 ptas.

10
Ternera en su Jugo
Champiñón
Patatas Fritas
Pan, Cerveza o Vino
350 ptas.

11
Escalope Vienés
con Ensalada del Tiempo
Pan, Cerveza o Vino
350 ptas.

12
Consomé
Callos a la Madrileña
Pan, Cerveza o Vino
400 ptas.

13
Consomé
Entrecot, Patatas y Pimiento
Pan, Cerveza o Vino
575 ptas.

14
Solomillo Plancha
con Guarnición de Seta o Cardos
Pan, Cerveza o Vino
950 ptas.

(↑) The menu for the visitors' café on the Alcalá-Meco prison grounds.

SAUDI ARABIAN STING

NG

OWARDES

Telephone call from American/Oriental accented male requesting home number of Howard and Judy.

Telephone call from same person identifying himself as Shepherd.

Telephone call from same person saying things were being done and someone would be coming over.

Dinner booking made in name of Kalid. Later confirmed by Valparaiso Hotel as being for Prince Kalid.

I was cooking Sunday lunch as usual and came into the dining room as work eased off. A tall, slim, dark-suited, sallow skinned, dark haired gentleman was sitting with a young attractive American blonde. On an adjacent table sat two shorter gentlemen: one was pleasant looking, grey-suited, and he introduced himself as secretary; the other was swarthier, slightly bulkier, and older, later identifying himself as a bodyguard. The blonde was told to leave the table. I was told to sit down amidst brief courtesies, then was told that he was under orders to help sort matters out and that a meeting at the Valparaiso would be essential to hold, the next day.

-1-

Sworn account of Bob Edwardes, the owner of a Welsh restaurant frequented by Howard and his family in the Mallorcan village of La Vileta, of communications between himself and persons claiming to be members of Saudi Arabia's royal family. The account refers to Howard's children being brought to meet these self-proclaimed Saudi Arabian princes in the Valparaíso hotel in Mallorca in 1988 ('1991' is a typo). It was a strange but unconvincing performance; the children expressed their sense of foul play when the robed gentleman in sunglasses outlined plans for rescuing Howard from prison by landing a helicopter on the prison roof. This account was prepared for Howard's defence, as an example of what Howard alleged to have been underhand tactics to obtain evidence (in this case, hidden money) against him. The yellow Post-it reading 'Saudi Arabian sting' is in Howard's handwriting.

HEROIN TRAFFICKERS, BLACK MARKET BENEFITS FROM CIA'S AFGHAN WEAPONS PIPELINE

Is The U.S. Being "Taken" Beyond All Reason?

N-C-D 27-4-88 (1)

Somewhere in the confines of the Covert Operations Directorate at CIA Headquarters in Langley, VA, a few officials are shaking their heads and hoping for the best.

While furnishing arms to Afghan rebels for their struggle against the Soviet Army, the CIA has — sort of — provided arms to a few other parties as well. It seems that people along the arms shipment pipeline have helped themselves.

In their efforts to get the Soviet Army out of Afghanistan, Covert-Ops has managed to successfully arm the rebels enough to obtain a "victory." The Soviet Army is withdrawing its troops. That's the good news.

Here comes the bad news. CIA and National Security Agency (NSA) officials estimate that about 20-30 percent of the weapons destined for Afghan rebels were "ripped-off." Other intelligence specialists say the stolen arms figures are much higher.

Former CIA Director Stansfield Turner said that he would be surprised if 20 percent of the arms got through the pipeline.

"Weapons are going to fall into the wrong hands. The Pakistanis are going to take something and the various Afghan factions are going to take their share, too," he said.

What weapons are being stolen and who is stealing them? For openers, the weapons taken were: AK-47 assault rifles and ammo, Stinger SAMs (surface-to-air missiles), and anti-aircraft guns, to name just a few. The weapons are being appropriated by:

- **Iranian revolutionaries:** They bought 12 Stingers and stole others. In one case,

of a "sales commission" — how much of a commission is unclear.

NCD 27-4-88 (5)

Heroin traffickers moved in and helped themselves, too.

A State Department official said: "There's been a tremendous proliferation of weapons all over the countryside. Every shepherd boy guarding his flock has got an AK-47. In the villages, you can rent an RPG."

The CIA forked out $1.7 billion in 1987 to run this operation. If 20 percent of the arms were stolen, that figures to be about $340 million. If half were stolen, $850 million was ripped off.

Intelligence agents are the first to say that they deal with corrupt officials when it comes to distributing arms. They know a percentage is going to fall into the wrong hands.

"But, you've got to keep your eyes open. You've got to ask yourself if the cost of the Stingers going astray, if the cost of what's being stolen, is more than it's worth. You have to ask yourself: 'Am I being taken beyond all reason?' " Turner said.

Ask the DEA agents who have taken cover from 7.62 mm rounds (the ammo used in AK-47s) while trying to bust a dope operation in Pakistan. ■

Stingers were launched at U.S. helicopter gunships in the Persian Gulf.

NCD 27/4/88 (2)

- **Corrupt Afghan rebel leaders** who sold weapons on the black market.
- **Pakistani soldiers** [namely Inter-Services Intelligence Directorate (ISID)] of Pakistan's military ruler, Gen. Mohammed Zia ul-Haq.
- **Drug traffickers in Afghanistan and Pakistan:** Pakistan is the number one source country for heroin.

The last group of arms self-helpers has agents and officials at the U.S. Drug Enforcement Administration (DEA), the State Department's Bureau of International Narcotics Matters (BINM), and USAID (Agency for International Development) hopping mad. Many of the sophisticated weapons have fallen into the hands of the world's most notorious heroin dealers. One drug agent said he has seen an anti-aircraft battery on the roof of a major heroin trafficker's house. Another agent said: "Every doper, down country, has got RPGs (rocket propelled grenades) and AK-47s. Where do you think these weapons come from — Allah?"

"The Cost ... Business"

A motive for murder: all the president's enemies

Sunday Times 21/8/88

AFTER 11 years of autocratic rule, President Zia ul-Haq of Pakistan accumulated an impressive list of enemies.

Some assassins had already tried and failed, others had threatened, and yet more were biding their time. In an earlier attempt one group used a surface-to-air missile, which narrowly missed Zia's aircraft.

Abu Nidal: Zia's sworn enemy

Perhaps his most deadly enemy was the Palestinian splinter group led by *Abu Nidal*. It had vowed to kill Zia for the sentencing to death of five of its gunmen for their part in hijacking a Pan Am jumbo jet at Karachi in 1986.

But, among Pakistani officials, the most likely culprit is believed to have been the Afghan secret police, the *Khad*. Its intention has been to destabilise Pakistan and stop Zia supplying arms to the mujaheddin. The group is already held responsible for 127 terrorist attacks in Pakistan last year, in which more than 100 people died.

There is also a feeling that the *KGB* may have been involved, given Moscow's anger about arms supplies to the rebels. However, this is discounted by most Western experts. They also believe suggestions of *India* playing a role are improbable.

Any assassin's problem was the tight security surrounding Zia. For any group to have planted a bomb on his plane or put a missile in his flight path required a "mole" inside *the military*.

Recently there have been rumblings in the army, especially among middle-ranking officers who thought too many resources were being diverted to the Afghan rebels.

There are other factions inside Pakistan which wanted Zia dead. Foremost among these are the *Shi'ites*, an extremist pro-Iranian Muslim faction who nurture resentments against Zia because of his links with America, and because he tried to impose Sunni orthodoxy.

They believe the general was behind the murder this month, near Peshawar, of Allama Arif Hussaini, leader of the main Shi'ite group. His supporters vowed revenge, and celebrated when they heard the news of Zia's death.

Zia had persecuted a sect called the *Qadianis*, closing down their mosques and arresting their leaders. After the crash, the Qadianis claimed victory and celebrated what they called the verdict of God.

Likewise, *Sindi* nationalists have fought a bitter campaign against the army in the Sind province of Pakistan. Groups of well-armed youths held Zia ultimately responsible for killing hundreds of Sindi political workers during the opposition campaign in 1983. They also celebrated his death.

Kamran Khan, Islamabad

Afghanista
It wou
FROM OUR SPECI
FOR an h
cans and
to escape the
a film at the
the film was
ghanistan. It
capist than i
heroics now
than life. To
of the Russ
judging by th
ists eager to
feeling amo
peace in th
squeezing lo
Afghani
tion of fiefs
The single-m
sian occupat
the 115,000
with the res
string of de
and the Rus
are resurfac
The mo
Mr Ahmad

Arm us
push u
THE Afghan
and hopeful.
gone, Pakistan m
to them. The ho
dling in the guerr
The guerrillas
decision to go o
after May 15th, w
to pull out of Af
decision in the fa
Soviet complaint
Geneva accord—
the private und
Americans and
would continue t
long as Russia w
the Kabul govern
But many of t
increasingly upse
policy. He appear
damentalist of t
Gulbuddin Heckr
kistan's Inter-Serv
military agency th
for carrying out Z
priority to the nee
followers have re
half of the weap

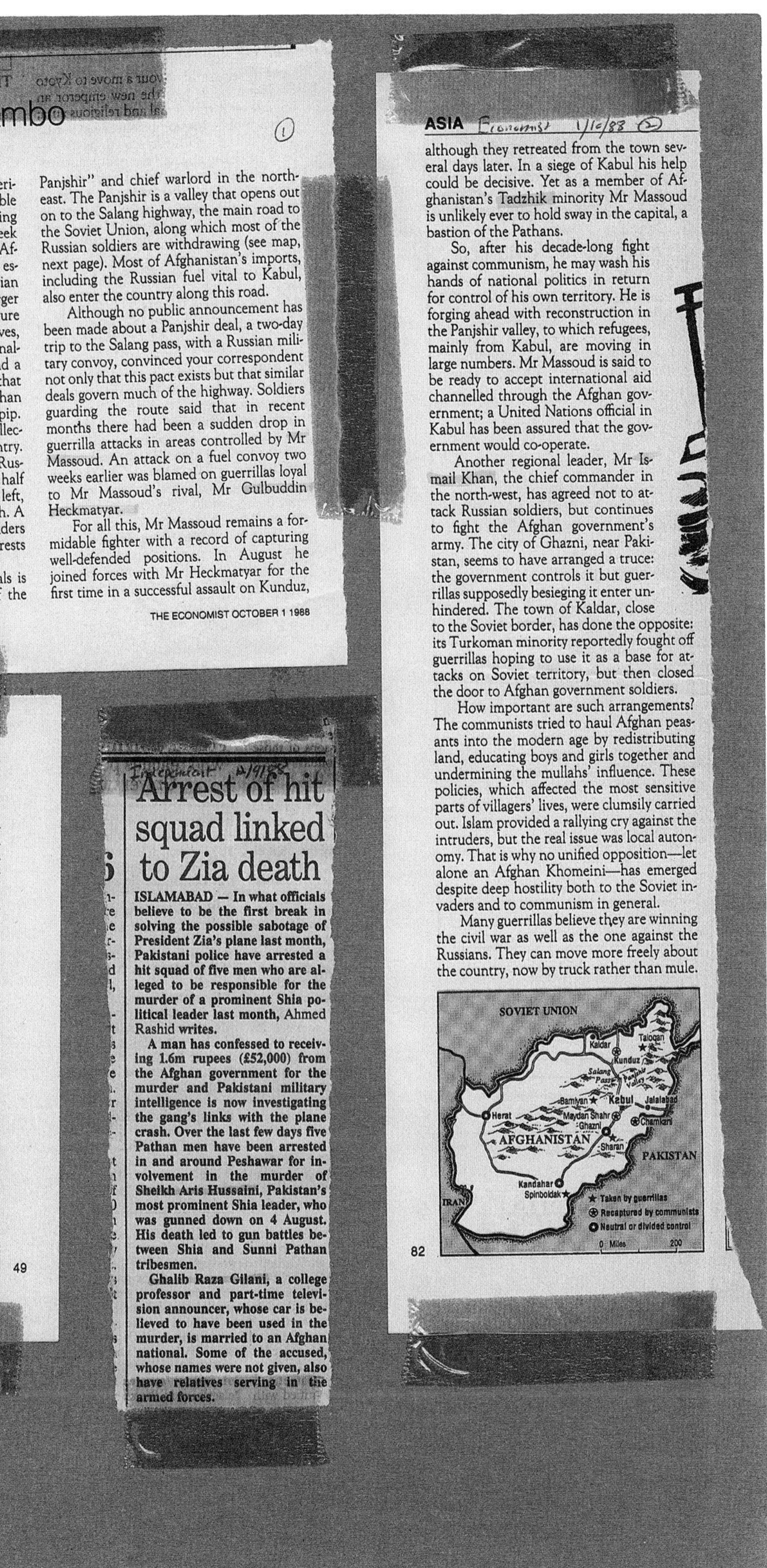

Panjshir" and chief warlord in the north-east. The Panjshir is a valley that opens out on to the Salang highway, the main road to the Soviet Union, along which most of the Russian soldiers are withdrawing (see map, next page). Most of Afghanistan's imports, including the Russian fuel vital to Kabul, also enter the country along this road.

Although no public announcement has been made about a Panjshir deal, a two-day trip to the Salang pass, with a Russian military convoy, convinced your correspondent not only that this pact exists but that similar deals govern much of the highway. Soldiers guarding the route said that in recent months there had been a sudden drop in guerrilla attacks in areas controlled by Mr Massoud. An attack on a fuel convoy two weeks earlier was blamed on guerrillas loyal to Mr Massoud's rival, Mr Gulbuddin Heckmatyar.

For all this, Mr Massoud remains a formidable fighter with a record of capturing well-defended positions. In August he joined forces with Mr Heckmatyar for the first time in a successful assault on Kunduz,

THE ECONOMIST OCTOBER 1 1988

ASIA Economist 1/10/88 (2)

although they retreated from the town several days later. In a siege of Kabul his help could be decisive. Yet as a member of Afghanistan's Tadzhik minority Mr Massoud is unlikely ever to hold sway in the capital, a bastion of the Pathans.

So, after his decade-long fight against communism, he may wash his hands of national politics in return for control of his own territory. He is forging ahead with reconstruction in the Panjshir valley, to which refugees, mainly from Kabul, are moving in large numbers. Mr Massoud is said to be ready to accept international aid channelled through the Afghan government; a United Nations official in Kabul has been assured that the government would co-operate.

Another regional leader, Mr Ismail Khan, the chief commander in the north-west, has agreed not to attack Russian soldiers, but continues to fight the Afghan government's army. The city of Ghazni, near Pakistan, seems to have arranged a truce: the government controls it but guerrillas supposedly besieging it enter unhindered. The town of Kaldar, close to the Soviet border, has done the opposite: its Turkoman minority reportedly fought off guerrillas hoping to use it as a base for attacks on Soviet territory, but then closed the door to Afghan government soldiers.

How important are such arrangements? The communists tried to haul Afghan peasants into the modern age by redistributing land, educating boys and girls together and undermining the mullahs' influence. These policies, which affected the most sensitive parts of villagers' lives, were clumsily carried out. Islam provided a rallying cry against the intruders, but the real issue was local autonomy. That is why no unified opposition—let alone an Afghan Khomeini—has emerged despite deep hostility both to the Soviet invaders and to communism in general.

Many guerrillas believe they are winning the civil war as well as the one against the Russians. They can move more freely about the country, now by truck rather than mule.

82

Independent 4/9/88

Arrest of hit squad linked to Zia death

ISLAMABAD — In what officials believe to be the first break in solving the possible sabotage of President Zia's plane last month, Pakistani police have arrested a hit squad of five men who are alleged to be responsible for the murder of a prominent Shia political leader last month, Ahmed Rashid **writes.**

A man has confessed to receiving 1.6m rupees (£52,000) from the Afghan government for the murder and Pakistani military intelligence is now investigating the gang's links with the plane crash. Over the last few days five Pathan men have been arrested in and around Peshawar for involvement in the murder of Sheikh Aris Hussaini, Pakistan's most prominent Shia leader, who was gunned down on 4 August. His death led to gun battles between Shia and Sunni Pathan tribesmen.

Ghalib Raza Gilani, a college professor and part-time television announcer, whose car is believed to have been used in the murder, is married to an Afghan national. Some of the accused, whose names were not given, also have relatives serving in the armed forces.

Two pages from Howard's collage of news cuttings on CIA operations and drug trafficking in Afghanistan, Nepal and Pakistan. This formed part of a fake defence created by Howard while fighting extradition in Spain. In the knowledge that he was likely to be extradited and that his belongings would be sent separately, Howard constructed a fake defence to mislead the DEA, one that involved drug-trafficking assignments on behalf of MI6 and the CIA, the sort of defence Howard figured he would be expected to run. Contained within the folder is a file entitled 'MI6'. This file contains a description by investigative journalist David Leigh of the training exercises conducted by British Secret Services:

'Bizarre training exercises in which policemen and justices' clerks up and down the country were persuaded to plant drugs on junior secret agents, arrest, charge and imprison them, and then remand them to prison at mock trials in local courtrooms. A key aspect of schemes, whose history dates back more than 15 years, was that attractive policewomen were used as "Mata Hari" figures to entrap junior agents, generally Oxbridge graduates in their early 20s. Large numbers of police and court officials were persuaded to cooperate under the cloak of the Official Secrets Act by telling them it was to test how British agents would behave if they fell into the hands of the Russians. They were told they were helping "national security" on behalf of a "nameless organisation". One source says he was told by a head of MI6 that police were becoming overenthusiastic. A provincial force started beating up the junior James Bonds once in custody. The trainee spies reacted angrily when told by their spymasters that the whole thing had been an MI6 ruse.'

EMERY AIR FREIGHT CORPORATION
EXECUTIVE OFFICES: W...TON, CONNECTICUT, U.S.A.

2751

NOT NEGOTIABLE AIR WAYBILL

AIR WAYBILL No. 77 AMS 51495

DESTINATION (AIRPORT OF) DETROIT

CONSIGNED TO	STREET ADDRESS	CITY AND COUNTRY
EMERY AIR FREIGHT CORP	33801 GODDARD ROAD	ROMULUS MICH 48174 U.S.A.

ALSO NOTIFY HOLD FOR PICK-UP BY : TRANS-ATLANTIC SOUND

No. OF PACKAGES	METHOD OF PACKING	NATURE AND QUANTITY OF GOODS	MARKS AND NUMBERS	COMM CODE	DIMENSIONS OR VOLUME	GROSS WEIGHT (Specify both Kilos and Lbs.)
29 PCS		SOUND APPARATUS	ADDR			1710 K 3762 #
PACKED IN ON ULD.						
		NYC- PLS SEN TROUGH DTT AS COMPLETE ULD				

ACCOUNT CODE 7.6900 — Special Instructions: ☐ GBL ☐ OTHER ☐ APS ☐ FMO / ☐ TCN ☐ FFD ☐ FREE DOMICILE

THESE COMMODITIES LICENSED BY U.S. FOR ULTIMATE DESTINATION .... DIVERSION CONTRARY TO U.S. LAW PROHIBITED

DOCUMENTS TO ACCOMPANY AIR WAYBILL: ☐ COMMERCIAL INVOICE: ☐ EXPORT DECLARATION: ☒ OTHER CARNET

SHIPPER'S DECLARED VALUE (Specify Currency) — For Customs N.V.D. — For Carriage N.V.D.

METHOD OF ROUTING AND CHARGES—Agreed stopping places are those places (other than the places of departure and destination) shown under Air Carriage, and/or those places shown in carrier's timetables as scheduled stopping places for the route. SEE CONDITIONS ON REVERSE HEREOF.

CHARGES ☒ Prepaid ☐ Collect ☐ Other ☐ GBL ☐ Comat

AIR CARRIAGE

		CHAR'BLE WEIGHT Specify Kilos or Lbs	RATE CLASSIFICATION	RATES	PREPAID	U.S. $	CHARGEABLE TO CONSIGNEE: AMOUNTS IN CURRENCIES AS CHARGED	U.S. $
Departure (Airport of) AMS	(Address of First Carrier)				DFL			
1. To DTT	First Carrier EAF	1710	4416	2.34	4001.40	1542.14		
2. To	Carrier							
3. To	Carrier							
4. Valuation Charge From	To:							
5. Valuation Charge From	To:							
6. INSURANCE: Amount Requested (Specify Currency)	$ 2328.-		0.25%		19.07	5.82		

If the shipper has requested Insurance as provided for on line 6 above, shipment is insured in the amount specified by the shipper (recovery being limited to actual loss) in accordance with Paragraph 8 on the reverse hereof. Insurance is payable to shipper unless another payee is designated in writing by the shipper.

OTHER CHARGES (SPECIFY): 7. At Origin—Pickup; 8. Advance; 9. Documentation; 10. FOB/TSC; 11. Fees (Specify) 22.50 8.67; 12.; 13.; 14.; 15.; 16. C.O.D. FEE; 17. SHIPPER'S C.O.D.

Department or Order Number

SHIPPERS C.O.D. IN WORDS NONE — TOTAL DFL 4042.97 1556.63

DISCOVERY MATERIAL ATTORNEY:

The shipper certifies that the particulars on the face hereof are correct and agrees to the CONDITIONS ON THE REVERSE HEREOF.

Carrier certifies above described goods were received for carriage SUBJECT TO THE CONDITIONS ON THE REVERSE HEREOF, the goods then being in apparent good order and condition except as noted hereon.

Shipper: TRANS ATLANTIC SOUND, 28 BROOK ST, LONDON W.1 ENGLAND

Executed on (Date) (At Place) — RECEIVED BY EMERY SEE FREIGHT AT: Shippers Door ☐ Emery Terminal ☐ Other Terminal ☐ EAF City Terminal ☐ — SPL Time 1800 / Date 9/7

Signature of Shipper — Name of Issuing Carriers — EMERY AIR FREIGHT CORPORATION

By Broker/Agent — Signature of Issuing Carrier or its Agent WJG

Third Party Billing

PTD IN U.K. FORM IT 2 — 14 Copies of this Air Waybill have been completed, of which Copies 1, 2 and 8 are originals and have the same Validity

(P093/09.08)

8 - ORIGINAL - CARRIER (EAF)

The 1973 Transatlantic Sounds shipments featured heavily in the paperwork against Howard, even though he had already served his time for this offence in England.

Howard and Judy fought their extradition tooth and nail, even confessing in a full-spread article in one of Spain's leading news magazines, *Panorama*, of shipping vast amounts of cannabis from the Far East, through Mozambique, into Spain, including detailed maps of smuggling routes. They wanted to be tried in Spain. Howard's lawyer Gustavo Muñoz even organised a private prosecution (*acción popular*) to keep Howard in Spain, where he faced a maximum sentence of 12 years, rather than being extradited to America where new sentencing guidelines meant he faced the possibility of consecutive life sentences without possibility of parole.

(→) The DEA's references to Howard as the Marco Polo of drug trafficking was a source of amusement to Howard. Spanish prisoners used it with fondness to call out to him within the prison compound.

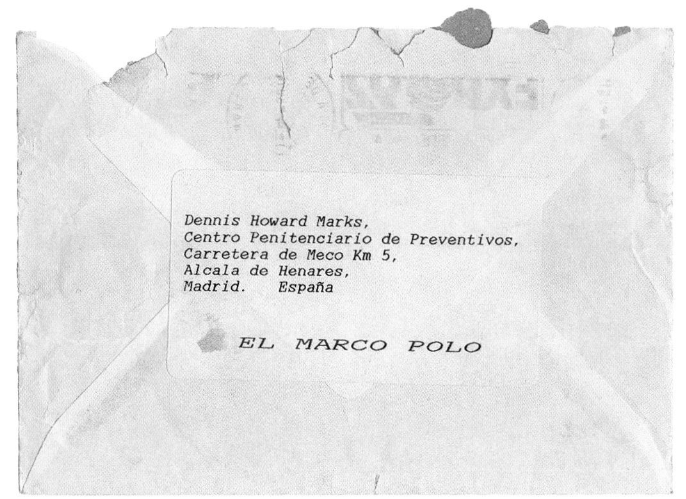

Dennis Howard Marks,
Centro Penitenciario de Preventivos,
Carretera de Meco Km 5,
Alcala de Henares,
Madrid. España
EL MARCO POLO

(↑) Photograph of the contents of a Transatlantic Sounds speaker, as included in the prosecution paperwork.

(↓) Telegram from Judy to Howard on 11 August 1989. After over a year in prison, first in Palma and later in Madrid, Judy agreed to go to the United States in the hope of securing her release from there. Several co-defendants, including the wife of Gerry Wills, had pleaded guilty and been immediately released on time served as a result. Three of Judy and Howard's co-defendants had just been found guilty in Florida. These included Judy's brother, Patrick Lane, who had been sentenced to a total of three years' imprisonment for his role in the 'Marks Cartel'. Ernie Combs, Howard's lifelong partner and friend, was sentenced to 40 years. Ernie's wife, Patti, was sentenced to eight years.

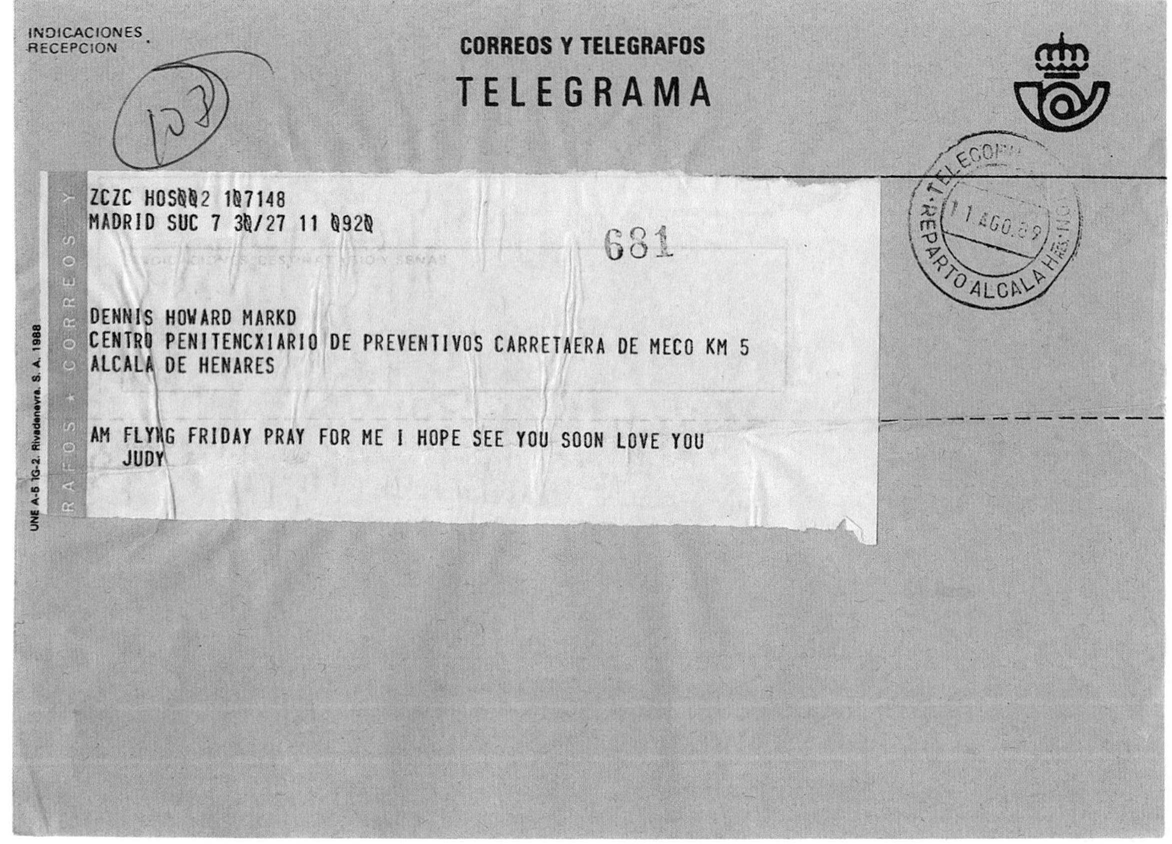
INDICACIONES
RECEPCION

CORREOS Y TELEGRAFOS

TELEGRAMA

ZCZC HOS002 107148
MADRID SUC 7 30/27 11 0920

681

DENNIS HOWARD MARKD
CENTRO PENITENCXIARIO DE PREVENTIVOS CARRETAERA DE MECO KM 5
ALCALA DE HENARES

AM FLYNG FRIDAY PRAY FOR ME I HOPE SEE YOU SOON LOVE YOU
JUDY

Howard's lawyer, Gustav Muñoz, continued bombarding every court he could with every application possible, but to no avail. Muñoz was outraged by what he saw as American judicial imperialism. So was Howard. On 13 October 1989, the Spanish court granted Howard's extradition request. Then a brief glimmer of hope appeared on the horizon when the German authorities looked like they were going to stake their own claim on Howard. Before the German proceedings completed their course, however, Howard was whisked away and on to a US-bound flight, outraging the defiant Muñoz once again.

On 12 December 1989, two months after Howard was flown to the US, and faced with a choice between going to trial – running the risk of being sentenced to 15 years with no parole – or pleading guilty with the promise of being home by Christmas, Judy pleaded guilty. She was sentenced to time served, having been in prison for 18 months, and flown home to her three children.

6

Defence Theory

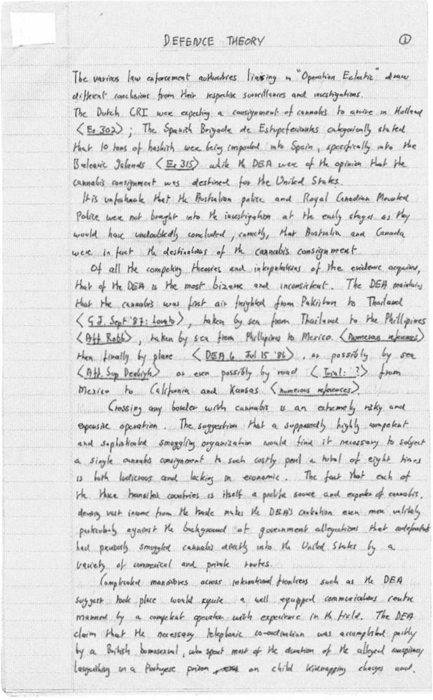
DEFENCE THEORY ①

The various law enforcement authorities liaising in "Operation Eclectic" draw different conclusions from their respective surveillances and investigations.
The Dutch CRI were expecting a consignment of cannabis to arrive in Holland <Ex 302>; The Spanish Brigada de Estupefacientes categorically stated that 10 tons of hashish were being imported into Spain, specifically into the Balearic Islands <Ex 315> while the DEA were of the opinion that the cannabis consignment was destined for the United States.
It is unfathomable that the Australian police and Royal Canadian Mounted Police were not brought into the investigation at the early stages as they would have undoubtedly concluded, correctly, that Australia and Canada were in fact the destinations of the cannabis consignment.
Of all the competing theories and interpretations of the evidence acquired, that of the DEA is the most bizarre and inconsistent. The DEA maintains that the cannabis was first air freighted from Pakistan to Thailand <G.J. Sept '87: Lovato>, taken by sea from Thailand to the Phillipines <Aff Robb>, taken by sea from Phillipines to Mexico. <numerous references> then finally by plane <DEA 6 Jul 15 '86>, or possibly by sea <Aff. Sup Denbigh> or even possibly by road <Trial: ?> from Mexico to California and Kansas <numerous references>.
Crossing any border with cannabis is an extremely risky and expensive operation. The suggestion that a supposedly highly competent and sophisticated smuggling organisation would find it necessary to subject a single cannabis consignment to such costly peril a total of eight times is both ludicrous and lacking in economic. The fact that each of the three transited countries is itself a prolific source and exporter of cannabis, deriving vast income from the trade makes the DEA's calculation even more unlikely particularly against the background of government allegations that codefendants had previously smuggled cannabis directly into the United States by a variety of commercial and private routes.
Complicated manoeuvres across international frontiers such as the DEA suggest took place would require a well equipped communications centre manned by a competent operator with experience in the field. The DEA claim that the necessary telephonic co-ordination was accomplished partly by a British homosexual, who spent most of the duration of the alleged conspiracy languishing in a Portugese prison on child kidnapping charges and.

With Judy now at home with the children, Howard got working in earnest on his defence. He was going to plead not guilty and he hoped to win. The source of the text for this chapter is Howard's handwritten outline of his defence.

The various law-enforcement authorities liaising in 'Operation Eclectic' draw different conclusions from their respective surveillances and investigations. The Dutch CRI were expecting a consignment of cannabis to arrive in Holland; the Spanish *Brigada de Estupefacientes* categorically stated that 10 tons of hashish were being imported into Spain, specifically into the Balearic Islands, while the DEA was of the opinion that the cannabis consignment was destined for the United States. It is unfathomable that the Australian police and Royal Canadian Mounted Police were not brought into the investigation at the early stages as they would have undoubtedly concluded, correctly, that Australia and Canada were in fact the destinations of the cannabis consignment.

Of all the competing theories and interpretations of the evidence acquired, that of the DEA is the most bizarre and inconsistent. The DEA maintains that the cannabis was first air freighted from Pakistan to Thailand, then taken by sea from Thailand to the Philippines before being taken by sea from the Philippines to Mexico and finally by plane, and possibly by sea, or even by road, from Mexico to California and Kansas. Crossing any border with cannabis is an extremely risky and expensive operation. The suggestion that a supposedly highly competent and sophisticated smuggling organisation would find it necessary to subject a single cannabis consignment to such costly peril a total of eight times is both ludicrous and lacking in economic sense. The fact that each of the three transited countries is itself a prolific source and exporter of cannabis, deriving vast income from the trade, makes the DEA's calculation even more unlikely, particularly against the background of government allegations that co-defendants had previously smuggled cannabis directly into the United States by a variety of commercial and private routes.

Craig Lovato, the DEA case agent in charge of the investigation, had four years' experience in the interdiction of drugs on the Mexican/Californian border. Despite such expertise and despite personally monitoring the telephone lines of the alleged organiser of the operation at the precise time the alleged importation occurred, the same case agent was unable to either seize any drugs entering the United States or determine the method by which any such entry was achieved. According to Lovato, a consignment of hashish is a rare occurrence in Southern California, and presumably even rarer in Kansas. One would therefore expect its consequences to be reported in, at the very least, an underground magazine such as *High Times*. No mention, however, is made of any availability of hashish from Pakistan in either California or Kansas during the relevant period (*High Times*, Feb to July 1986). The only seizure purported to be of any relevance was that of one small crumpled-up slab of hashish which the DEA conceded may not have been related to the consignment in question.

This failure to seize hashish is truly remarkable when one considers that the suspects were the targets of an investigation utilising the cooperation of law-enforcement teams from 14 different countries. Surveillance teams were activated in at least 10 of these countries; wiretaps were initiated in at least four of these countries (Spain alone had a minimum of 14 lines intercepted) and the services of at least 11 cooperating individuals were enlisted. The excuse offered by the DEA for this lack of success is that they

Defence Theory — Supplement (2)

NNIC 88 p18 The THC content of hashish is approximately 3.32% while the THC content of American produced sinsemilla has reached levels of
NNIC 88 p9 18.83%. [Sinsemilla comprises 42% of American cultivated marijuana which in turn comprises 25% of the total marijuana consumed in the United States]

Given the absence of any mention, it is assumed that seizures of black pakistani hashish during 1986-88 were negligible. However it may be the case that they are included in the tables given for marijuana. [The report is unclear on this] if it is they clearly must form part of 'other' marijuana as the remaining marijuana is all from South America + Caribbean. 'Other' would include cannabis from Pakistan, Afghanistan, Lebanon, Morocco, Turkey, India, Thailand, Laos, Cambodia, Vietnam, Africa and the Phillipines.
NNIC 87 p18 Cannabis from all these regions totalled 8% of the gross quantity of cannabis available on the United States market. This again implies that seizures of Pakistani hashish and more importantly the availability of Pakistani hashish during 1986 was determined, by the various American intelligence and law enforcement agencies compiling the report to be negligible.

The government occasionally conjectures that in the instant case, hashish was taken by plane from Mexico to the United States. This conjecture should be viewed in the light of the following quotation:— "The majority of Mexican marijuana is smuggled into the United States by vehicle. The use of private aircraft for smuggling Mexican marijuana into the United States was sporadic accounting for only 5% of the total marijuana seizures along the US/Mexico border" <NNIC 87 p 13>

Thai Marijuana in Canada during 1987

Thailand's share of the illicit marijuana market in 1987 was estimated
NDIE 87/88 p89 at 20%. No country had a greater share [but Jamaica was equal]
" than this. during 1987

Of a total of 29 major Canadian related marijuana seizures 1986-1988, 3 were seized
NDIE 86/87 p100 in the United States bound for Canada. None were described as having been
" 87/88 p109 seized in Canada bound for the United States, despite at least 3
NDIE 87/88 p 9, 90, 109 specific mentions of the seizure in the instant case.

Thai Marijuana in the United States during 1987

Thai marijuana is included under 'other' <ie non South American non

One of several hundred pages prepared by Howard to contest DEA allegations.

were continually outwitted by the sophistication of the organisation.

A far more plausible explanation is that the alleged importation into the United States did not occur. Supporting this is the speed at which this particular load of cannabis was sold. The consumption of cannabis is greater in the United States than in the remainder of net importing countries in total. DEA statistics show that the annual consumption in the United States amounts to 8,000 tons. The greater the consumption, the faster the speed of selling. Had it been the case that this particular load of cannabis was imported to the United States then the sale would have been over within a matter of days. The evidence shows that the sale took many months, strongly implying that the cannabis was imported to a country with an extremely small cannabis-consuming population. There are three other areas of the world where the demand for cannabis necessitates importation – Canada, Europe and Australasia. In each of these areas the retail price of cannabis is higher than in the United States. None of the countries begins to deploy anything like the vast resources for drug interdiction that the

UNICOR FEDERAL PRISON INDUSTRIES INC.
LEAVENWORTH KANSAS

U.S. DEPARTMENT OF JUSTICE
Federal Bureau of Prisons

INMATE REQUEST TO STAFF MEMBER

[RECE]IVED

DATE: NOVEMBER 5, 1989

TO: THE WARDEN
(Name and title of officer)

[W]ARDEN'S OFFICE
M.C.C. MIAMI

SUBJECT: State completely but briefly the problem on which you desire assistance, and what you think should be done (Give details).

Dear Sir, I have been informed both verbally and in response to my cop out that the making of international telephone calls is prohibited by prison policy.
I am a British subject. My elderly parents and children live in Europe. I have no friends or family in the United States. It will prove extremely expensive and inconvenient for anyone to visit me.
A few days ago I received my (Use other side of page if more space is needed) first letter from my family. They had been informed both by the prison staff here and the British Consul in Atlanta that I am allowed to telephone Europe anytime I wish. My inability to communicate has therefore further increased their anxiety. Most foreigners incarcerated here have friends in the United States able to provide them with a 3-way telephone facility but I do not. Given the above, would you please allow me to periodically telephone my family.

NAME: DENNIS HOWARD MARKS   No.: 41526-004

Work assignment: UNASSIGNED   Unit: F

NOTE: If you follow instructions in preparing your request, it can be disposed of more promptly and intelligently. You will be interviewed, if necessary, in order to satisfactorily handle your request. Your failure to specifically state your problem may result in no action being taken.

DISPOSITION: (Do not write in this space)   DATE: November 7, 1989

This is in response to your request for permission to make international telephone calls to your family in Europe.
According to our current policy, inmates incarcerated at this facility are not allowed to make international phone calls. However, we will make provisions to inmates that can substantiate an emergency need to communicate overseas.
In the mean time we encourage you to correspond with your family in writing.
Your request is therefore denied.

Mel Collins, AW(P)
Officer

Original – File
Canary – Inmate

On arrival in the United States, Howard was told he was not allowed to phone Europe, where all his family resided. Howard made countless motions and applications on his own and others' behalves, fully engaging in a bureaucracy of which he was no fan, writing home, 'It is extraordinary that the more automated a society gets, the greater the amount of red tape there is for people to deal with. Bureaucracy is a horrible monster, feeding on itself and others; perfected, of course, in America.'

United States does. Another factor considered by smuggling groups is the distance which the load, continually under risk, has to be transported. This explains why most imported cannabis in the United States originates in South America, while that in Europe originates in Africa and that in Australia comes from the Far East and Indian subcontinent. For reasons of geographical proximity, economic feasibility, avoidance of detection and minimisation of punishment, the United States would be the last logical choice of destination. The first choice would be Australia. These considerations would be unlikely to be overlooked by a 'highly sophisticated international drug smuggling cartel' with sources of supply in the Far East.

For obvious reasons of traceability, security, etc, smuggled goods are normally sold for cash. Throughout the world virtually all black-market transactions are conducted using United States dollars as their currency. Whether eggs are smuggled from Bangkok to Singapore, or heroin from India to Nigeria, prices are quoted in and paid for by United States dollars. It is estimated that 80% of all Federal Reserve banknotes circulate in the black markets of the world. One of the major problems facing smugglers who wish to enjoy the fruits of their labours is how to convert these piles of cash into apparently legitimate assets. Although the banks of some countries such as Hong Kong, Panama and the Caribbean are often prepared to accept large volumes of dollars in cash form, those of typical cannabis-importing western nations are not. A suitcase of dollars is an embarrassment in any country that lacks an entrenched or sophisticated infrastructure at the interface between smuggler and financial institutions. The United States, however, has had at least 70 years' experience of dealing with hot money in cash form; initiated by the proceeds of illegal alcohol sales during prohibition, developed by proceeds resulting from the repressive legislature concerning gambling and prostitution, and perfected by the proceeds of recent decades of rampant illegal drug consumption. This, combined with contributions from billion-dollar clandestine arms deals, kickbacks to foreign officials and nationwide evasion practices, have rendered the disposal of hot money in the United States a simple and frequent practice.

One obvious solution for the smuggler's suitcases of dollars in any part of the world is therefore to transfer them to the United States and inject them into the banking system. Indicative of the widespread occurrence of this practice is the attached publication *Money Laundering and the Illicit Drug Trade* prepared by special sections of the DEA and RCMP, which gives details of five specific instances of individuals transporting United States dollars into the United States from Canada in amounts ranging from $30,000 to $250,000. The same publication makes reference to a US Customs Service report entitled *Comparison of Currency Transported through Canada and Mexico into the United States 1980–1986*, which would presumably give further examples of this practice. Aside from direct transportation as exemplified above, cash dollars generated in a foreign currency also reach the United States through numerous underground banking systems. These are normally organised by members of an immigrant group prevalent both in the United States and the country in which the cash was generated. Chinese and Pakistani immigrants are particularly active in this field. The dollars generated in the foreign country are given to the underground banking organisation, which enables a representative of the provider of the dollars to pick up the same amount, less any fee charged, from members of the underground banking organisation in the United States. Should the cash generated by the sale of smuggled goods in any particular country not be in dollars, currency export restrictions and cash movement monitoring procedures imposed by that country often force the smuggler to adopt similar methods to those outlined above, leading him to possess cash dollars in the United States. Australian authorities are particularly vigilant of cash movements, making the procedures described above attractive to those engaged in smuggling contraband into that country. The possession of cash dollars within the United States does not therefore imply that the currency derives from contraband sales within the United States; it could have come from anywhere.

The indictment states that the amount of cannabis in question was 15,000lb, but the government gives no justification for this conjecture. There are three units of measure used when dealing with weights of Pakistani cannabis: the British pound; the kilo (= 2.205lb); and the Pakistani unit of seet, which is less than 1kg but greater than 2lb. Slabs of cannabis were exported from Pakistan in weight from 1lb to ½kg. The amount of cannabis actually obtained in Pakistan was meant to be 5,000kg, 3,000 of which was for the Australian/American members of the transporting, importing and selling group and 2,000 of which was for the Pakistani/British members of the exporting group. The load was destined for importation into Australia where some of it would be sold, while the remainder would be transported to Canada and sold there. There was no importation into either Mexico or the United States. □

Transcript Errors (5)

(2). Prior Knowledge of Co-conspirators' Names and Aliases (Cont'd)

Ex	Page	Disc	Tape	Transcript	Explanation
34	68	2056	Balendo	Lowe	Balendo Lo
35	21	2113	Oh	John	John Denbigh
35	49	2141	Podge	Touch	G. Wills *aka* Touch
				[plus the following]	
04	44	0277	try to	Howard	Howard Marks
25	68	1324	0	John	John Denbigh

When the symbol '0' appears in the Tape column it signifies that the transcribed word is simply inserted without any correlating word, phonetically similar or otherwise, to be found on the tape.
'UI' signifies that the word or words on the tape are unintelligible.

(3). Prior Assumption of Distribution of Hashish and/or Marijuana and Collection of its proceeds.

Ex	Page	Disc	Tape	Transcript
03	3	0163	UI	a little grass
03	25	0187	drag	drug
03	28	0188	drag	drug
05	29	0321	presence	prices
05	29	0321	afterwards	ounces
05	30	0322	you think best	we sell things fast
05	31	0323	direct to Tony on it	per ton unit
05	39	0331	Tim	ten
05	45	0337	down there	twenty percent
05	46	0338	it is want he wants	quality is well kept
18	26	0791	hush hush	hash hash
22	38	1043	statue	stuff
22	65	1070	Tony	ton
24	74	1219	north and south	we all have stock
24	74	1219	have worked it out	I bought stock
25	45	1301	400 pounds	100 dollars
28	22	1435	total	million
31	23	1682	pretence	percent
31	29	1688	start	stuff
32	27	1802	bun	pot
32	50	1825	courting	counting
32	56	1831	cats	cash
32	56	1831	cats	cash
32	56	1831	cats	cash
32	56	1831	cats	cash
35	50	2142	out of the way	hashed away
35	55	2147	serves	seven
35	69	2161	this other nonsense	seven done
25	34	1290	sort of	seven

(4). Prior Assumption of Sea Smuggling Venture Taking Place

Ex	Page	Disc	Tape	Transcript
03	53	0213	bread	boat
09	3	0485	after sheep	off at sea
14	36	0615	book	boat
25	51	1307	wait until next year	walk away from that ship
26	10	1347	out there	captain

Attorney Bobby O'Neill fought hard against Howard's co-defendants' attempts to exclude Lovato's 'expert' interpretation of the phone taps from evidence. At first, the judge said that only the recordings themselves could be played, and the jury would be invited to draw their own conclusions from them. This had been perceived as a near-fatal blow to the prosecution:

'It was almost better not to play the tapes at all than to have the jury listen to hours and hours of conversations in which the words "hashish", "marijuana", or "drugs" were not mentioned once.' HMP

O'Neill was successful and the judge reversed his ruling. Lovato would be allowed to present his 'expert' opinion as to what was being said. Howard made meticulous notes on thousands of telephone recordings, pointing out obvious errors, important omissions, apparent fabrications, inconsistencies (tickets are decoded as 'dollars' in one transcript and as 'hashish' in others) and multiple examples of perceptual bias in Lovato's version. Lovato had provided sworn testimony that the person speaking in a particular transcript was Mr Malik. Howard points out that Mr Malik has a 'pronounced Pakistani accent', whereas the speaker in question has an 'extremely heavy cockney accent'. In another note, Howard provides evidence supporting what he had come to believe explained errors in the transcription; Lovato's reading of *High Times*.

Transcript Errors (6)

(4). Prior Assumption of Sea Smuglling Venture Taking Place (Cont'd)

Ex	Page	Disc	Tape	Transcript
26	21	1358	boy	bay
26	48	1385	of course yeah	at the coast line
28	2	1415	see if I can do	chief officer
34	55	2043	bloke	boat
35	5	2097	fits in with your	that big shipment of yours

(5(. Prior Assumption of Non Specific Criminality

Ex	Page	Disc	Tape	Transcript
04	21	0254	overlapping	mobile operative
05	32	0324	date	deal
05	37	0329	most ideal	worst part of the deal
12	15	0534	grand	gun
23	56	1132	schedule	deal
24	12	1157	due	deal
26	18	1355	I realise that	the deal is on
24	84	1229	modelling agency	other nations *(false passports)*
30	27	1564	give you another	did you make a deal
30	36	1573	of course	court
30	38	1575	concentrate	counsel
30	117	1656	or sensible	was sentenced
32	35	1810	bastard	busted

The high degree of perceptually biased mistranscriptions evidenced above drastically increases the potential for prejudicial error created by the introduction of these inauthentic transcripts to the trier of fact.

Prejudicial error was created by innacurate transcripts in US v Robinson.

> *"Accuracy of the transcript should be checked by the court outside the presence of the jury"* People v Feld

Non prejudicial error was created by inaccurate transcripts in US v Bryant

Other cases stressing the necessity of authenticating the transcripts are:- US v Sutherland, US v Rochan, and US v Onori.

Howard noted every error in transcription.

The DEA claimed American jurisdiction over the seizure of Vietnamese cannabis by the Royal Canadian Mounted Police in Vancouver because it, as well as cannabis seized in California, bore this logo on it. The DEA maintained that the Bird of Prey logo was a hallmark of the 'Marks Cartel' and that the bird in question was a sparrowhawk, Sparrowhawk being the surname of Howard's connection, Philip, in Bangkok. There was ample evidence that this logo belonged to a totally unconnected group of cannabis smugglers and this should have been enough to undermine the DEA claim. Howard went the extra mile of conducting an elementary ornithological study on the characteristics of birds of prey, including the key differences between sparrowhawks and eagles.

Part (6)

BIRD OF PREY

LOVATO consistently refers to this logo as being exclusive to me and known throughout the "narcotics trade as a symbol of quality"

One can only presume that this absurd ~~notk~~ notion took root in his imagination as a result of SPARROWHAWK's name also being that of a bird of prey.

An elementary Ornithological study reveals that there are three main categories of birds of prey – hawks, eagles and owls. The logo is clearly not an owl. The distinguishing characteristics of hawks are long pointed wings, short tails and narrow legs. Those of eagles are big broad wings, big broad tails and extremely stout legs. Additionally eagles are the only birds of prey which have "crowns" on top of their heads.

It is abundantly clear from the above that the bird of prey in question is an eagle not a Sparrowhawk

To be more precise a Sparrowhawk (or American Kestrel) is a member of a subgroup of hawks called falcons

There are four main subgroups of eagles – Golden Eagles, Bald Eagles, Ospreys and Siberian Sea Eagles. That depicted in the logo more closely resembles a Siberian Sea Eagle than any of the others

Defence
They
US

N32

HOWARD MARKS FALSE PASSPORT APPLICATIONS

GUIDE TO USE OF THIS BOOKLET

Where there are similarities between passports a colour is used to identify the area concerned,further information on the relevant point will be contained within the comments column at the end of each applicants line.The colour used is consistent throughout both booklets on each particular similarity as in some cases there are overlaps between the true and false applications .

THIS BOOKLET IS TO BE USED IN CONJUNCTION WITH THE HOWARD MARKS TRUE APPLICATION CHARTS THE INTELLIGENCE MUST BE TREATED WITH THE UTMOST CAUTION AND NOT BE DISSEMINATED WITHOUT PRIOR AUTHORITY FROM DETECTIVE CHIEF SUPERINTENDENT NDIU.

NDIU 1988

(↑↗) Cover pages of the *Howard Marks False Passport Applications* and *Howard Marks True Passport Applications* booklets for investigators participating in 'Operation Eclectic'. Howard's observations on the material, from his preparations for trial, include this: 'Fifteen of the twenty-nine genuine passports exhibited are unknown to me. It is worth noting that the government describes anyone who has obtained a false passport from James Newton [who makes a business of this activity] as a member of my syndicate.'

N319

HOWARD MARKS TRUE PASSPORT APPLICATIONS

GUIDE TO USE OF THIS BOOKLET

Where there are similarities between passports a colour is used to identify the area concerned,further information on the relevant point will be contained within the comments column at the end of each applicants line.The colour used is consistent throughout both booklets on each particular similarity as in some cases there are overlaps between the true and false applications.

THIS BOOKLET IS TO BE USED IN CONJUNCTION WITH TH HOWARD MARKS FALSE APPLICATION CHARTS. THE INTELLIGENCE MUST BE TREATED WITH THE UTMOST CAUTION AND NOT BE DISSEMINATED WITHOUT PRIOR AUTHORITY FROM DETECTIVE CHIEF SUPERINTENDENT NDIU.

NDIU 1988

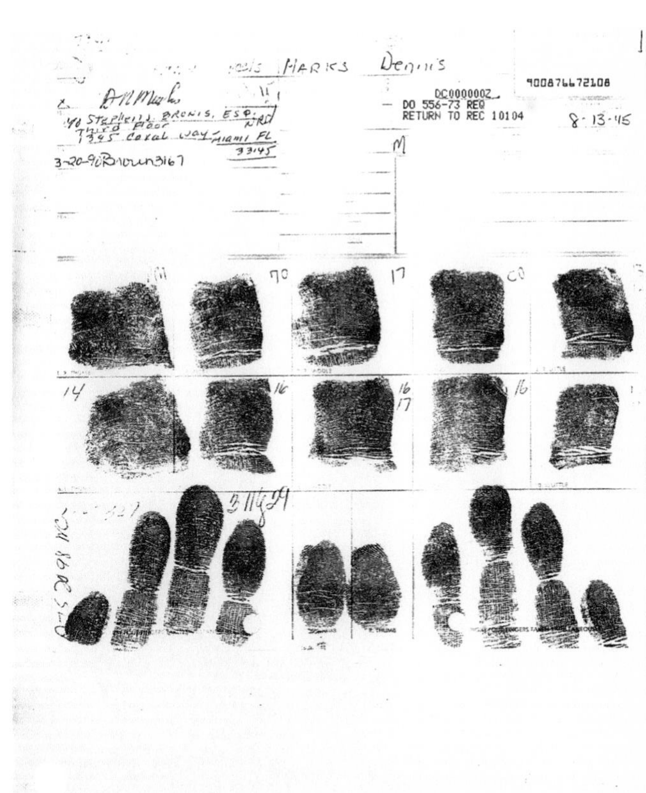

(→) Howard had to prove his identity by providing his fingerprints in order to obtain responses to his various Freedom of Information Requests.

King of Cannabis

JAY SCHADLER, ABC News: For starters, forget everything you ever imagined a drug-smuggler to look, think or sound like. Now, meet Howard Marks.

HOWARD MARKS, Accused Drug Smuggler: I think the stereotype of a drug dealer is probably wrong. I've certainly met many charming, engaging, intelligent people within the marijuana trade. Most of them don't get caught, as why perhaps I am, exposed rather more than the others.

SCHADLER: *[voice-over]* If Mr. Marks seems uncommonly cheerful for someone in the slammer, perhaps that's because there's nothing common about him.

STEPHEN BRONIS: Howard is a fascinating person. He's charming, he's engaging, he's brilliant.

SCHADLER: *[voice-over]* That's Marks's defense attorney, Stephen Bronis, talking. Remember, this is a man who has seen lots of drug dealers.

Mr. BRONIS: But I've never met anybody quite like him.

SCHADLER: *[voice-over]* And even a less sympathetic observer, like Tom Cash, the U.S. drug agent largely responsible for busting marks, offers this back-handed compliment.

TOM CASH: I described Mr. Marks from all the travels that he had as the Marco Polo of the drug world.

Mr. MARKS: I hate the word "drug" for marijuana, but then if I describe myself as a herb smuggler, that seems as if, you know, I'm trying to make a point which is not going to go down too well, but I do regard marijuana as a harmless herb which has a relaxing effect.

SCHADLER: But you're not exactly a weekend gardener either.

Mr. MARKS: No, no.

SCHADLER: *[voice-over]* Marks may be the only federal defendant whose IQ matches his eight-digit prison number. During the 1960's, he earned three advanced degrees from England's prestigious Oxford University, but seduced by the era's peace, love and drugs anthem, the scholar turned smuggler — very radical, very quotable.

[interviewing] During the 1960's, you were talking about your ambitions for the future, and you said the only avenues seemed to be rock 'n' roll, marrying a rich chick, being a professor or becoming a crook.

Mr. MARKS: Yes, yes.

SCHADLER: How many of those four have you achieved?

Mr. MARKS: None of them.

SCHADLER: You've never been a crook?

Mr. MARKS: I've been a crook, but I don't think I was a successful crook.

SCHADLER: *[voice-over]* You'd never convince police agencies around the world of that. They say he parlayed a pot-smoking pastime into a world class drug ring spanning six continents and netting $175 million in total revenue. Marijuana grown in Middle and Far Eastern fields was turned to hashish in a factory in Karachi, Pakistan. Beginning in 1970, he reportedly shipped 75,000 pounds of marijuana and 40,000 pounds of hashish into the U.S. and Canada, often to the sounds of rock 'n' roll.

Mr. MARKS: Hash would be into the speakers and taken out in America.

SCHADLER: So in the speakers of a rock 'n' roll band sat pounds of marijuana or hashish.

—8—

(pp.140–142) Howard acceded to media requests, surmising in a letter home, 'I cannot now reverse the attention on me but must use it to the best advantage. It is important to me to expose the DEA lies and the US government's political manipulation in my case. I also want to do what I can to legalise marijuana. Believe me, I've done some deep soul-searching on this and feel it's almost like a mission.'

This episode of *PrimeTime Live* (above and overleaf) aired on ABC News throughout the United States on 5 April 1990, as Howard prepared for trial. Viewing ratings for the programme were the highest that it had ever attained, the presenter telling the audience at its end, 'When Howard Marks finally walks into a

Mr. MARKS: That's right, yes.
SCHADLER: Any rock 'n' roll bands that we might know?
Mr. MARKS: Emerson, Lake and Palmer, Eric Clapton, Genesis, Pink Floyd.
SCHADLER: *[voice-over]* Though Marks says the bands never knew of the scam, British Customs did and first arrested him in 1973, but he disappeared before his trial, eluding the police for the next six years. Add "international fugitive" to his resumé.

[interviewing] Describe the six years you were a fugitive.
Mr. MARKS: Probably the best six years of my life, I think, a wonderful six years — never having to be on call for anyone, never having to give one's phone number to anyone, changing identities as often as I wished. I found it fascinating.
SCHADLER: *[voice-over]* Call it Howard's Walter Mitty phase. Marks alias Donald Nice, alias John Goddard, alias Roy Green, and with each fake passport, a new persona.

[interviewing] What was your favorite personality?
Mr. MARKS: I think the film producer. I enjoyed being a film producer very much.
SCHADLER: Why?
Mr. MARKS: Oh, just for the reasons that anyone enjoys being a film producer, I mean, lots of glamour, lots of famous people, and I produced a film called *Life After Elvis*, which was always one of my ambitions, so I could exploit some of my fantasies, basically, before they exploited me.
SCHADLER: *[voice-over]* But his fantasy ended abruptly in 1981. Arrested at an English pub and put back on trial, he then stunned prosecutors by revealing and proving he held yet another occupation, British spy. Recruited by a classmate from his Oxford days, marks persuaded the jury his drug smuggling schemes were just a front used to help his government uncover arms smuggling by the Irish Republican Army. The jury acquitted him.

[interviewing] We have an expression here, I don't know if you have it in England, "playing both sides against the middle." Is that what you were doing in part?
Mr. MARKS: No, I wasn't playing either side against each other or the middle. I mean, I had to give a true account of my activities, and— which included my work for British Intelligence, and that brought sympathy from the jury.
SCHADLER: Should you not have been acquitted?
Mr. MARKS: Oh, I think the system of British justice should be upheld. I wouldn't criticize it for a second.
SCHADLER: You say that with a smile—
Mr. MARKS: You bet.
SCHADLER: It sounds like you think you're a criminal.
Mr. MARKS: Pardon? I think I was lucky to get acquitted, and I was surprised to get acquitted. I think that's all I need say about that.
SCHADLER: *[voice-over]* His acquittal gave Marks legendary status in the British press. Brits loved it, the police hated it, and when a book came out detailing Marks's bravado and the government's bungling, drug cops around the world could only smolder.

[interviewing] And the fact that he was so vocal and so public with his escapades as a dealer, was he sort of rubbing your noses in all of this?
TOM CASH, DEA Agent: No, I don't think— I don't think he rubbed our

—9—

Florida courtroom later this year to begin his trial, you can expect some surprises. After all, he seems to like it that way. Remember in his 1981 trial in England, he pulled a legal rabbit out of the hat by convincing jurors he was a British spy. Well, this time, with his act playing on an American stage he's already hinted to us that there's another trick up his sleeve… Marks will reportedly claim that drug shipments, including one that brought 4,800lb of hashish into the Alameda Naval Stations in California, were arranged with the complicity of unnamed US military officials.'

Shortly after the programme aired, Howard was moved to a different cell block and every member of the former block petitioned to have Howard returned.

nose in anything.

SCHADLER: One of the peculiar arguments that Mr. Marks makes is that the marijuana drug trade is sort of a kinder, gentler version of the cocaine-heroin drug trade. Do you buy that argument?

Mr. CASH: I have not seen any part of the narcotics traffic that was, as you say "kinder and gentler." I would like to find the first less violent narcotics trafficker so that I could put him in the Smithsonian.

SCHADLER: *[voice-over]* To finally put Howard Marks in a federal prison required an elaborate trap. At Marks's new home on the Spanish island of Mallorca, DEA agents wire-tapped his phone, recording what they say are his cryptic drug deals.

> **Mr. MARKS**: *[transcript]* This seems to be the quickest and easiest way of doing it, no?
>
> **CALLER**: Yeah.
>
> **Mr. MARKS**: I mean, I don't want to do it for the obvious reasons.

SCHADLER: *[voice-over]* Then Anthony Moynihan, an old chum of Marks and a notorious English lord implicated in everything from white slavery to murder, was brought in as a government informant. That's him on undercover videotape, arriving at a meeting he set up between Marks's brother-in-law and a DEA agent.

> **Mr. MOYNIHAN**: You don't mind if I join in your conversation?

SCHADLER: *[voice-over]* It was the sting that finally stung Howard Marks.

[interviewing] Lord Anthony Moynihan, you used to call him a friend, a good friend. What would you call him now?

Mr. MARKS: A bad friend.

SCHADLER: *[voice-over]* Eventually, a jury will have to decide which of these two old friends to believe, the admitted drug smuggler or the convicted con artist. Either way, if Marks takes the stand—

Mr. BRONIS: I would pay to be admitted to that portion of the testimony. He certainly won't be boring, I can assure you of that.

SCHADLER: When Howard Marks finally walks into a Florida courtroom later this year to begin his trial, you can expect some surprises. After all, he seems to like it that way. Remember, in his 1981 trial in England, he pulled a legal rabbit out of the hat by convincing jurors he was a British spy. Well, this time, with his act playing on an American stage, he's already hinted to us that there's another trick up his sleeve.

Mr. MARKS: One has to remember that something like 7,000 tons of marijuana get into this country every year, and the government doesn't know how? Of course, they know how.

SCHADLER: Marks will reportedly claim that drug shipments, including one that brought 4800 pounds of hashish into the Alameda Naval Station in California, were arranged with the complicity of unnamed U.S. military officials.

[interviewing] More than one military official involved?

Mr. MARKS: More than one, yes.

SCHADLER: And what happened in one military base undoubtedly happened at others?

Mr. MARKS: Yes, or in this case, happened in the same military base or naval station more than once.

SCHADLER: *[voice-over]* Though you might expect the DEA to deny that, don't.

[interviewing] If a military base is not secure from drugs, where can any-

(↓) Included in the prosecution case was this composite drawing made of the man seen delivering crates of cannabis to the American President Line at Karachi Wharf in 1984. An account of what happened next is given in *Hunting Marco Polo*, which was researched and written with the collaboration of DEA agents and British law enforcement, while Howard awaited trial:

'Harlon Bowe walked over to the desk and glanced at the picture. Then looked again, intently. "Christ," he said, "That's Howard Marks."' HMP

Michael Stephenson of Her Majesty's Customs and Excise (the man whom Lord Jeremy Hutchinson had enjoyed cross-examining in 1981 about his proclaimed ability to identify Howard through the keyhole of a hotel room) was now Britain's Drug Liaison Officer in Karachi, the first British drug agent to be stationed overseas. Stephenson, like Bowe, had taken one look at the composite drawing of 'Mr Dennis' and identified him as Howard Marks. Howard was beginning to look forward to his trial. It wasn't him who had delivered the crates, though it was meant to have been, and he could prove it.

Also, to Howard's joy, Old John had been freed in Canada. The courts in Vancouver refused to extradite him to the United States after discovering that the DEA had withheld evidence favourable to the defence.

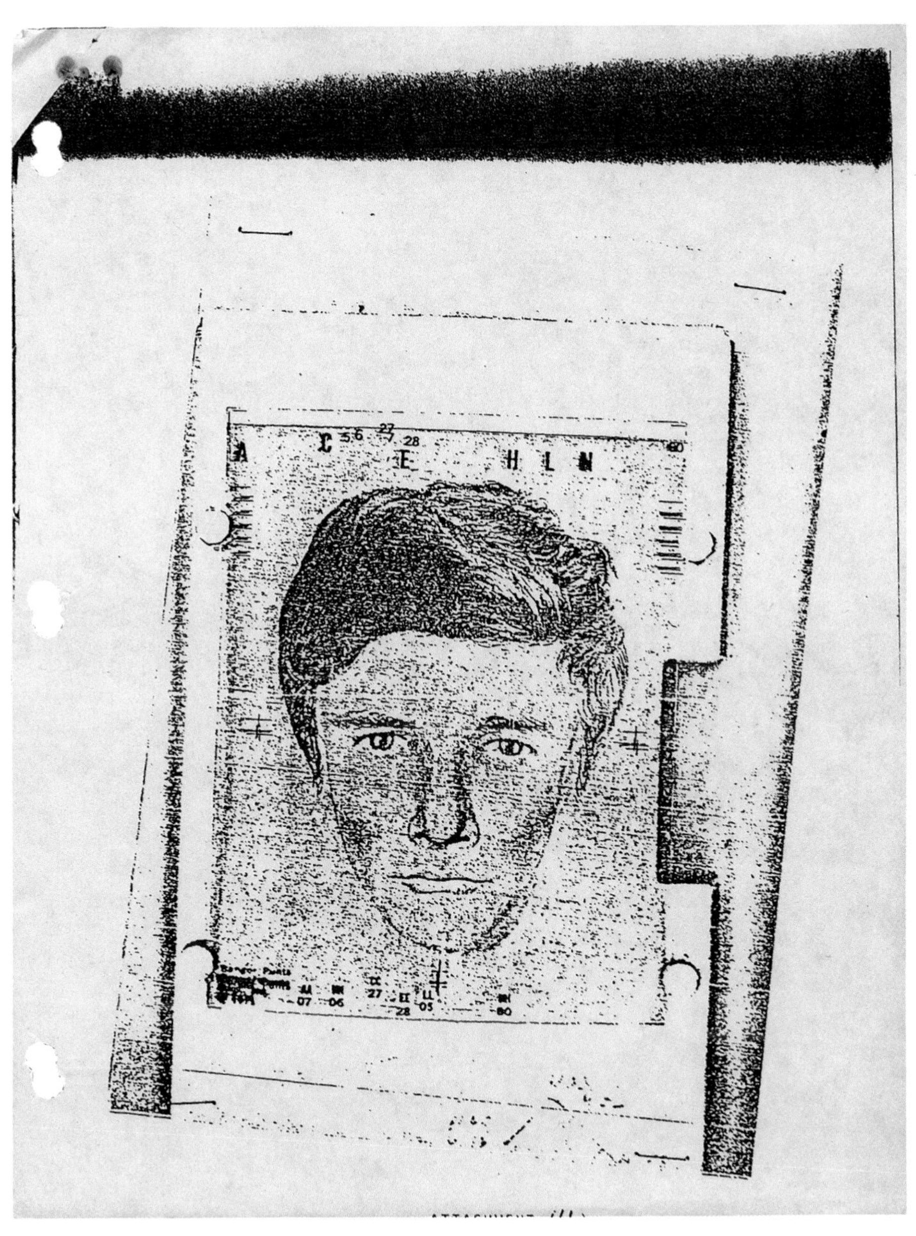

16

quantity of approximately 13,000 pounds of marijuana, a Schedule I non-narcotic controlled substance."

[Viva voce evidence from Vancouver witnesses - see chronology (Authorities, Appendix I).] The previous pattern of importing from Holland to the United States and from Mexico to the United States allow an inference this load was going from Vancouver to the United States. In addition, Marks' comments to Moynihan that California was the only serious market in the world. In addition, the presence of Alexander, Light, Allen, and Wills, all Americans, in Vancouver lead to an inference the load was destined for the United States.]

B. Acts of racketeering involving the distribution and possession with intent to distribute hashish in violation of Title 18, United States Code, Section 841(a)(1)

Date:

4.B. "on or about April 9, 1986"

Location:

4.B. "in Los Angeles, California, United States of America, and elsewhere"

Defendants:

4.B. "Ernest Franz Combs, Jr.
Patricia Ann Hayes
and others known and unknown"

Offence:

4.B. "knowingly and intentionally did possess with the intent to distribute and did distribute and did cause others to possess with the intent to distribute and did distribute a quantity of approximately one pound of hashish, a Schedule I non-narcotic controlled substance."

[Affidavits of Robert C. Arnold, Julie Desm, Peter M. Shigeta - see also chronology (Authorities, Appendix II, pp.13-14).]

C. Acts of racketeering involving the importation of hashish in violation of Title 21, United States Code, Section 952

This is from the paperwork Old John sent to Howard, with John's observations scribbled on it in pen.

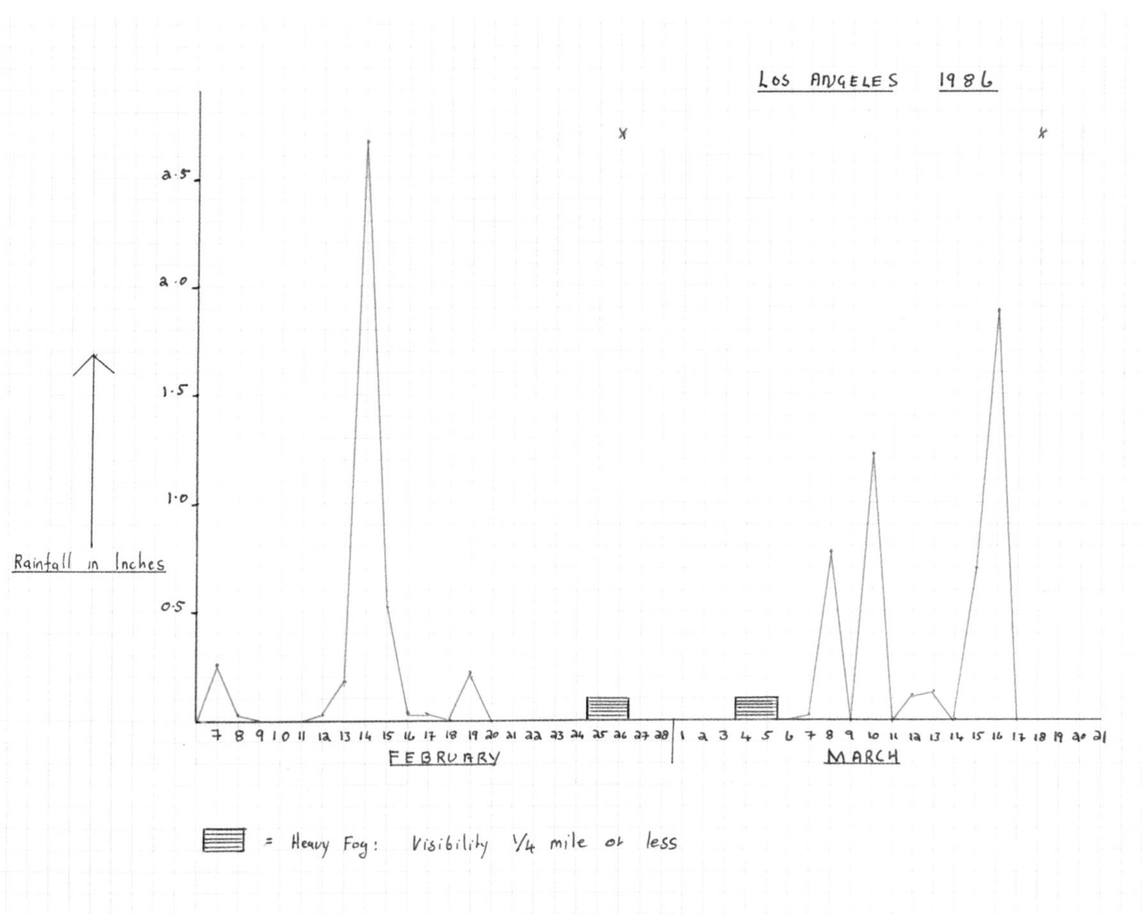

In support of his defence (that the cannabis was destined for Australia, not the United States), Howard obtained meteorological data showing that comments made by him and his co-defendants on DEA phone taps referred to a particularly severe storm off the Australian coast. Howard created this chart with a pen and ruler to explain graphically the weather conditions. Shortly before his trial was due to commence, Howard was informed that Ernie had agreed to give evidence against him, in exchange for his own wife's freedom. Howard realised he now did not stand a chance of succeeding with his defence.

In West Palm Beach Courthouse on 13 July 1990, Howard pleaded guilty to racketeering and conspiracy to racketeer and was sentenced to 25 years' imprisonment. The judge recommended that he be housed in Butner, Northern Carolina, which was particularly suited to prisoners wishing to pursue academic studies, and that he be considered for a transfer to serve an appropriate portion of his sentence in an institution in the United Kingdom.

In his sentencing remarks, HHJ Paine said:

'It is apparent, Mr Marks, that you regard the use of marijuana and its derivatives as consistent with sound moral principles, and it is also apparent that you have been quite willing to violate laws which prohibit or control use, possession or commercial transactions with respect to marijuana. You have been quite willing to ignore, or studiously violate the laws of many countries. You have demonstrated that you have little respect for the rules of society as expressed by criminal laws which do not conform to what you believe to be acceptable conduct. While there is a large body of opinion that use of marijuana is not addictive, does not impair health in an unacceptable way, and should not, therefore, be illegal, there is, also, a large body of opinion to the contrary as to these matters. Further, and more importantly, federal statutes prohibit trafficking in marijuana. These statutes have been enacted by the Congress of the United States, and are enforced by the executive branch of the government by initiation of court action and otherwise. I have taken an oath to administer justice, perform all duties agreeable to the laws of the United States. So, even if I agreed that laws controlling use and sale of marijuana are inappropriate, even foolish, I would have to abide by them until Congress has repealed them. These are rules of society which the courts are bound to apply – whether you agree or not that these laws should be in place.'

Howard's friends and family were shocked and devastated, organising several petitions and campaigns. Howard later wrote to his father, sensing his annoyance at the iniquity of the length of time violators of the cannabis laws were sentenced to:

'Maybe the enclosed news cutting of a few days ago indicates that the pendulum has at last reached the extremity of its amplitude and is, ever so slowly, reversing its swing. As you know from your own studies of the simple harmonic motion of the tides, the reversing of direction of motion is what takes the longest time. Rationality should assert itself and eradicate such injustices. There is no doubt that cannabis will one day be regarded for what it is. I expected it to happen over 20 years ago.'

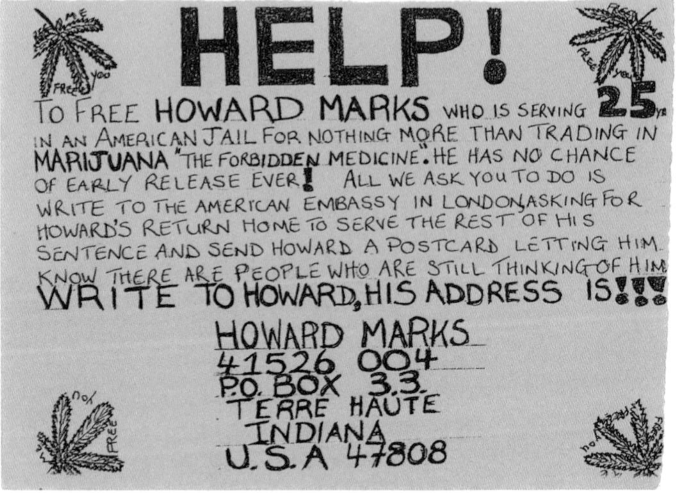

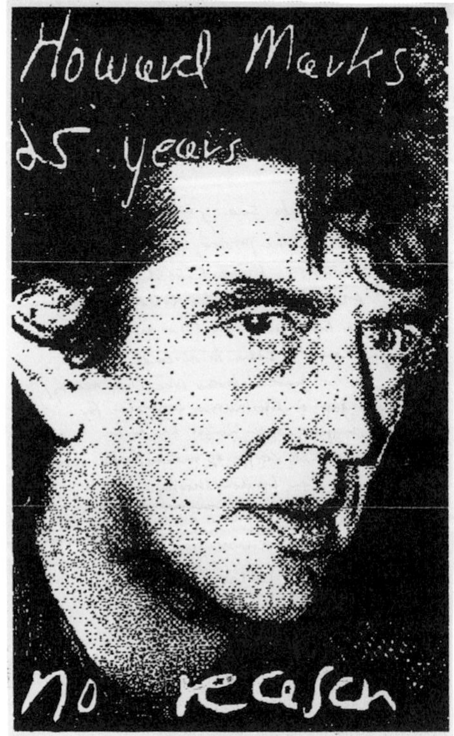

7

Terror Hut

Several hurt in brief prison fight

By John Wright
Tribune-Star

A fight in the U.S. Penitentiary at Terre Haute on Wednesday morning left a staff member hospitalized and other employees and inmates injured.

Bill Gerth, public information officer, said the fight between two groups of inmates broke out about 6:30 a.m., during breakfast in the dining room.

A foreman in food service at the prison was admitted to Terre Haute Regional Hospital. Gerth said he did not have authorization to release his name. The employee's condition was unavailable late Wednesday.

See "Prison," Page A3

1-20-94

Prison

• Continued from Page A1

Several inmates were stabbed and two other members of staff were injured, Gerth said. Gerth said he did not know if any inmates were admitted to the hospital. The other employees were treated and released.

Order was restored within 10 minutes after the fight started. "All inmates are locked in their cells," Gerth said Wednesday afternoon of what is known as a "lockdown."

The lockdown, put in effect immediately after the fight, is expected to last until at least today. Inmates are confined to the buildings where they are housed, not allowed to go to their prison jobs and denied visitors during lockdowns.

Gary Wills, a food service employee, was one staff member injured. He was treated and released from Terre Haute Regional Hospital.

Gerth said he did not have authorization to release the names of others injured.

Gerth said he did not know why the fight started. Forty staff members attending a training session at the prison were brought in to help secure the institution.

"We had enough men to get it under control in a matter of minutes," he said.

The FBI is investigating the fight by interviewing the 1,300 inmates in the institution, Gerth said.

TRIBUNE-STAR • Thursday, March 24, 1994 • A

Penitentiary inmate stabbed to death

3-24-94

An inmate in the U.S. Penitentiary at Terre Haute died Tuesday after being stabbed with a homemade knife, Vigo County Coroner Dr. Roland Kohr said.

The single stab wound in the middle of Perrydean A. Poquette's back severed a large artery, causing the inmate to bleed to death, said Kohr, who performed an autopsy Wednesday.

Prison officials said Poquette, 23, of St. Alban, Vt., collapsed in the main hallway of the prison at 3:42 p.m. Tuesday. He was taken to Terre Haute Regional Hospital and pronounced dead at 4:45 p.m. by emergency room doctors.

Prison public information officer Bill Gerth said Poquette was seen by staff walking in the hallway before he collapsed at the hallway's east end.

Poquette was serving a 15-year sentence for possession of firearm by a convicted felon.

Gerth said all inmates wer[e] locked in their cells for a fe[w] hours Tuesday before the priso[n] returned to normal operations.

Prison staff and FBI agent[s] from Terre Haute conducted sev[eral] interviews at the priso[n] Wednesday. FBI Agent Marti[n] Riggin said the investigatio[n] into Poquette's death could las[t] several days.

One dead, two injured in fight at penitentiary

4-7-9[4]

By David Kaye
Tribune-Star

For the second time in two weeks, an altercation in the U.S. Penitentiary at Terre Haute has resulted in an inmate's death.

Roosevelt Daniels, 42, of Chicago was one of three inmates assaulted in the prison's dining hall at noon Tuesday. Daniels was transported to Terre Haute Regional Hospital and pronounced dead by emergency room personnel at 12:40 p.m.

The prison released the information at 5:45 p.m.

Vigo County Coroner Dr. Roland Kohr will perform an autopsy today to determine the cause of death. Kohr said it was an apparent stabbing.

The second inmate is in critical condition at Terre Haute Regional Hospital. The third inmate was treated for minor injuries at the prison.

Prison officials and FBI agents interviewed some of the 1,300 inmates to try and determine the motive of the attack and who was involved, according to Bill Gerth, the prison's public information director.

Gerth said the prison will remain "locked down" until further notice. During lockdowns, inmates are confined to buildings where they live and not allowed to work or have visitors.

Gerth would not provide any more details about the incident or the identities of the two injured inmates.

Daniels was serving 40 years for criminal enterprise, racketeering and selling cocaine.

See "Inmates," Page A3

FBI Agent Marty Riggen said there are 400 to 500 inmates to interview.

Daniels' death came 14 days after Perrydean Poquette, 23, of St. Alban, Vt., was stabbed to death with a homemade knife. Poquette was serving a 15-year sentence for possession of a firearm by a convicted felon.

"It's starting to be a problem out there," said Riggen. "Hopefully, we can get this one straightened out and also the previous one." Riggen said he was optimistic about finding the person — or persons — responsible for Daniels' death.

The dining hall has been the site of other problems recently in the prison.

A fight between two rival groups of inmates occurred in the dining hall Jan. 19. Several inmates were stabbed and three prison staff members were injured during the incident.

The prison was then locked down for more than 24 hours.

Although HHJ Paine had recommended he be housed in a low-security prison, Howard was sent to Terre Haute, a high-security penitentiary in Indiana. He was shocked and terrified by the news. But by January 1991 he felt able to write home, 'the place is far better than I expected and there are plenty of good interesting people here. I've already played dozens of games of chess winning, I guess, about 50% of the time. The standard here is far higher than any other prison I've been to.' In May 1991 Howard wrote of his visit from the British Consul: 'He's a very nice man. He will monitor the progress of my application for international transfer, chase up about my being allowed to participate in a degree course and find out who exactly is responsible for preventing me from "officially" making international telephone calls. The weather is now beginning to get hot and sticky, which apparently is normal for Indiana spring and summer. Chipmunks are tearing round the prison grounds and are surprisingly tame and friendly. There are a variety of birds – red-haired finches, starlings, giant robins, jackdaws, bluejays and kites and pigeons and a less attractive variety of insects.'

This is a collection of cuttings used by Howard in support of his applications for transfer to a lower security institution and the United Kingdom.

In the spring of 1991 John Jones, Dean of Balliol, struck up a correspondence with Howard, and Howard agreed to write an account of his time at university for John's records. In October, Howard wrote to John, 'Since I last wrote to you, there has been a murder committed a few yards away from me, approximately twenty-five miraculously non-fatal stabbings, and a daily occurrence of one or more vicious fights. It's very hard to get rehabilitated in a gladiator school. The United States' so-called Department of Justice, in full exercise of its limited wisdom, has denied my application to serve the rest of my sentence in Great Britain. Quite why it is preferred that I be incarcerated at American rather than British expense is puzzling. It's also depressing, particularly for my family who are either too old, too young, or otherwise prohibited from visiting the United States. I can, however, reapply in a year or so. To make matters worse, the Federal Government is attempting to confiscate my home in Spain. This is not being done on the basis of the property having been bought with illicit proceeds – but on the basis that I furthered my wicked actions by making telephone calls from there. The prospect of my wife and kids having to take to the streets is a gloomy one.'

The report below recommends time off (30 days being the maximum deduction available) for Howard's good behaviour.

U.S. DEPARTMENT OF JUSTICE
Federal Bureau of Prisons

EXTRA GOOD TIME RECOMMENDATION

Institution: USP–TERRE HAUTE, INDIANA	Date: JUNE 26, 1991	
NAME (Last, First, Middle): MARKS, DENNIS HOWARD	Number: 41526-004	Assignment: EDUCATION

[X] Recommend Meritorious Good Time Effective: APRIL 1, 1991 (The effective date can not be retroactive any more than three months, excluding the month in which the recommendation is made).

[ ] Recommend Termination of Meritorious Good Time Effective: ____________

[ ] Recommend Disallowance of Extra Good Time For The Calendar Month of: ____________

[ ] Recommend Lump Sum Award of ____________ Days: Date of act or termination of activity for which the recommendation is made ____________

JUSTIFICATION: INMATE MARKS HAS WORKED AS A TUTOR FOR THE GED PROGRAM FOR THE PAST 3 MONTHS. HE HAS DONE AN OUTSTANDING JOB SINCE HIS ASSIGNMENT TO THE EDUCATION DEPARTMENT. HIS HIGH DEGREE OF EDUCATION AND TRAINING HAS MADE HIM OF EXCEPTIONAL VALUE IN ASSISTING IN PROGRAM PLANNING AND CURRICULUM DEVELOPMENT. HE EXHIBITS A POSITIVE ATTITUDE TOWARD HIS WORK; EVEN AN ENTHUSIASM TOWARD TUTORING AND TEACHING. HE HAS ALWAYS CARRIED OUT HIS DUTIES OR WHATEVER WAS ASKED OF HIM TO THE BEST OF HIS ABILITIES AND WITH NEVER A COMPLAINT. HE HAS ESTABLISHED AN EXCELLENT RAPPORT, NOT ONLY WITH THE INMATE STUDENTS THAT HE TEACHES BUT ALSO WITH THE OTHER INMATE TUTORS AS WELL AS OTHER STAFF MEMBERS. HE HAS PROVED VERY ADEPT ALSO AT RECRUITING NEW STUDENTS AND HAS BEEN A POSITIVE INFLUENCE ON MANY OF THE OTHER INMATES IN THE DEPARTMENT. HIS KNOWLEDGE, ATTITUDE AND SELF-MOTIVATION HAVE MADE HIM AN EXTREMELYVALUABLE ADDITION TO THE EDUCATION DEPARTMENT AND IN MY OPINION INMATE MARKS IS VERY DESERVING OF APPROVAL FOR THE AWARD OF MERITORIOUS GOOD TIME.

Work Supervisor: [signature]

Approved By: (Name) [signature] acting SOE

Chief Executive Officer or Committee: [signature]

Date: 7-16-91

Sentry Release Date Adjusted by: [signature]
Legal Technician Signature

Date 7/22/91

Original – J & C
Canary – Central File
Pink – Work Supervisor

Previously BP-REC

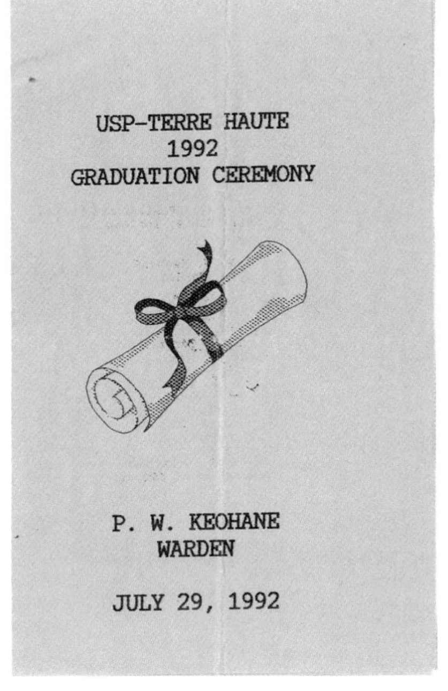
USP-TERRE HAUTE
1992
GRADUATION CEREMONY

P. W. KEOHANE
WARDEN

JULY 29, 1992

Howard obtained his High School Diploma, required for him to teach inmates, on account of the prison system's inability to recognise foreign qualifications. He achieved the highest mark ever awarded to an inmate and came within the top 5% of the country as a whole. In March 1991, Howard's appointment as a tutor was approved by various prison supervisors, 'It seems that my fate is teaching English grammar rather than mathematics which is a surprise. American education is pretty appalling which makes me believe that they're actually dedicated to producing an uneducated populace, stupefied by TV and basketball, so that the people won't revolt against the clearly corrupt administration. It was in the 60s that American education standards were at their highest and the students brought an end to warmongering in Vietnam. The powers that be won't let that happen again.'

By autumn 1991, Howard was working on a punctuation guide for the education department in the prison and receiving handmade birthday cards from his students, writing home of it: 'They aren't the sort of people one expects that sort of gesture from, which makes it all the more appreciated... eventually, I'll have a single cell though that may take about a year. My present cell mate is a real gentleman – 61 years old, a counterfeiter who was once the General Superintendent of the construction of Sears Tower, Chicago, the tallest building in the world. The weather has taken an incredibly sudden turn. Three days ago it was 95°F at midday. Two days ago, at 5am, it was 33°F, the lowest it has been for 70 years for this time of year. This, apparently, is how winter announces itself in Indiana. The summer has suddenly disappeared. At the beginning of the week we were in shorts, now we're in Long Johns... A large skunk patrols the prison grounds at night. I can't see him, but I often smell him as he marks out his territory – what an amazing weapon it has to defend itself.'

①

Monday October 12th, 1992

Today is Columbus Day, and we are not required to work. It's now 10.00am. I was going to play tennis at 9.30 am with Fiacconi, but my left leg is hurting – not the knee itself, but the rest of it.

The night before last I watched the Michael Jackson concert in Bucharest. Apparently my son Patrick is obsessed with Michael Jackson. He'll be six years old soon, and I've not seen him for over 3 years. This gets harder to bear everyday. I couldn't watch Michael Jackson without thinking of Patrick. When he sang Billie Jean and walked backwards, I had so many feelings of nostalgia; we used to have that track on tape – Amber and Francesca loved it.

Last night I watched most of the first presidential debate – in the library, as the tv's in the cell block were showing a cowboy film and a football game. It was disappointing, partly because Clinton didn't come off as well as I'd hoped, but more so because he stated he was adamant about not legalising drugs stating that his brother would be dead if drugs had been legal.

I have no real idea why I decided to write today – something to do with maybe one day writing a book and something to do with being irritated with forgetting things. Apparently old men have to write down everything.

My main preoccupations are whether my parents will live to see me free, whether Judy will start living with someone else, and whether my children will be too old to need a father before I get out.

My cell mate, Dan, has motion sickness. He's had it since Friday, and now sleeps on the bottom bunk.

I've been in this cell for a year, 4 months with Bateman, 3 months with Scott Brady, and 4 months with Dan. I've just moved the desk to the centre, as the radiator's too hot. Dan likes it hot. Some like it hot.

I'm waiting to find out whether or not I'm to be transferred to an FCI – which one and when. I'm scared

(↑) A rare diary entry by Howard, while suffering a bout of sadness. He wrote home of how he dealt with depression when it got the better of him in prison:

'I cope with it, or try to cope with it, on four fundamentally different levels. The first is my attempting to get physically fit by walking lots, playing tennis and twisting myself up in yoga positions. I should really give up smoking as well. Secondly, I try to do good by helping people. This is partly just a method of survival and partly my conscience. Thirdly, I try to make use of my time by studying new subjects like history, genetics and law.

Lastly, I meditate to try to grasp what various religions refer to as the "inner self", something we all have but not many are aware of having. I've yet to encounter an explanation of "inner self" which is easy to convey. Think of individuals as balloons full of air. When a balloon bursts, the skin doesn't go to heaven or hell, it just rots into nothing. But, the air inside the balloon carries on. Some of it might get inside another new balloon. It is, was, and always will be air. The "inner self" is something like that air. That's the best I can do.'

(↓) Howard kept his family up to date on his reading and having finished the copy of Richard Dawkins' *The Selfish Gene*, sent him by Julian Peto, he wrote disparagingly '... treating human beings as mere "survival machine systems" for genes which are immortal passing from one generation to another, callously discarding bodies when they become useless for their purposes – an interesting viewpoint.'

In response to John Jones's kind enquiry regarding Howard's access to current affairs publications, Howard replied:

'I do get the newspapers. Each day, I borrow *USA Today* (America's *Daily Express*); each week, I get a copy of the *Manchester Guardian* (an excellent weekly containing the best of *The Guardian*, *Washington Post* and *Le Monde*) for which Julian Peto gave me a gift subscription; each fortnight, Steve Balogh sends me the current *Private Eye*; and each month, I get sent a copy of *Gentleman's Quarterly*, courtesy of its deputy editor, David Jenkins. Accordingly, I'm reasonably up to date with what's happening and aware of the Dickensian nature of modern-day English life. It does seem rather hopeless.'

(↗) In May 1992, Howard wrote home, 'In the sense of avoiding casualties I too am glad that the LA riots have subsided. In another sense, I'm disappointed as it's high time that the iniquitous justice system in this country was subjected to serious, meaningful attack.'

In the autumn of 1992 Howard wrote to John Jones, 'The clearly ill wind Andrew, despite proverbial wisdom, performed the invaluable service of levelling two Florida prisons, including one which housed me for several months. Apparently no one escaped, and the 2,000 inmates were the first of 250,000 homeless to be found accommodation. This, however, was not accomplished without throwing the Department of Justice into hopefully permanent disarray. Andrew should stand for president.

You may be amused to learn that I have been asked by the prison's supervisor of education to teach an evening class in philosophy beginning next January. The idea of teaching mafia hit-men and Hell's Angels the finer points of Leibniz's theory of monads has its disturbingly surreal aspects; nevertheless, I'm looking forward to it.'

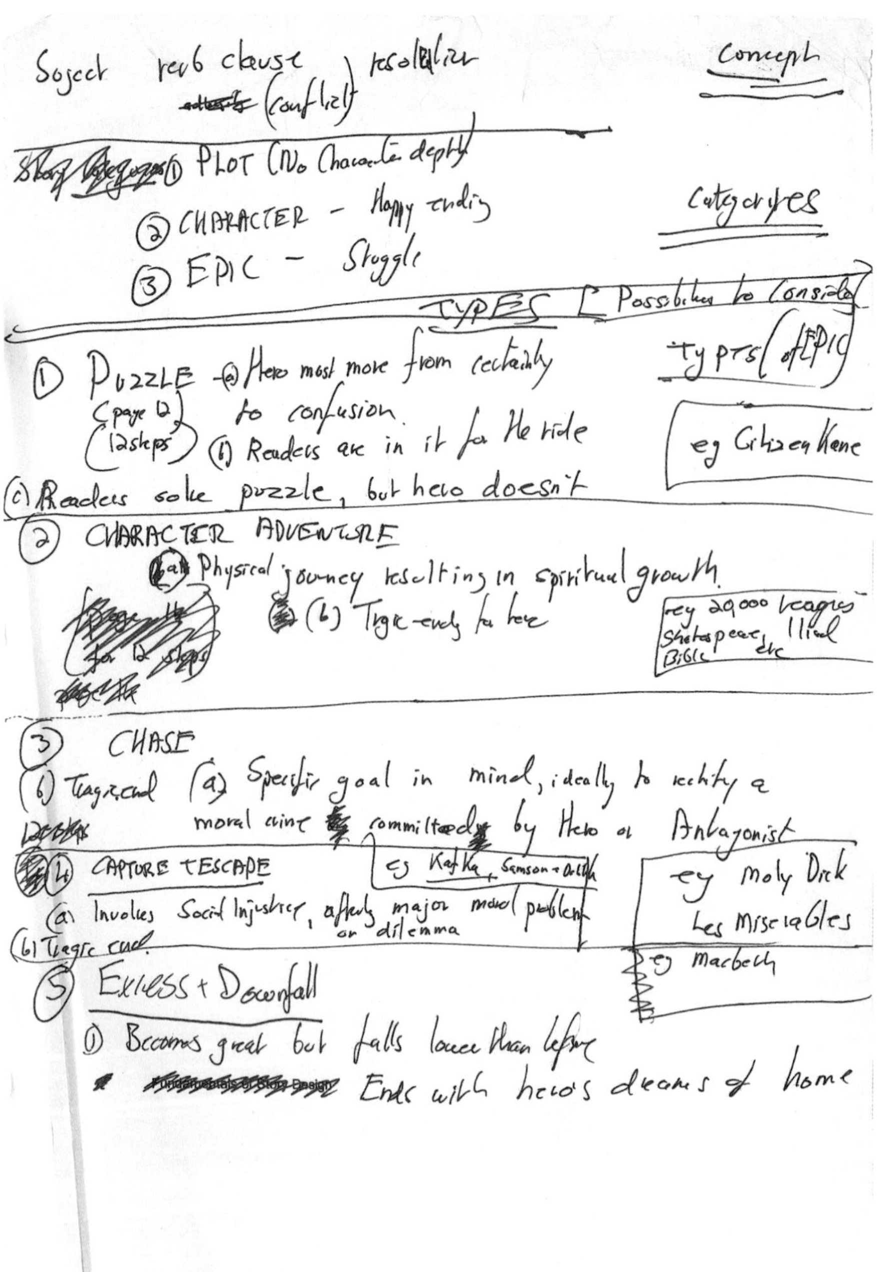

Subject verb clause (conflict) resolution

Concept

① PLOT (No Character depth)
② CHARACTER – Happy ending
③ EPIC – Struggle

Categories

TYPES [Possibilities to Consider

Types (of EPIC)

① PUZZLE (a) Hero must move from certainty to confusion.
(page 12) (12 steps) (b) Readers are in it for the ride
(c) Readers solve puzzle, but hero doesn't

eg Citizen Kane

② CHARACTER ADVENTURE
(a) Physical journey resulting in spiritual growth.
(b) Tragic-end for hero

eg 20,000 leagues Shakespeare, Iliad Bible etc

③ CHASE
(a) Specific goal in mind, ideally to rectify a moral crime committed by Hero or Antagonist
(b) Tragic end

④ CAPTURE + ESCAPE eg Kafka, Samson + Delilah
(a) Involves Social Injustice, affecting major moral problem or dilemma
(b) Tragic end.

eg Moby Dick Les Miserables

eg Macbeth

⑤ Excess + Downfall
(a) Becomes great but falls lower than before
Ends with hero's dreams of home

(↑) Howard's notes from a writing class in prison.

(↗) Sports news for Terre Haute. The last paragraph is about 'Howard (The Englishman) Marks'.

SPORTS NEWS

DON'T MISS ANOTHER ISSUE

SPORT MAGAZINE STAFF

L. FARRELL, REC. SUPV.

OFFICER GRIMES, REC. SPECIALIST

MIKE GRIFFIN, EDITOR

JOHN BONNER, REPORTER

Wednesday, December 11, 1991

VARSITY NEWS

VARSITY
USP SPURS

VS.

PICK-UP TEAM
'THE DREAM TEAM'

Last night we were expecting a team from the street to come in and play, but seems like they fear our VARSITY TEAM so much that they all keep leaving their I.D. home. If you have seen our VARSITY TEAM then you could maybe understand their fear. These guys are truly awesome.

They had worked up a sweat practicing, so we decided to pick-up a group of guys and give the VARSITY TEAM a game. AND WHAT A GAME IT WAS!!! The final score was 237-236! Yes, this was truly an offensive showing by both teams. I'll bet you are wondering who won this game. Well, hold your horses and wait!

The PICK UP TEAM consisted of "The Patch Barry, Nay Nay, Truck, Howard "Marco Polo" Marks, the "Dynamo" Savage-El, "The Rocking Moraccan" Sidi. We all chuckled when the game started, until they sent their tallest man out for the opening tap. . . it was Nay Nay! It was like one of those Japanese Kung Fu movies, Nay Nay jumped up 15 feet into the air to get the opening tap.

The VARSITY had their normal scoring balance. Big rock had 33 pts (plus 5 sacks), Pearl had 27 pts & 4 body-slams, Steve jumped clean over Savage-El 13 times for 19 pts, Overton-Bey "Rock" had 23 pts and his voice was blown-out completely. Coles scored one (1) point, had

[illegible]

146 steals, 432 assists. Clea had 46 rebounds. Lumpkin sank 11 three pointer out of 47 attempts. Baskins hit 123 free throws in a row. Tony jumped so high we had to help him down from the top of the back board. Randy, House, and Dana, all three stuffed Savage-El into the basket for 39 points. Charles Rogers had 75 steals. And finally the last member on this team, Tex, scored 8 points and he was not even there!!! Didn't I tell you it was a hell of a game!! Well just wait, there's more to come.

Truck was a one man gang scoring 87 points, 23 steals with 33 assist! (How is that Truck? enough points so you can send the paper home?) Nay Nay was like Meadowlark Lemon, dribbling the ball all over the court. I mean all over the court! Shoot??? - he would not pass the ball to anybody - his own team put Savage-El on Nay Nay. During all of his dribbling, he still found enough time to score 37 points. Sidi and Savage-El combined for 2 rebounds and 474 shots. Talk about bricks, these two guys had enough to build a house. They both had 4 slam dunks apiece, leaping 8 to 10 feet in to the air hovering over the basket before they slammed the ball into the basket. Only problem, they were at the wrong end of the court.

The game come down to the last few seconds and the PICK UP TEAM having only two men left on the floor. There were a lot laying on the sidelines, but only two playing! Barry called Howard (the Englishman) Marks out of the Law Library to help him get the ball up court. Howard did not know a slam dunk from a dribble, so he picks up a book on basketball on the way to the gym. With law books in hand, Howard and Barry start up the floor. With only 14 seconds left in the game, Barry & Howard scored 52 points! With 1 second left on the clock, Barry goes up high for a rebound and 10 feet in the air, turns and fires a perfect pass to a streaking Marks. The ball left Mark's hand as the buzzer sounded. The PICK UP TEAM needed 3 points to win, The ball hit the rim with a thud (reminded me of a weekend in Orlando) YES!! Howard Marks sinks a 96 foot shot for the winning score!!! What a game!

See you the next time. See what you miss when you don't come out to see the basketball games?!

HEALING FROM THE INSIDE

I HAVE LIVED the past twenty-four years of my life as a federal prisoner with the Bureau of Prisons' number 35316-136 appended to my name.

For those of you who have never been inside a maximum security penitentiary, it might be difficult, if not impossible, to imagine it as a place where the plaintive sounds of shakuhachi [Japanese bamboo flute] can be heard. Ah! But it is true.

I am honored and happy to be able to share with you a story about a young man (whom doctors had told would never walk again) and a piece of bamboo. This is a story of the human spirit and will at their finest, and a story of the healing power that is within shakuhachi.

In 1987, this young man (let's call him Punchy) was shot in the back in Detroit, Michigan. The shot and subsequent operation left him completely paralyzed from the waist down. Call it coincidence, fate or simply the way things happen, but in that very same year I was introduced to shakuhachi by a man named Monty H. Levenson, shakuhachi maker and now dear friend.

Three years later, in the recreation yard of Terre Haute Federal Penitentiary in Indiana, I first saw Punchy—he, being pushed in his wheelchair around the quarter-mile track; me, sitting under the shade of a lone tre blowing my shakuhachi. I closed my eyes and continued to blow The song in my heart reflected what I had just seen and m shakuhachi began to cry.

After about two weeks of watching Punchy go for his daily ride I made arrangements through one of his "drivers" to meet him I explained to Punchy that I practiced an ancient art calle "Hands-on Healing". I explained about Touch for Health Acupressure, Tsubo Therapy, Shiastsu Therapy, Jin Shin Do Massage Therapy and Meditation Healing using sounds an colors. We talked about ch'i and the circulation of energy chakras, stretching, as well as other kinds of physical therap and exercise. I looked into his eyes and told him I'd like to try t help him. Although he had never heard of such things and wa unable to hide his skepticism, he agreed.

Where? How to begin? That was the burning question in m mind as we made arrangements to meet the following afternoon I knew that I would have to examine his entire body from hea to toes and would have to work with him daily for quite a lon time. We would both have to be committed—to each other an to ourselves. This would involve much work, way beyon physical therapy.

As agreed, we began the following day. After a solid month (days a week, 2 1/2 hours a day) of breathing exercises acupressure treatments, and stretching, we were basically wher we were when we started. Punchy was locked up inside of himse where I could not touch. I knew that unless he would allow m to come in, unless he could open up and share with me hi deepest pain, no amount of massage and manipulation c muscles, no amount of stimulation of nerves, no amount c stretching, no amount of anything would result in a improvement of his condition.

Were the doctors with their professional diagnosis correct i their approach? Or was Punchy—a young man, who had s much energy inside himself—being sentenced to a wheelcha for the rest of his life? Is it true that the solution (if there is solution) to any problem lies *within* the problem itself?

A breakthrough was needed.

I had recently started conducting meditation sessions wit members of our Rastafarian Community in the chapel durin which I blow shakuhachi. I asked Punchy to attend. For th special session I gathered together seven men, all physicall strong and emotionally and spiritually well-balanced. The seve men would represent the Sun, the Moon, Mother Earth and th Four Directions (North, East, South and West). I explained t them Punchy's condition and what was needed of each man a well as all of them as a collective body. The following is part of "Self-Monitoring Cross-Consciousness" account of our fir

14

(↑↗) One of Howard's dearest friends in Terre Haute was Veronza Bowers, the author of this article. Veronza was a member of the Black Panther party and was convicted of the murder of a US park ranger in 1973, on the word of government informants. He continues to deny involvement in the killing and is by now one of the longest serving prisoners in the US justice system. His family continue to petition for his release. In spite of exemplary behaviour throughout his decades of imprisonment, his applications for release on parole continue to be rejected. Veronza cured Howard of various ailments during incarceration.

In autumn 1993 Howard wrote to John Jones how '[a] rather chilling development is that the one and only federal Death Row and execution chamber is to be housed within these walls. Although individual states' justice systems have been enthusiastically executing minorities for some considerable time, the federal death penalty has not been implemented for decades. Bush engineered its comeback, and the

by Veronzo Bowers jr

meditation healing session written immediately following the session by Darrell, one of the participants.

"A wounded Brother was placed on his back in the center of the room. We were instructed to form a circle around him, lying on our backs with our heads nearest to him and focus upon channeling positive energy so that he might be healed.

"We were instructed to breathe in a rhythmic and harmonious flow, inhaling deeply to the count of five and exhaling deeply to the count of five until we were in perfect unison. A flute began to play... With my eyes closed, I can hear the melody uttering words of transient delight, making it hard to resist complete relaxation. I have given myself totally to the Wounded One.

"There was a light. I used it to focus on as I attempted to channel my energy towards the Wounded One. I concentrated on the lower half of his body, for he was unable to walk. The light was drawing near and growing dim, the musical sounds freeing me from anxiety... The light now, ever so near and dimmer still, as the sounds of winds from the flute hovered over my body. I am conscious as my body releases the tension from the controlled breathing and begins to act upon its own to recover its natural pace...The hollow sounds of beauty making me ever so comfortable as the dimness of the light slowly turns to a red.

"The flute player is standing over me. I am aware of his presence, but why am I moaning?... Why can I not respond to acknowledge him? Where am I?... Can I help my wounded Brother, and who and where are the drummers? My body won't respond, but I am conscious... I can hear everything and the breaths of everyone; we are all breathing out of time... Everyone has lost the rhythm except the flutist. He has acted as a tour guide down the pathway of total redness, almost leading me towards serenity, if it weren't for the pain. What pain?... Whose pain?... So much pain, but why am I still moaning? Where am I?

"It appears that I have allowed the flutist, the tour guide, to take me beyond the realms of my control. I can sense serenity, but the pain... Oh! The pain! And why do I feel as if I'm not alone. The corridor, or pathway, which has turned blue some time ago is now glowing and has a strange aura.

"The silence broke. 'Rub your hands together.' It was the familiar voice of the tour guide, and I made motions with my hands, which was all I could do to make him aware that the command had been heard. I didn't quite know how to function, for I was distant, incoherent and a slight bit delirious; but I could sense that he knew, for I was still trapped in space. 'Rub your hands together so that they generate energy, and then rub the warmth over your face... wash your face with energy.' I was able to comprehend the fact that this was, no doubt, a command, and I found myself obedient, my body began to respond, my eyes opened... it was over."

After the session had ended and everyone else had "returned" to this plane, Punchy was still out. When he finally "awoke", he blurted out, "What happened? Where have I been?" Everyone laughed.

I was terribly excited and anxious to talk with the Brother who had been moaning and groaning and rolling his head back and forth. I needed to know what he had "seen", what he had "experienced". He and I got together immediately after everyone had left the chapel. As I blew shakuhachi at the top of the stairwell, he recorded what you have just read.

Ah! The breakthrough! On so many levels. A small piece of bamboo, 1.8 feet long, had opened doorways which had previously been welded shut.

Shakuhachi had done in one and one-half hours what no human being had done in three years. Shakuhachi had made it possible, via Darrell's psychic bonding with Punchy, to connect with and to deeply understand Punchy's psychological and spiritual pain. During our next working session, Punchy and I discussed all that we had both learned, and for the first time he opened up completely.

From then on, we began each working session with shakuhachi. Numerous approaches—healthy diet with vitamins; a combination of disciplines mentioned earlier; meditation and circulation of ch'i; weightlifting for upper body strength; stretching, stretching and more stretching for leg strength (the strength of the Tiger lies in his flexibility); and a determined will—all combined, so that by the end of the summer (10 months after our first meditation healing session), Punchy could do 100 full squats non-stop, walk five steps on his own, walk behind his wheelchair with *me* sitting in it and push me one full lap around the quarter-mile track in the yard.

I wish I had more space to share with you the details of this inspiring struggle of a young man determined to walk again and the never ending mystery that is shakuhachi.

I am eternally grateful to shakuhachi for so graciously accepting my breath and for allowing me to be an extension through which healing can pass.

In addition to studying and practicing meditation and the ancient healing arts of China and Japan, Veronzò Bowers Jr is an accomplished musician and composer of original pieces for the shakuhachi. This story will also appear in Volume II of the Annals of The International Shakuhachi Society (Wadhurst, Sussex, TN5 6PN, England; phone 0892-78-2045.

15

'95 AUTUMN ISSUE: NOETIC SCIENCES JOURNAL

numbers awaiting execution are growing. The federal Death Row has to be located in a maximum security penitentiary where the surrounding community have no objection. A telephone poll conducted in Terre Haute indicated an approval rate of 93%. I have always believed the death penalty to be one of mankind's greatest abominations, and the presence here of a modern day gallows will do little to improve the already sadly lacking ambience...

I've just been reading articles by and about the Mayor of Baltimore, Kurt Schmoke (Balliol, 1971). Mayor Schmoke started calling for a debate on decriminalization of drugs in 1988, and any day now, he is hosting an international drug summit in Baltimore, to which he has invited the mayors of 75 cities throughout the world. He has been meeting regularly with administration types, including on at least one occasion, Our Lady of Good Counsel, Attorney General Janet Reno. His beliefs include treating drugs as a health rather than a criminal justice programme and reserving prison for violent offenders.'

Howard became close friends with Laurent 'Charlot' Fiocconi, the Corsican who worked as chemist to Pablo Escobar, but who is better known for his involvement in 'the French Connection' drug operation in the 1960s. In early December 1992, Howard wrote home, 'The nicotine craving is getting less, but I'm now smoking in my dreams – isn't it ridiculous? My Corsican friend (who gave up smoking a few weeks before I did) and I have gone on a diet to counteract the weight we've put on as a result of our abstention. We're watching each other like hawks and each has his spies ready to report any transgression like eating chocolate or biscuits on the side. He's very pleased with me because I did some legal work for him and got his sentence reduced by 15 months. He's up for parole next year as a result... In an hour I have to teach my voluntary English class – capitalisation, and the use of the period, ellipses, question mark and exclamation point. The class still gets almost full attendance. I dropped out of sign language – no time.'

Howard wrote home, 'We have had quite a bit of snow, but it has now cleared completely, though the weather is still sub-zero. It's not so much the snow actually falling that's hazardous in Indiana, but the high winds that follow a snowfall causing blizzards and rearranging the level snow into huge drifts... It's good that attitudes to marijuana in Europe are generally softening, but I wish Labour would be more courageous. In this country, unfortunately, attitudes are still hardening. Bush is politically incapable of admitting his errors. Despite a Washington court ordering the DEA to allow physicians to prescribe marijuana, the government, instead, are insisting they prescribe Marinol, a synthetic analogue to marijuana which is not nearly as effective. It's ironic that Bush is now suffering from glaucoma, for which the only known cure is marijuana.'

January 1992

Dearest Mam and Dad,

Don't be fooled. They didn't really let me go for a night out in New York.

All my love
Your devoted son
—Howard.

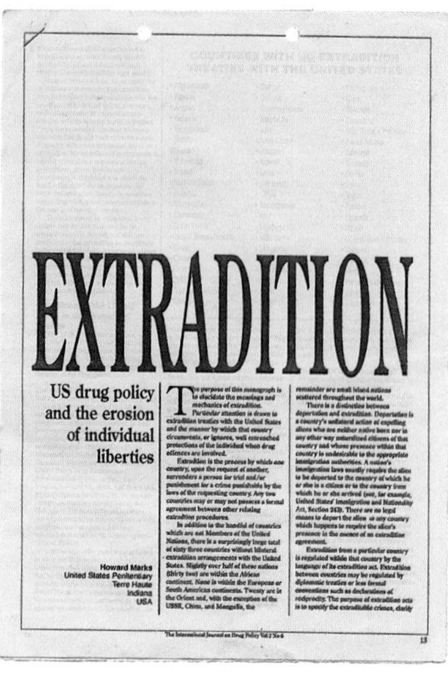

EXTRADITION

US drug policy and the erosion of individual liberties

Howard Marks
United States Penitentiary
Terre Haute
Indiana
USA

The purpose of this monograph is to elucidate the meanings and mechanics of extradition. Particular attention is drawn to extradition treaties with the United States and the manner by which that country circumvents, or ignores, well entrenched protections of the individual when drug offences are involved.

Extradition is the process by which one country, upon the request of another, surrenders a person for trial and/or punishment for a crime punishable by the laws of the requesting country. Any two countries may or may not possess a formal agreement between other relating extradition procedures.

In addition to the handful of countries which are not Members of the United Nations, there is a surprisingly large total of sixty three countries without bilateral extradition arrangements with the United States. Slightly over half of these nations (thirty two) are within the African continent. None is within the European or South American continents. Twenty are in the Orient and, with the exception of the USSR, China, and Mongolia, the remainder are small island nations scattered throughout the world.

There is a distinction between deportation and extradition. Deportation is a country's unilateral action of expelling aliens who are neither native born nor in any other way naturalized citizens of that country and whose presence within that country is undesirable to the appropriate immigration authorities. A nation's immigration laws usually require the alien to be deported to the country of which he or she is a citizen or to the country from which he or she arrived (see, for example, United States' Immigration and Nationality Act, Section 243). There are no legal means to deport the alien to any country which happens to require the alien's presence in the absence of an extradition agreement.

Extradition from a particular country is regulated within that country by the language of its extradition act. Extradition between countries may be regulated by diplomatic treaties or less formal conventions such as declarations of reciprocity. The purpose of extradition acts is to specify the extraditable crimes, clarify

The International Journal on Drug Policy Vol 2 No 6 13

Dennis Howard Marks
41526-004

United States Penitentiary
P.O. Box 33
Terre Haute
INDIANA 47808

January 1st, 1992.

The Editor
Sunday Telegraph
Peterborough Court
South Quay Plaza
Marshwall
London E. 14.

Dear Editor,

It was such a wonderful and much needed Christmas surprise to read in your columns that I am the owner of fifty million pounds which are concealed in Caribbean and/or Eastern Bloc bank accounts [Dec. 8th]. I was totally unaware that I had this loot. All they say about the damaging effects of cannabis on the memory must, it seems, be true.

Federal Bureau of Prison rules preclude my ability to sensibly and responsibly use this money. Providing, therefore, you undertake to pay my federally imposed fine, settle my wife's mortgage, keep my family from starving to death, and pay for my children's school fees, I would be delighted to transfer these funds to any purpose you choose.

Please let me know whether or not you are interested. If so, I will send you a duly notarised power of attorney form granting you access to any and all funds of mine held in any bank account in any country. You may prefer to send me your own form for me to sign. This is equally acceptable.

Incidentally, there were a couple of errors in your report: I am incarcerated in a federal penitentiary, not a jail, which is in Indiana, not Florida. Also, I was fined fifty thousand dollars, not a hundred thousand pounds. Still, that's all the more for you if you take advantage of my offer.

Trusting and hoping these were the only innacuracies,

I remain yours sincerely,

Howard Marks.

(↑→) Throughout his sentence, Howard used what he perceived as injustices against him to argue the case for legalisation, adherence to treaties on the treatment of prisoners and to undermine the demonisation of marijuana smugglers.

In the spring of 1993, Howard wrote to John Jones, 'My philosophy teaching has been enormously successful. The class proved to be very popular, and preparing for it has really kept me on my toes. We've dealt with the Ancient Greeks, the Scholastics and the Renaissance. This week, it's Hobbes. Next week, it's Descartes. It's the fastest crash course ever. Other news is not good. The United States Department of Justice has again denied me the opportunity of serving my sentence in the United Kingdom. This time, the application was made by the Home Office and the Directorate of Her Majesty's Prisons. Enclosed is the relevant letter of mine recently published by the *Nation*.'

March 20, 1996

Ignore drug baron

MARKS: MPs' sympathy

I READ recently that Howard Marks, jailed for drug smuggling in America, has won the support of Members of Parliament to bring him home to serve his sentence.

Is the quoted MP going to foot the bill for his stay in prison in this country and what feeling has the righteous MP for the victims of the drugs supplied who have now probably gone onto hard drugs?

R Healy
Lynmouth Crescent
Rumney, Cardiff

Lynne Parry
Letters Editor
Wales on Sunday

Dear Ms. Parry:

It would, of course, be most inappropriate for me tc even attempt to speak on behalf of those Members of Parliament who have so kindly and courageously supported my application to be transferred to a British prison. I can, however, inform R. Healy (WoS Mar. 20) that the question of who pays what when prisoners are returned to serve sentences in their own countries was resolved during 1985 when Great Britain and 22 other countries became signatories to the Council of Europe's Convention on the Transfer of Sentenced Persons (Strasbourg). The cost of my incarceration in Britain would be paid by the British government, while costs of incarcerating prisoners transferred from Britain would be paid by the governments of the countries to which they were transferred.

R. Healy also makes reference to those individuals to whom I have supplied marijuana, labelling them as "victims" and speculating that they are now probably taking hard drugs. A victim is someone who has been killed, injured, or otherwise harmed. During thousands of years of marijuana usage, there is no record of anyone ever being harmed by this herb. The escalation (stepping stone) theory has been thoroughly discredited by innumerable studies. Any progression from marijuana usage to the taking of dangerous drugs can be attributed to the irrational prohibition of an innocuous, medically beneficial, and recreationally useful herb, which forces the marijuana user to encounter purveyors of illegal merchandise.

In November 1993, Howard wrote home, 'I've now been nine days in my single cell. Life is certainly a lot better when living alone, which I haven't done for over three years. My routine has changed as a result both of the single cell and the very definite presence of winter. I now get up at 6am, have a shower, do a series of dynamic yoga exercises and have breakfast. I then clean up my cell and work from 7.30–10.30. Next comes a series of static yoga exercises followed by some reading (usually Eastern religion or philosophy) and lunch. I work again from 12–3. From 3–5 I usually attend to my mail, from 5–6 I eat and walk, and from 6–8.30, I usually work in the library or attend (or teach) the inmate evening classes.'

It was as a result of Ernie's agreement to give evidence against Howard that Howard decided he had no option other than to plead guilty, but Howard and Ernie remained good friends and both did all they could with each other's various motions, applications and attempts to publicise government corruption in the war on drugs. Ernie's sentence would eventually be reduced. In May 1994, Howard wrote to John Jones:

'At last, I have what might be some good news. My sentencing judge has set a hearing with respect to my 3½-year-old motion to reduce sentence and has ordered me to be present. The hearing has been set for 13 July and any day, I will begin my Odyssey to West Palm Beach, Florida.

For unknown reasons, the judge simply sat on the motion for all this time. I had almost given up waiting for his ruling. As he could have easily denied the motion without a hearing at any time since 1990, his requirement of my presence is to be taken as an encouraging sign. Perhaps the denial of my transfer to the UK, coupled with the prevention of my wife's entry to the US, has got to him. One cannot, of course, let any hopes build up when dealing with the US Department of Justice. I will ensure you know the outcome as soon as possible after it has been made, which might be some time after the hearing.'

COUNTY OF Maricopa }
SS:
STATE OF ARIZONA }

AFFIDAVIT

I, Ernest Franz Combs, being first duly sworn, do hereby depose and state the following:

1. that I had not heard of Dennis Howard Marks until May 1973;

2. that I have no reason to believe that Dennis Howard Marks was involved in any hashish or marijuana importation into the United States that took place before May 1973;

3. that I have no reason to believe that Dennis Howard Marks, at any time before May 1973, procured hashish at the direction of Graham Plinston, as alleged on page 7 of the Pre-sentence Investigation Report (hereinafter PSI) of Dennis Howard Marks;

4. that Dennis Howard Marks neither participated in nor was aware of any of the hashish importations into the United States during 1970 that involved the use of Wolkswagen vehicles and that are referred to on pages 7 and 9 of the PSI of Dennis Howard Marks;

5. that Dennis Howard Marks did not participate in any of the following importations of hashish into the United

-1-

States that occurred during 1973 and that are referred to on pages 7, 8, and 9 of the PSI of Dennis Howard Marks: March 14th - Paris to New York, April 11th - Vienna to Philadelphia, and July 12th - Vienna to Chicago;

6. that I met Dennis Howard Marks for the first time during September 1973;

7. that Dennis Howard Marks's knowledge of hashish and/or marijuana importations that took place between 1975 and 1979 at John F. Kennedy Airport, New York and that are referred to on pages 7, 8, 9, and 16 of the PSI of Dennis Howard Marks were limited to that concerning 5 (five) of those importations; and

8. that at no stage during any of the hashish/marijuana importations that took place between 1975 and 1979 at John F. Kennedy Airport, New York and that are referred to on pages 7, 8, and 9 of the PSI of Dennis Howard Marks did Dennis Howard Marks take care of any arrangements at Ireland or at Rome as alleged on page 8 of the PSI of Dennis Howard Marks.

I swear under penalty of perjury that the preceding statements are true to the best of my knowledge and belief.

DATED:

ERNEST FRANZ COMBS 1-7-93

SUBSCRIBED AND SWORN TO before me this 7th day of January, 1993.

NOTARY PUBLIC

My commission expires on My Commission Expires April 9, 19

-2-

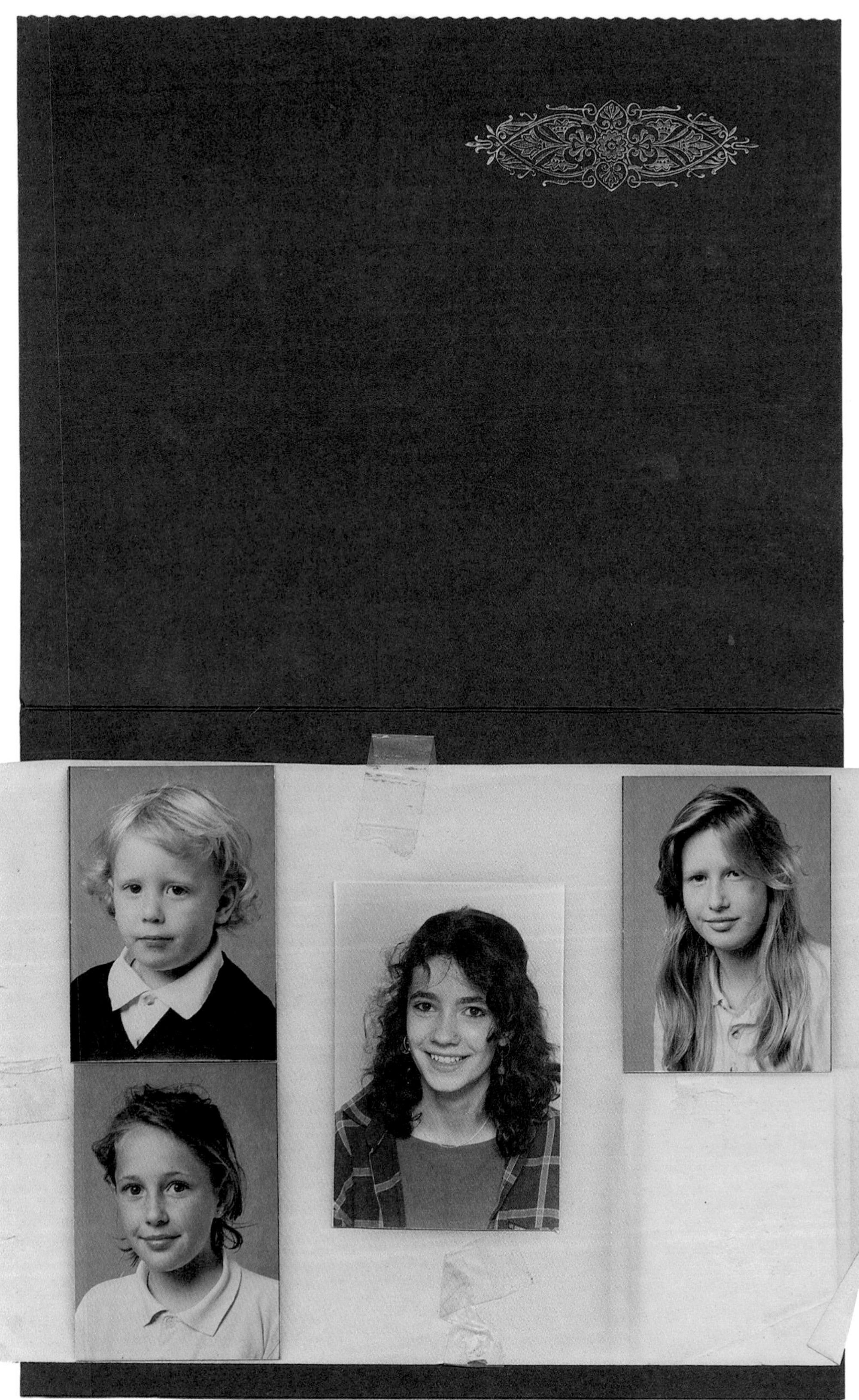

(↘) In February 1994 Howard wrote to John Jones:

'During November, Julian Peto performed the exceptional kindness of bringing over my two youngest daughters to see me. It was the first time I had seen them in five years, and although the visits were absolutely wonderful, parting at the end of the final one was the most heartbreaking sorrow I have ever experienced. Spending time with them had forcefully demonstrated just how much I was missing, and seeing them leave was like being arrested all over again. Consequently, I've been rather depressed, which of course, happens to us all for one reason or another, but now, I'm quite definitely on the mend.

Unfortunately, despite all sorts of promises from the United States Attorney's Office and others involved in my prosecution, my wife, Judy, has been well and truly forbidden from visiting me by the Immigration and Naturalization Service.

The petition which you and other College members very kindly signed is doing well. Various MPs have signed, and I'm pleased with its success. The same cannot be said of my letters to various senators, and various congressmen, none of whom has sent any acknowledgement.

At present, I am fulfilling my agreement to teach a 14-week course in linguistics. I knew nothing about the subject and am simply keeping a lesson ahead of my students. Still, I'm enjoying it, and, with luck, I may get another 30 days knocked off my sentence. This year has produced the coldest weather I've ever experienced −40°F wind-chill factor on top of a temperature of −30°F and the worst eruption of prison gang violence that has occurred during the three years I have been here. However, it seems quiet now, and today's temperature is an extraordinary 63°F.'

(←) Pictures of his children, which Howard was allowed to keep in his cell throughout his incarceration.

BUREAU OF PRISONS CENTRAL FILE

In the Bureau of Prisons Central File relating to me, I am described as an "extreme escape risk." It is stated that this information came from the Assistant United States Attorney [B1]. I have never escaped or attempted to escape from anywhere and have been totally unsuccessful in determining why I am described as any kind of escape risk. Being so described has all sorts of unpleasant consequences: handcuffed in a "black box" when moved, kept in "the hole" when in transit, and condemned to incarceration in high security facilities.

In its Program Statement PS 5100.04 (6-15-92), the Bureau of Prisons has designed a point system of classifying those in its custody. My points have been calculated as 15 [B2]. Prisoners with classification scores of 11-18 are normally housed in medium security federal correctional institutions, while those of scores of 19+ are normally housed in penitentiaries [B3]. The Mid-Atlantic region of the Bureau of Prisons has insisted that I remain housed on a penitentiary because of an unspecified "security management variable" [B2]. I do not know if this is due to the above erroneous escape allegations, stemming from an Assistant United Sttaes Attorney, or due to the Southern District of Florida Attorney's Office requirement that I remain 12 years incarcerated in a United States Penitentiary (see pleading to the Court dated November 1993) (see also exhibit T7 in the section dealing with Transfer to the United Kingdom) or due to some other reason.

Howard continued to make applications to be transferred to a less secure institution where he hoped he would witness less violence. Howard was 'black boxed' every time he was moved to attend a court hearing. In May 1994, Howard wrote to John Jones:

'I've just arrived back at Terre Haute after a most exhausting tour of United States penal facilities. It's odd, if not slightly disturbing, to feel relief at returning to a maximum security penitentiary, but is undoubtedly my feeling. Perhaps I'm institutionalised, but I doubt it.

The 13 July hearing went as well as could be expected. The judge, however, decided not to rule on the motion to reduce sentence until he had thought some more about it, so I'm now anxiously waiting for the result. Goodness knows how long it might take. I'll keep you informed. My trip from here took me to El Reno, Oklahoma. This is the Crewe or Swindon of the federal prison's transport system. Virtually every travelling convict passes through. The turnover is several hundred a day, which encourages unending chaos. After a week there, I was flown via New Orleans to Miami and then taken by bus to West Palm Beach County Jail, where I remained for many weeks. It was a thoroughly disgusting, depressing place; and it is best forgotten. Before eventually arriving back at Terre Haute, I spent two miserable weeks in segregation in a Miami prison (I'm classified as an "extreme escape risk") and another week in El Reno (less than 24 hours from Tulsa).'

On 6 October 1994, HHJ Paine ruled on Howard's motion to have his sentence reduced. Howard wrote to inform John Jones of the outcome:

'There has indeed been some news: the judge reduced my sentence from 25 to 20 years and recommended that I be immediately considered for transfer to the United Kingdom.

Although I had hoped for a greater reduction, I also dreaded none at all; and in today's climate, the frequency of sentence reductions is not as great as that of other miracles.

Unfortunately, the judge does not have the authority to ensure his recommendations are enforced, and the DEA will continue to obstruct in all manner of ways. My application, has, however, been rendered that much more persuasive.

The five-year reduction is etched in stone (I think) and means that if I remain incarcerated in the United States without relief, I will be released in the year 2000. It means that I become eligible for release on parole (which in my case translates to deportation, but not to a British prison) in March 1995, which is remarkably soon.

Sadly, parole decisions are made almost wholly on the basis of the current political perception of the gravity of the offence underlying the sentence. Institutional conduct and participation in rehabilitation and education programmes tend not to be taken into consideration unless they are extremely bad. Nevertheless, there is always a chance, and I have decided to appear before the Parole Commission during January to take full advantage of the judge's recent comments. (Hearing examiners visit the prison every few months.)'

hundred thousand dollars was made available to the defendant as a result of his smuggling activities. The defendant's role in the smuggling organization was characterized as being that of organizer and planner of the criminal activity.

Court's Findings and Conclusions

At the hearing on defendant's motion to reduce and/or modify his sentence held on July 13, 1994 considerable evidence was introduced by both the defendant and the government. Materials made available to the court through the presentence investigation, many letters from friends, associates and relatives of the defendant have been received by the court. The circumstances of defendant's imprisonment since the date of his arrest were revealed by documents introduced into evidence at the Rule 35 hearing.

It is difficult to conclude that the defendant has been fairly incarcerated in a maximum security facility because of the comment of another inmate that the defendant was speaking about plans for an escape. The reliability of such a statement by a fellow inmate appears suspect. This occurrence should not have so drastically affected the place of imprisonment ordered by the Bureau of Prisons.

Having considered all of the foregoing, it is

ORDERED and ADJUDGED

(a) Defendant's sentence of imprisonment as to count 2 is hereby reduced from the previously imposed sentence of 15 years to 10 years consecutive to the ten year sentence of imprisonment as to count 1. Defendant's aggregate sentence of imprisonment is reduced to 20 years, the total as to counts 1 and 2. The fines imposed as to each of counts 1 and 2 are to be treated as non-committed rather

5

(↙↓) Famous biker James 'Big Jim' Nolan of the Outlaws resided at Terre Haute. Unlike numerous other gangs within the prison, biker gangs such as the Hell's Angels, the Pagans and the Outlaws did not fight each other while incarcerated. Jim and Howard became good friends. Jim cut Howard's hair for his parole hearing, scheduled for January 1995. Howard explained to his family, 'I'm not actually eligible for parole until March but will appear for a hearing in January. They will set a parole release date for in-between March 1995 and somewhere in 2000. Shortly after January, I will know whether they will release me. I very much doubt it.'

(↗) In February 1994, Howard was informed that he would be released at the earliest possible release date, the following month, and an open plane ticket was purchased on his behalf.

PASSENGER TICKET AND BAGGAGE CHECK
SUBJECT TO CONDITIONS OF CONTRACT
NOT TRANSFERABLE

SITI

ARC FLIGHT COUPON

TOUR CODE 1154457810 AGENT CODE

ISSUED BY CONTINENTAL AIRLINES 1 OF 1 A33872300

NAME OF ISSUING AGENT THE TRAVEL PEOPLE NEW YORK NY US08MAR95

NAME OF PASSENGER MARKS/DENNIS HOWAR RMKNLN/AA Y23E 6 0011/

X/O FROM HOUSTON INTL IAHCO OPEN Y

X/O TO LONDON GATWICK X/ M361*BH

ENDORSEMENTS/RESTRICTIONS

FP MC5424180283913082*0396/ 703992 /FCHOU CO LON

Q5.00 841.00Y23E NUC846.00END ROE1.00

FARE USD 846.00

TAX US 6.00

TOTAL USD 852.00

EQUIV. FARE PD.

STOCK CONTROL NO. TX 889 CK 37147145593

CPN DOCUMENT NUMBER CK 1 005 1154457810 4

ABH

BOARDING PASS

NAME OF PASSENGER MARKS/DENNIS HOWARD

FROM HOUSTON INTL IAH

TO LONDON GATWICK

CARRIER CONTINENTAL AIRLI

CO OPENY

GATE SEAT SMOKE

PCS WT UNCKD BAGGAGE ID NUMBER

1 005 1154457810 4

AA33872300

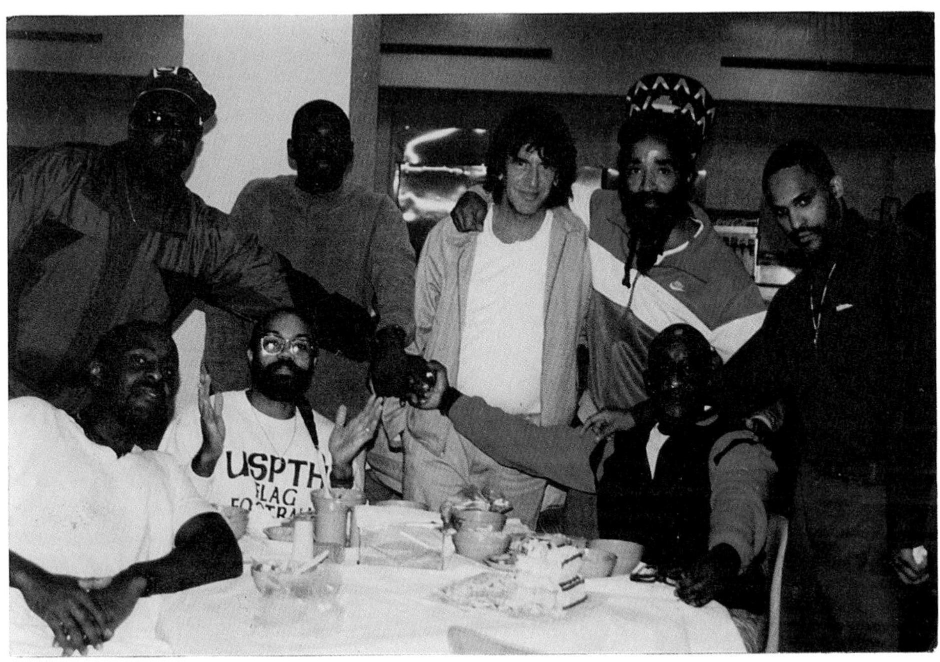

(↗) Howard's stay in Terre Haute penitentiary had come to an end. He had befriended hundreds from a wide range of backgrounds and communities: he edited the Sports newsletter produced by the prison's basketball club and the weekly law page for the Muslim community news journal; he taught fellow inmates, attended the classes of fellow inmates, worked as jail house lawyer and received kindness in the form of cards, cooked food and healing from the likes of Veronza Bowers, pictured with his arm around Howard in this photo.

He knew that of those with whom he had been imprisoned, at least half would never be released. He explained to his family how, 'It was strange leaving Terre Haute. I was obviously not feeling sad for myself, but felt extremely sad for many of those I was leaving behind. I expected there to be a lot of resentment and malicious envy at my good fortune, but there was nothing other than well wishing – a great deal of it – with comments like "At least one person has survived it," and "A part of me is going free with you." There is something so very very wrong with this country's relentless and unnecessary deprivation of people's freedom.'

On 24 February 1995 Howard wrote home, 'Here I am for the fourth time in the dreaded El Reno. The journey here from Terre Haute took several hours and was via stops in Chicago, Michigan and Minnesota. Departures from here are shrouded in mystery and there's no telling when I'll leave. I doubt if it will be before March but trust it'll be no later than 8 March and trust there'll be no further stopovers between here and Oakdale. Conditions here are pretty grim. Apart from one hour each weekday for outdoor exercise, we are kept in cages surrounded by perpetually blaring televisions. Because this facility in El Reno is due to be completely closed down next month, the conditions are worse than usual – blocked sinks and toilets, cockroaches, etc. There are no books this time. In the unit I'm in, there are five telephones serving 400 people. Two of the phones don't work. You can imagine the problems.'

On 18 March he wrote again: 'This is the first letter I've written since I left Oklahoma. It's been a strange couple of weeks. I was very surprised to be called on 3 March (1.30am) and told I was leaving. Air lifts are gruelling at the best of times. Luckily this had only one stop, Memphis, Tennessee – and we arrived at Alexandria Airport, Lousiana, at about midday. An hour's bus journey took us to the prison. Typically my arrival presented enigmatic circumstances: I hadn't finished my sentence, but I would finish it before the Federal Correctional Institute would have been able to put me through the so-called "Admission and Orientation Program". Whenever in doubt, the Bureau of Prisons places one in the hole, and I have already communicated to you the disadvantages of such accommodation. The lack of information and the contradictory nature of the small amount imparted were immensely frustrating. Some of these frustrations continue. Although I know my airline ticket has arrived, I cannot confirm whether my passport has.'

On 25 March 1995, Howard was released from prison and flown to Gatwick, London. He managed to get an emergency passport at the airport and he flew directly to Judy and their children in Palma de Mallorca.

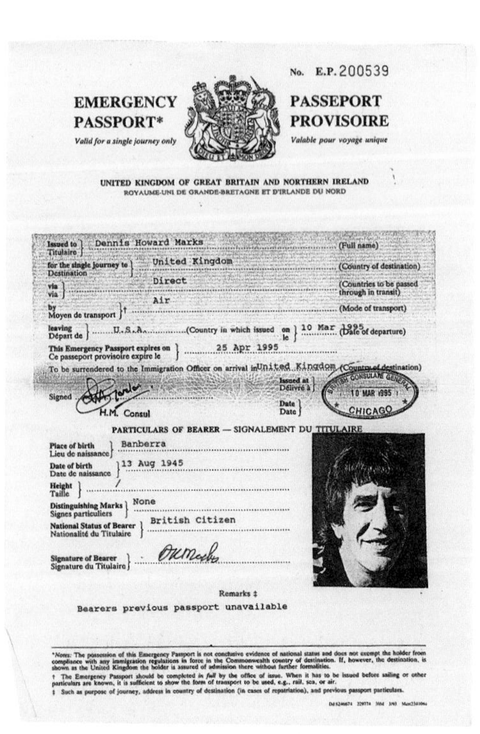

No. E.P. 200539

EMERGENCY PASSPORT* — PASSEPORT PROVISOIRE

Valid for a single journey only — *Valable pour voyage unique*

UNITED KINGDOM OF GREAT BRITAIN AND NORTHERN IRELAND
ROYAUME-UNI DE GRANDE-BRETAGNE ET D'IRLANDE DU NORD

Issued to / Titulaire: Dennis Howard Marks (Full name)
for the single journey to / Destination: United Kingdom (Country of destination)
via / via: Direct (Countries to be passed through in transit)
by / Moyen de transport†: Air (Mode of transport)
leaving / Départ de: U.S.A. (Country in which issued) on / le: 10 Mar 1995 (Date of departure)
This Emergency Passport expires on / Ce passeport provisoire expire le: 25 Apr 1995
To be surrendered to the Immigration Officer on arrival in United Kingdom (Country of destination)
Signed: H.M. Consul
Issued at / Délivré à: BRITISH CONSULATE GENERAL 10 MAR 1995 CHICAGO
Date / Date

PARTICULARS OF BEARER — SIGNALEMENT DU TITULAIRE

Place of birth / Lieu de naissance: Banberra
Date of birth / Date de naissance: 13 Aug 1945
Height / Taille: /
Distinguishing Marks / Signes particuliers: None
National Status of Bearer / Nationalité du Titulaire: British Citizen
Signature of Bearer / Signature du Titulaire: DHMarks

Remarks ‡
Bearers previous passport unavailable

*Notes: The possession of this Emergency Passport is not conclusive evidence of national status and does not exempt the holder from compliance with any immigration regulations in force in the Commonwealth country of destination. If, however, the destination, is shown as the United Kingdom the holder is assured of admission there without further formalities.
† The Emergency Passport should be completed *in full* by the office of issue. When it has to be issued before sailing or other particulars are known, it is sufficient to show the form of transport to be used, e.g., rail, sea, or air.
‡ Such as purpose of journey, address in country of destination (in cases of repatriation), and previous passport particulars.

8

Mr Nice

NEWS OF THE WORLD
THE WORLD'S LARGEST SUNDAY SALE

1 VIRGINIA STREET, LONDON E1 9XY
Telephone: 071-782 4000
Telex: 262136

Howard – hope you're all well and this finds you in good form.

I enclose proofs of the first draft for your amusement.

As you can see, I got them to cut out your "odious smirks" once it was reduced to 2 pages, but alas apart from that they were still intent on painting you as a fiend in human form.

Nevertheless your quotes stood & I think it ended on an up-beat note.

Registered Office: News Group Newspapers Ltd, P.O. Box 495, Virginia Street, London E1 9XY
Registered No. 679215 England

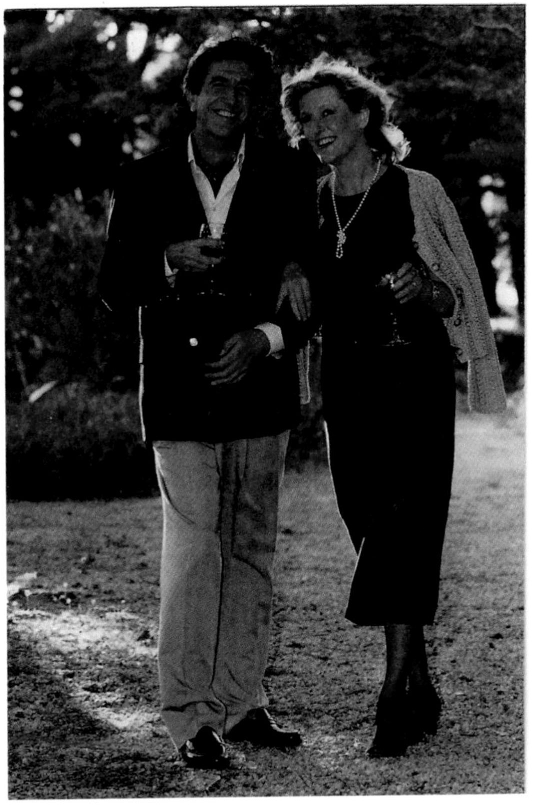

Howard's release was greeted by yet another media frenzy, some publications celebrating Howard's reunion with his family, but many determined to demonise him as an unrepentant drug pusher gobbing in the face of justice. The *News of the World* was willing to pay for the opportunity to blacken his name, and Howard and Judy agreed to be styled by the newspaper to give the impression that they were bathing gleefully in ill-gotten gains. Chris Blythe, the journalist sent by the *News of the World* to interview Howard and his wife, became a dear friend of the family. The letter above is from Chris, written shortly before his tragic and untimely death.

SUPER FURRY ANIMALS
SOMETHING 4 THE WEEKEND

"ARA DEG MAE DAL IÂR"
SONGS/CANEUON: SFA
PUBLISHED BY/CYHOEDDWYD GA
POLYGRAM MUSIC PUBLISHING
PRODUCTION/CYNHYRCHU:
GORWEL OWEN/SFA
ENGINEERING/PEIRIANNU:
GORWEL OWEN, ANDY WILKINSON
RECORDED/RECORDIWYD:
STIWDIO OFN, LLANFAELOG
ROCKFIELD STUDIOS*
DESIGN/CYNLLUN: TOBY EGELNIC
IMAGES/DELWEDDAU: MICRODOT
1. SOMETHING 4 THE WEEKEND
2. WAITING TO HAPPEN
3. ARNOFIO/GLÔ IN THE DARK
4. SOMETHING FOR THE WEEKEND*
SUPER FURRY ANIMALS SOMETHING 4 THE WEEKEND
1. SOMETHING 4 THE WEEKEND
2. WAITING TO HAPPEN
3. ARNOFIO/GLÔ IN THE DARK
4. SOMETHING FOR THE WEEKEND
5 017556 702352

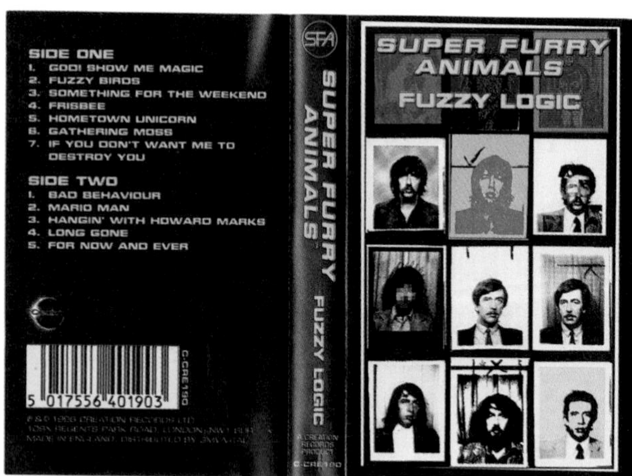
SIDE ONE
1. GOD! SHOW ME MAGIC
2. FUZZY BIRDS
3. SOMETHING FOR THE WEEKEND
4. FRISBEE
5. HOMETOWN UNICORN
6. GATHERING MOSS
7. IF YOU DON'T WANT ME TO DESTROY YOU
SIDE TWO
1. BAD BEHAVIOUR
2. MARIO MAN
3. HANGIN' WITH HOWARD MARKS
4. LONG GONE
5. FOR NOW AND EVER
5 017556 401903
SUPER FURRY ANIMALS
FUZZY LOGIC
SUPER FURRY ANIMALS
FUZZY LOGIC

SUPER FURRY ANIMALS
FUZZY LOGIC
THE DEBUT ALBUM
OUT NOW
CD · LP · CASSETTE
INCLUDES THE SINGLES:
HOMETOWN UNICORN
GOD! SHOW ME MAGIC &
IF YOU DON'T WANT ME TO DESTROY YOU
A CREATION RECORDS PRODUCT

July 96

12 RYDER ST
CANTON
CARDIFF
CF1 9BR

ANNWYL HOWARD,

Thanks again for your warm welcome at palma and for filling our days and nights with plenty of action! the badly timed fever that knocked me out vanished after a couple of days rest, ready to take the tank out

for its first festival I enclose a press cutting here's some people freaking out on top of the tank in front of a large crowd. cians inside with his decks (at one point he d.J'd non-stop for nine hours!) I also enclose the album by J5 that includes a song about you

(←) Up and coming Welsh band the Super Furry Animals had no idea Howard was due to come home when they decided to release a song about him, 'Hangin' with Howard Marks'. On hearing the news they asked if they could use his false passport photographs as their debut album cover. The album climbed swiftly up the charts and Howard and the band became lifelong friends.

(↑) An extract from lead singer Gruff Rhys's letter to Howard after visiting his family home.

(↓) On hearing of Howard's release, Geoff Mulligan, an editor at Secker & Warburg, asked a mutual friend if he could meet Howard to discuss a possible autobiography. The word came back: 'He's expecting you Wednesday.' Mulligan had intended to use a ghost writer, but after several days spent in Howard's company, he was convinced that Howard should write the book himself.

Howard wrote daily, completing the manuscript within six months. The Corsican Laurent 'Charlot' Fiocconi wrote to Howard from Terre Haute to congratulate him for the offer he had received to write an autobiography. 'The irrational guilt you experienced for being selected from hundreds of thousands of us for release is due to your good heart and great feelings. Be fortunate; enjoy life to the maximum. In life, nothing is damnation or blessing; everything is a challenge. Perhaps the biggest challenge of all is to enjoy life; to be fortunate; to be happy. Sometimes overcoming adversity seems more easy of a challenge. We are very happy and proud for the offer you received from the British publishers.'

On completion of Howard's autobiography, Geoff Mulligan met

12-1-96

Hey Mr. Nice,

The name is perfect! No one that I know would disagree. Did you send Webbter an autographed copy? I bet he is still grinning. I have someone looking for the book here, but so far no luck. An article appeared in one of the Spanish magazines and a lot of the guys asked about it. Everyone is pulling for you and are very happy for your freedom and your sucess. In the article it spoke of all of your friends. That is oh soooo true.

Anyway - enough kissing up here to [illegible]!! How have you and Judy been doing? Are you traveling around promoting the book? Let me know who to contact for a copy or send me an autographed one!! You knew that was coming didn't you!! Do let me know where I can get one for myself! Hmmm - did you make some good money off of this? You know me - money - money - money. Money H--- - give me women and freedom!!

Things here are still the same.

with him in The Eagle pub in Farringdon, London, to discuss what to call it. Mulligan asked Howard to list the numerous identities adopted during his time as a fugitive (1974–80). Donald Nice was Geoff's favourite and he suggested calling the book *Mr Nice*. The publication of a convicted criminal's autobiography was controversial in the political climate at that time (no publisher in the USA would even consider it). The supply of cannabis was portrayed in the media as morally abhorrent, and 'drug dealers' an evil scourge of society. Mulligan believed that the average Middle Englander would assume the worst of a man who had spent so long in such a high-security prison, and was confident that Howard's account would confound their expectations: the summary on the front of the book, written by Geoff, reads: 'He was Britain's most wanted man. He spent seven years in America's toughest penitentiary. You'll like him.' Entitling the autobiography *Mr Nice* was a value-laden statement and a direct challenge to the media portrayal of cannabis smugglers as immoral degenerates. Howard's friends in Terre Haute stayed in touch; they thought the name Mr Nice apt.

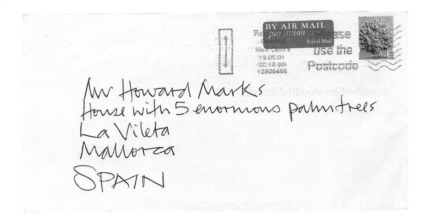

(↑→) Howard began receiving fan mail from dozens of strangers at his home in Mallorca, all of whom were invited to visit or were provided with his support. He gave an early reading from his book in Deia, Palma de Mallorca. Musician Tomas Graves (son of poet Robert Graves) made the cassette recording pictured.

MEGATRIPOLIS
brought to you with Pronoia
March 7th
Cathedral
Marco Arnaldi, Russ Cox & Richard Grey
Cauldron
The Binky Bonk Drummers
The Telling Cave
Dr. John Beresford ~talks of US Prisoners of the war on drugs
March 14th
Cathedral
Vonton, Mark Allen & James Monro
Cauldron
Dan Morris & Marco Arnaldi
The Telling Cave
Himalayan Healer ~ Amchi Tsewang Smania talks of his work in reviving the methods of traditional tibetan healing.
March 21st
EQUINOX CLEBRATIONS
Cathedral
Marco Arnaldi, Alex Knight & JOEY BELTRAM
Cauldron
The Binky Bonk Drummers
The Telling Cave
HOWARD MARKS - The life & times of the infamous cannabis smuggler.
March 28th
GODDESS NIGHT
Cathedral
Jane Travis, Brenda Russell & Lulu
Cauldron
Emma Hamilton, Charlotte & Giselle
The Telling Cave
High-Dee Unlikely ~ Unlikely stories of reality seen through rose tinted spectacles
£3 BEFORE OR £5 AFTER 11PM WITH THIS FLYER OTHERWISE £7/£5 (CONCS)
at HEAVEN, under The Arches, off Villiers Street WC1, every Thursday 20.30 - 03.00
For info phone: 0181-960 0030 Web site - http://www.southern.com/megaT/
...as we enter the imagination age...we are the children of light.

Avalon Promotions Presents
AN EVENING WITH
HOWARD MARKS
"A folk legend...he sounds like Richard Burton and looks like a Rolling Stone" The Daily Mail
"A man most wanted...his one man show is the biggest draw in town" James Rampton, The Independent
DUE TO ENORMOUS PUBLIC DEMAND
EXTRA DATE
Friday December 5th at 8.00pm
Box Office: 0171 924 9999
At the height of his career he was smuggling consignments of up to fifty tons of marijuana and had contact with organisations as diverse as MI6, the CIA, the IRA and the Mafia. Following a worldwide operation by the Drugs Enforcement Agency, he was busted and sentenced to 25 years in America's toughest prison.
Come and meet him. You'll like him.
LIVE AT THE SHEPHERDS BUSH EMPIRE
Friday 7th November 1997 at 8pm
SOLD OUT
Box Office 0171 924 9999

NIGEL McINTYRE & TONY DOBSON by arrangement with APOLLO MANAGEMENT LTD proudly present
HOWARD MARKS
An Audience with MR NICE
Howard's legendary cutting edge stand-up returns with a BRAND NEW SHOW. More dangerous and more revealing than ever before, Howard will be recounting stories never previously heard, ranging from dealings with the CIA to the Italian Mafia to MI6. The new show format includes multimedia video footage spanning over 3 decades, projecting both the fascinating story and the many faces of the "maverick phenomenon" (Sunday Times)
October 2001
11 RETFORD Majestic 01777 706 866
12 WORKSOP Regal Centre 01909 482 896
13 SHEFFIELD City Hall 01142 789 789
14 BEVERLEY Picture House 01482 867 430
16 CLEETHORPES Beachcomber 01472 349 222
17 STOCKTON Arc 01642 666 600
18 EDINBURGH Liquid Rooms 0131 220 3234
19 GLASGOW Garage 0141 248 8089
31 IPSWICH Corn Exchange 01473 433 100
November 2001
01 EPSOM Playhouse 01372 742 555
02 ALDERSHOT Princes Hall 01252 329 155
04 NOTTINGHAM Rock City 01159 588 484
05 NORWICH UEA 01603 508 050
06 WATFORD Colosseum 01923 445 000
09 HIGH WYCOMBE Town Hall 01494 512 000
10 BRISTOL Anson Rooms 08704 444 400
11 FROME Cheese and Grain 01373 455 420
12 EXETER Phoenix Arts Centre 01392 667 080
13 CROYDON Ashcroft Theatre 0208 688 9291
22 NEWCASTLE Tyne Theatre 0191 232 0899
23 MORECAMBE Platform 0152 458 2803
24 MANCHESTER Lowry 0161 876 2000
25 YORK Opera House 01904 671 818
27 CHESTER Telfords Warehouse 01244 390 090
28 COVENTRY Colosseum 02476 226 176
30 LONDON Ocean 0207 314 2800
UNDER THE INFLUENCE is the first major release from Bothered Records - Howard Marks's own record label. This compilation album features acts who have written tracks with or about Howard, together with a selection of brand new signings to Bothered. This 13 track album includes tracks by STEREOPHONICS, SUPER FURRY ANIMALS, SHAUN RYDER, Mew from ELASTICA, Dan Glendining from HEADSWIM, D:Fariq from SONA FARIQ, Richard Norris from THE GRID, the DOPE SMUGGLAZ and the LEVELLERS.
MR NICE
Available nationwide from all good record stores www.bothered.net

MR NICE
AN AUDIENCE WITH HOWARD MARKS
Smuggler, MI6 Agent, TV Personality, Folk Hero, Travel Writer, Campaigner
"The narcotic Tommy Cooper"
"A folk legend. Howard Marks has huge charisma"
Howard Marks, a 1960's Oxford University postgraduate, rose to become the most sophisticated drugs baron of all time. Recruited by MI6 (Her Majesty's Secret Service), he orchestrated major cannabis importations with members of the CIA and the Italian MAFIA. He had 43 documented aliases and 25 international companies as cover for his smuggling empire. Howard now writes travel articles for The Observer and The Times, while his one man show remains the biggest draw in town.
"A maverick phenomenon. Marks is the Guv'nor!"
OCTOBER 2007
03 NORWICH Arts Centre 01603 660 352
04 CAMBRIDGE Junction 01223 511 511
05 ANDOVER The Lights 01264 368 368
06 ALDERSHOT West End Centre 01252 330 040
07 BLACKBURN King Georges Hall 01254 582 582
09 LINCOLN Drill Hall 01522 873 894
10 KENDAL Brewery Arts Centre 01539 725 133
11 BURY Met 0161 761 2216
12 NEWPORT Riverfront Arts Centre 01633 656 757
13 BUILTH WELLS Wyeside Arts Centre 01982 552 555
14 LUDLOW Assembly Rooms 01584 878 141
16 HULL Truck Theatre 01482 323 638
19 TUNBRIDGE WELLS Trinity Arts Ctre 01892 678 678
20 INVERNESS Iron Works 0871 7894 173
21 ABERDEEN Lemon Tree 01224 642 230
23 BIRMINGHAM Glee Club 0870 241 5093
24 LLANGOLLEN Royal Pavilion 01978 860 111
26 ST ALBANS Maltings 01727 844 222
28 ST IVES Theatre 01736 797 007
29 LYME REGIS Marine Theatre 01297 442 138
30 BOURNEMOUTH The Landmark 01202 589 888
NOVEMBER 2007
08 HALIFAX Square Chapel 01422 349 422
09 HARLECH Theatr Ardudwy 01766 780 667
WWW.HOWARDMARKS.CO.UK

Nigel McIntyre and Gilded Balloon Productions Present
MR NICE LIVE
PREVIEWING A NEW SHOW FOR HIS AUTUMN UK TOUR
'The narcotic Tommy Cooper' Evening Standard
'A man most wanted... his one man show is the biggest draw in town' Independent
'Frequently hilarious, occasionally sad, often surreal' GQ
'An absolutely hilarious show' Observer
'A folk legend... he sounds like Richard Burton and looks like a Rolling Stone' Daily Mail
'A maverick phenomenon... Marks is the guv'nor!' Sunday Times
HOWARD MARKS
An Audience with
MR NICE
EDINBURGH QUEENS HALL
MONDAY 18th and TUESDAY 19th AUGUST 2003
On Stage 10.30pm · Tickets £12 (£11)
Available from
Metro Gilded Balloon Box Office 0131 226 2151
and Queens Hall Box Office 0131 668 2019
METRO
GILDED BALLOON

SWANSEA GRAND THEATRE
Kenfig Hill very own
Mr Nice
Howard Marks
16 YEARS & OVER ONLY!
An Audience with Mr Nice
"Hilarious" - GQ
MWED 10th MAY 7.30PM
Box Office 01792 475715
CITY AND COUNTY OF SWANSEA • DINAS A SIR ABERTAWE

NIGEL McINTYRE & TONY DOBSON in assoc. with ARROW & by arrangement with GILES COOPER proudly present
HOWARD MARKS
MR NICE LIVE
"An absolutely hilarious show" Observer
"A maverick phenomenon" Sunday Times
THE TRAIL OF DEAD ROACHES TOUR
OCTOBER 2002
02 MANCHESTER Lowry 0161 876 2000
03 GLASGOW Queen Margaret's SU 0141 339 8525
10 LEEDS City Palace of Varieties 0113 243 0808
12 LEICESTER University 0116 912 9000
13 DERBY Assembly Rooms 01332 255 800
15 HASTINGS White Rock Theatre 01424 781 000
16 BRIGHTON Dome Corn Exchange 01273 709 709
17 SWINDON Wyvern Theatre 01793 524 481
19 NEWTON Theatr Hafren 01686 625 007
20 CARDIFF Coal Exchange 02920 230 130
25 BELFAST Waterfront 02890 334 455
27 BIRMINGHAM Alexandra Theatre 0870 607 7533
29 CHESTER Telfords Warehouse 01244 390 090
30 BURNLEY Mechanics 01282 664 400
31 WHITEHAVEN Civic Hall 01946 852 821
NOVEMBER 2002
01 LIVERPOOL Royal Court 0151 709 4321
02 KEELE University 01782 713 145
05 HAYES Beck Theatre 0208 561 8371
07 HARLOW Playhouse 01279 431 945
08 HITCHIN Town Hall 01462 453 722
09 BARNSTAPLE Queens Theatre 01271 324 242
10 SOUTHAMPTON The Brook 02380 555 366
18 WORTHING Assembly Halls 01903 206 206
19 BOURNEMOUTH Int. Centre 01202 456 456
21 GLOUCESTER Guild Hall 01452 505 089
22 LONDON Shepherds Bush Empire
29 LONDON Astoria Theatre
'101 USES OF A DEAD ROACH' by SIMON BOND & HOWARD MARKS
published by ARROW. Available from 31st October 2002 priced £5.99
'MR NICE - THE ALBUM' out October 2002 on COLUMBIA/SONY | MRNICE.net

MR NICE
is back: Di 5. Sept.
HOWARD MARKS IM KOMBINAT DARMSTADT

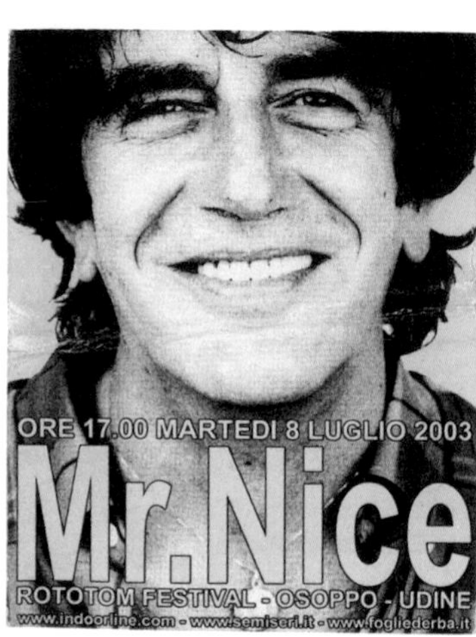
ORE 17.00 MARTEDI 8 LUGLIO 2003
Mr.Nice
ROTOTOM FESTIVAL - OSOPPO - UDINE
www.indoorline.com - www.semiseri.it - www.fogliederba.it

(←↘) Howard's publishers first appreciated they had a major bestseller on their hands when the organisers of a book signing by Howard in Alchemy Culture Shop on Portobello Road in Notting Hill ordered 50 hardback copies (hardbacks do not usually sell in such large numbers) and then rang back during the event to order a further 120, selling all copies at the event. This was unheard of. It soon topped all the bestseller charts in the UK and went on to be translated into several languages including French, German, Spanish, Italian, Russian and Hebrew: *Mr Nice: Every Jewish Mamma's Nightmare (But He's All Right Really)*. The audience that both Howard and his publishers expected to buy the book had been those of Howard's generation. In fact, the book chimed most with the generation of people in their twenties, tapping into a growing undercurrent of opposition to the criminalisation of cannabis that Howard, in his promotion of *Mr Nice*, brought into mainstream news, university debating halls and political debates, and eventually into a one-man show that sold out at venues across the United Kingdom, Germany, Spain and Norway in a series of tours between 1998 and 2014. *Mr Nice* has been included on a reading list for school children (A levels, that is age 16–18) and Howard was invited to give talks in schools, including in the Oratory School.

Despite the media furore with which his provocatively titled book was received, Howard eventually succeeded in charming the public, transforming his personal experiences into a political challenge to the drug laws:

'The man used to be one of the world's biggest drug dealers. They also say he's a really nice guy… In an age in which anyone connected with the drug trade is painted as evil incarnate, Howard Marks should be one of the most reviled people in the world… Yet it is impossible not to like the man. His charm is legendary.' ('Inside Dope', *The Sunday Age*, Melbourne, Australia, 5 January 1997).

'Never before has Reading's Waterstones bookshop erupted with rapturous applause on the arrival of a guest, especially a convicted criminal… If you can put aside the rights and wrongs of marijuana use, you will find it difficult not to like Mr Nice himself.' ('Con in demand', *Reading Chronicle*, 27 July 1997).

The use of the name 'Mr Nice' for a well-known and avowedly unrepentant convicted cannabis smuggler meant that the public could not put aside the rights and wrongs of cannabis in his promotional activities, and Howard thereby succeeded in making the legalisation of cannabis a mainstream news topic. A summary of the reaction of the British press was printed in the *Majorca Daily Bulletin*:

'To begin with, the title *Mr Nice* seems to have irritated most reviewers, even though the book makes clear that it is in fact one of the pseudonyms Marks used during his criminal career… Marks describes the illegal trade [in cannabis] as "transporting beneficial herbs from one place to another"…' ('Who said Mr Nice was pleasant?' *Majorca Daily Bulletin*, 17 September 1996).

Journalists reviewing his book for the press, who opposed the legalisation of cannabis, referred to him as 'Mr Nasty' ('Mr Nice, more like Mr Nasty', *The Evening Telegram*, Canada, 18 May 1997; 'Nasty, Not Nice', *Sunday Business Post*, Dublin, 8 September 1996). The right-wing press expressed fury at what they called the 'deification' of Marks ('Deification of a dirty drug dealer', *Daily Mail*, 6 September 1996).

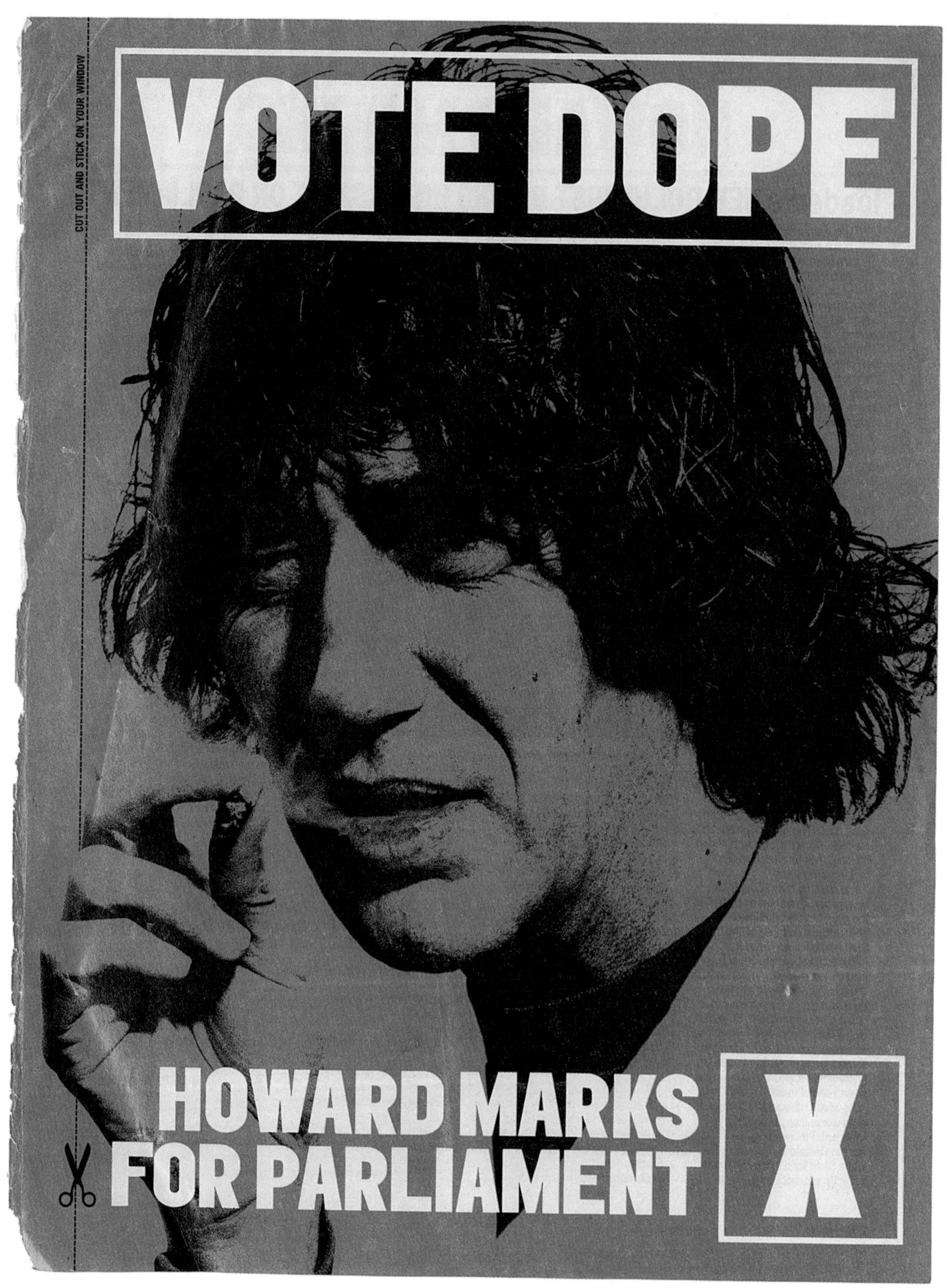

CUT OUT AND STICK ON YOUR WINDOW
VOTE DOPE
HOWARD MARKS
FOR PARLIAMENT
X

(↑→) Howard was hired as a columnist for *Loaded* and used his media platform to further the cause of cannabis legalisation. In the UK's general election in 1997 he stood as a candidate in four separate constituencies (Norwich South, Norwich North, Neath and Southampton) on the single issue of the legalisation of cannabis, catalysing the formation of the Legal Cannabis Alliance, and participated in debates with candidates from Britain's mainstream parties on television and radio.

LEGALISE CANNABIS

"The smoking of cannabis, even long term, is not harmful to health." **The Lancet, November 1995.**

"Having reviewed all the material available to us we find ourselves in agreement with the conclusion reached by the Indian Hemp Drugs Commission appointed by the Government of India (1893-4) and the New York Mayor's Committee (1944) that the long-term consumption of cannabis in moderate doses has no harmful effects."
The Wootton Report, (UK) (1968-70): Cannabis – Report by the Advisory Committte on Drug Dependence (Hallucinogens Sub-Committee)

Quotes on the safety of cannabis refer to its use in pure form and not when smoked with tobacco.

For further election information, please contact
Derek Williams, Election Agent, The Legalise Cannabis Party, 29 St Augustine Street, Norwich NR3 3BY (Tel: 01603 766854)

Published by Howard Marks,
The Legalise Cannabis Party, 29 St Augustine Street, Norwich NR3 3BY

Printed by Xavier Press,
Unit D6, Barwell Business Park, Leatherhead Road, Chessington, Surrey KT9 2NY

Designed by Lifework (0171 603 0732)

PRINTED BY PHANTOM PRESS 01603 486014

WHAT SORT OF GOVERNMENT WOULD BAN

**A SAFE MEDICINE,
A NON-POLLUTING FUEL,
A NATURAL RESOURCE,
A NUTRITIOUS FOOD,
A SACRAMENT,
A SAFE RECREATIONAL ~~DRUG~~ RELAXANT,
A HARMLESS HERB,
AN ECOLOGICALLY SOUND & ENVIRONMENTALLY BENEFICIAL PLANT**

LABOUR WOULD, TORIES WOULD

CANNABIS IS ALL THESE, YET IT IS BANNED IN FAVOUR OF DANGEROUS, EXPENSIVE AND WORLD DESTROYING ALTERNATIVES

VOTE FOR YOUR LEGALISE CANNABIS CANDIDATE

HOWARD MARKS

23/04 '97 WED 15:44 FAX 01703 424770 ECHO RECEPTION 002

MR NICE

HOWARD MARKS

Legalise Cannabis Party

SOUTHAMPTON TEST ☒

" I, AS AN INDEPENDANT, AM ABLE TO SAY THINGS THAT PARTY POLITICIANS CANNOT. I REGARD THE LAWS BANNING CANNABIS USE AND CULTIVATION TO BE UNSOUND, UNJUST & UNREALISTIC.
ALL MAJOR GOVERNMENT REPORTS ON CANNABIS HAVE SUGGESTED SOME FORM OF LEGALISATION, YET POLITICIANS REFUSE TO OPENLY DEBATE OR DISCUSS THE MATTER. I AM STANDING TO GIVE YOU THE OPPORTUNITY OF EXPRESSING JUST HOW IMPORTANT YOU KNOW THIS ISSUE TO BE. " - HOWARD MARKS

YOU CAN MEET HOWARD AND DEBATE THE ISSUES @

X Howard Marks
VICTORY PARTY • MAY 1ST

Don't forget to vote for Howard Marks on Election Day!

Room1

from Cambridge
CLUELESS SYSTEM
with special guests:
DJ Touch and
Noel Watson
No-U-Turn Records
'TORQUE' LP/CD out now!

Room2

PSE
SOUND SYSTEM
Reefer Bill
Andrew Lagerland
With Special Reggae Guest: Mr. Ting
Roots Ting Sound System

Thursday 1st May, 9pm-2am • Venue: The Talk, Oak Street., Norwich

Tickets: £5 on door/advance from:
Paradox Delights & Legalise Cannabis Party: 01603 441 178
Matrix, Norfolk: 01603 447 447
Soundclash, Norwich: 016030 761004
MellowDee, Great Yarmouth: 01493 745 554
Hedgehog, Ely: 01353 668898
Red Eye, Ipswich: 01473 256 922
Clueless System
Off Your Face

FROM THE ACTING MASTER AND MASTER-ELECT

BALLIOL COLLEGE
OXFORD
OX1 3BJ

Tel: 01865 277710
Fax: 01865 277764

E-mail: masters.secretary@balliol.ox.ac.uk

2 February, 2001

Howard Marks Esq
Unit 7
Apollo House
18 All Saints Road
Notting Hill
London, W11 1HH

Dear Howard

This is just a brief note to thank you for speaking at the Master's Seminar last Thursday. But, brief though it may be, it comes with my warmest thanks. These seminars depend critically on the contributions by speakers and, in particular, in introducing the topic in a clear, thoughtful and provocative manner. You spoke very eloquently and presented a strong and convincing argument which helped to generate a very lively and informed discussion. I am most grateful.

You may also like to know that quite a number of the people to whom I talked later in the evening felt this had been one of the most successful of these seminars.

Very best wishes

Yours

Andrew Graham

So nice to see you back in a Balliol environment.

(↑↗) Howard must have debated the legalisation of cannabis at almost every university student union in Britain, and at the prestigious Master's Seminar at Balliol College.

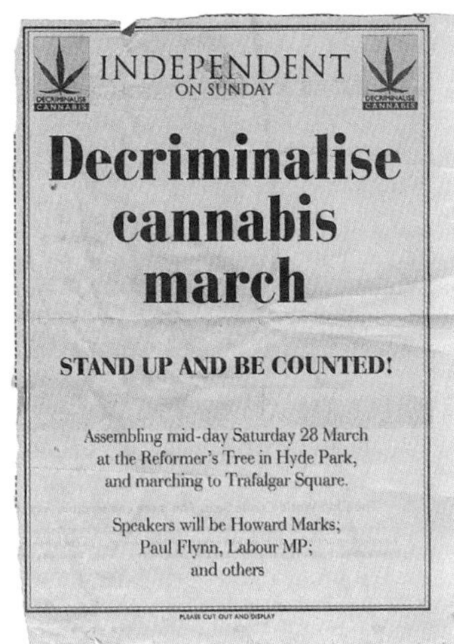

INDEPENDENT ON SUNDAY

DECRIMINALISE CANNABIS

Decriminalise cannabis march

STAND UP AND BE COUNTED!

Assembling mid-day Saturday 28 March at the Reformer's Tree in Hyde Park, and marching to Trafalgar Square.

Speakers will be Howard Marks; Paul Flynn, Labour MP; and others

PLEASE CUT OUT AND DISPLAY

Should Cannabis be Legalised?

DEBATE

Special Guest - Howard Marks

Falkirk College Assembly Hall
Tuesday 20th April 1999
Doors open at 7.00pm
Tickets £2 - all proceeds to FSU RAG

FALKIRK STUDENT UNION

END PROHIBITION RALLY

DR. JOHN MARKS
(LIBERAL PARTY CANDIDATE)

WITH

***MR NICE* - HOWARD MARKS**
(Legalise Cannabis Party, Ex-drug Smuggler)

DANNY KUSHLICK
(Campaign to TRANSFORM Drug Policy and Legislation)

... PLUS GUESTS ...

OTHER CANDIDATES INVITED

TIME	**1-2 pm:** ***Rally***	**2-3 pm:** ***Questions to Candidates***
DATE	**Saturday 26 April 1997**	
VENUE	**Large Lecture Hall, Crosby Library, Crosby Road North, Crosby L22**	

NO GUEST LIST **NO SPITTING**

CONTACT: Stella Cairns (0151) 708-5277 or Danny Kushlick (0117) 972-7428

PUBLISHED BY STELLA CAIRNS, 162 CHATHAM STREET, LIVERPOOL L7 7BA
Printed by: Northwest Printing & Design, 96 Duke Street L1 5AG

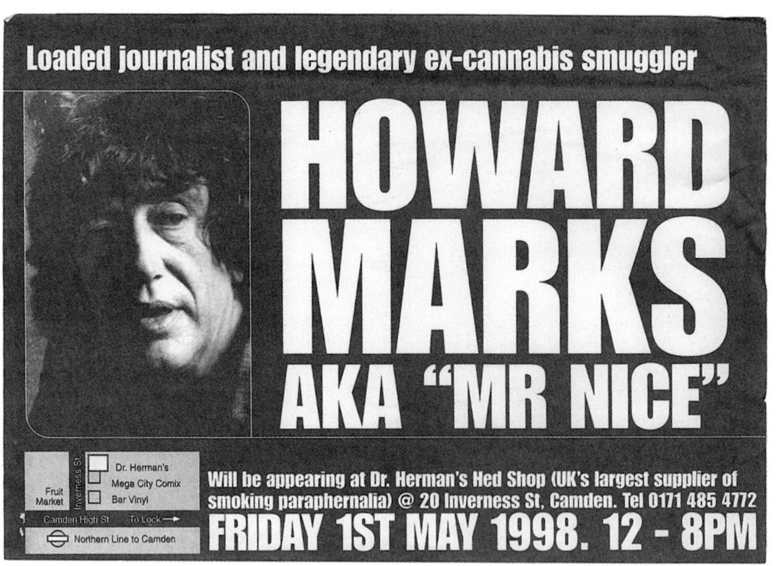

NORML UK

WORKING TO REFORM CANNABIS LAWS

Mission statement

NORML-UK seeks to gain recognition for the rights of people to peacefully pursue activities relating to cannabis without unwarranted intervention by the authorities.

A voice for responsible cannabis users

Founded in 1970 in the USA, NORML is an international organisation representing cannabis users worldwide. NORML-UK is is a non-partisan, non-profit organisation working for more research into the benefits of the uses of the cannabis plant for all purposes. We aim to provide a support network to those seeking the normalisation of cannabis users and to influence a positive transformation to laws to enable responsible medical, spiritual, recreational and industrial uses in the UK.

Our founding member are a diverse group of people from all walks of life who have one thing in common, we are all passionate about individual freedom, responsibility and liberty.

Medicinal cannabis user Des Humphrey and Howard Marks are proud to launch NORML-UK at the Global Marijuana March 2012 in Cardiff, Wales.

WWW.NORML-UK.ORG

(↑→) Howard supported the emerging semi-legitimate cannabis industry, founding one of Spain's first cannabis associations in Mallorca, joining others, speaking at cannabis trade fairs.

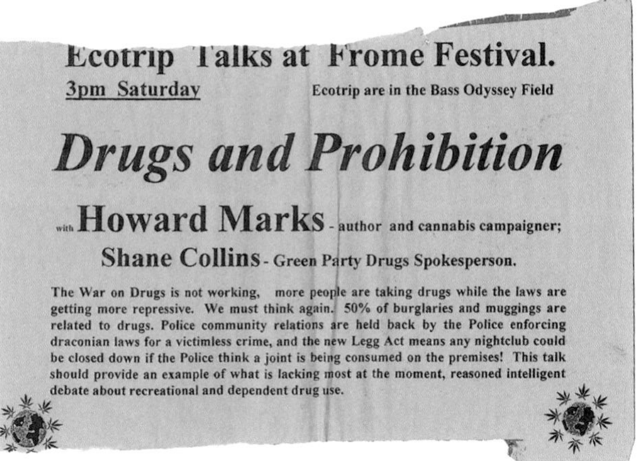
Ecotrip Talks at Frome Festival.
3pm Saturday Ecotrip are in the Bass Odyssey Field

Drugs and Prohibition

with **Howard Marks** - author and cannabis campaigner;
Shane Collins - Green Party Drugs Spokesperson.

The War on Drugs is not working, more people are taking drugs while the laws are getting more repressive. We must think again. 50% of burglaries and muggings are related to drugs. Police community relations are held back by the Police enforcing draconian laws for a victimless crime, and the new Legg Act means any nightclub could be closed down if the Police think a joint is being consumed on the premises! This talk should provide an example of what is lacking most at the moment, reasoned intelligent debate about recreational and dependent drug use.

Associació
Calada de Mar
E-mail: caladademar@gmail.com
Telèfon: 603545263
Website: www.caladademar.org
Calella

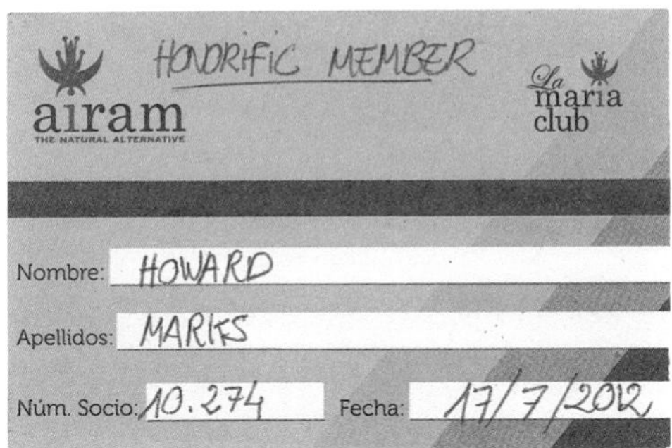

HONORIFIC MEMBER
airam
THE NATURAL ALTERNATIVE
La maria club
Nombre: HOWARD
Apellidos: MARKS
Núm. Socio: 10.274
Fecha: 17/7/2012

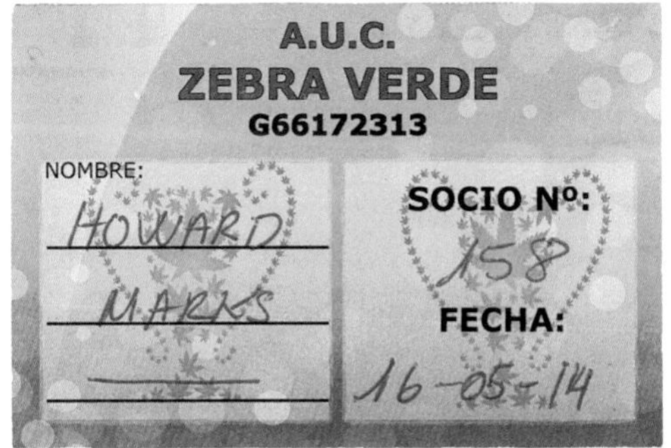

A.U.C.
ZEBRA VERDE
G66172313
NOMBRE:
HOWARD
MARKS
SOCIO Nº:
158
FECHA:
16-05-14

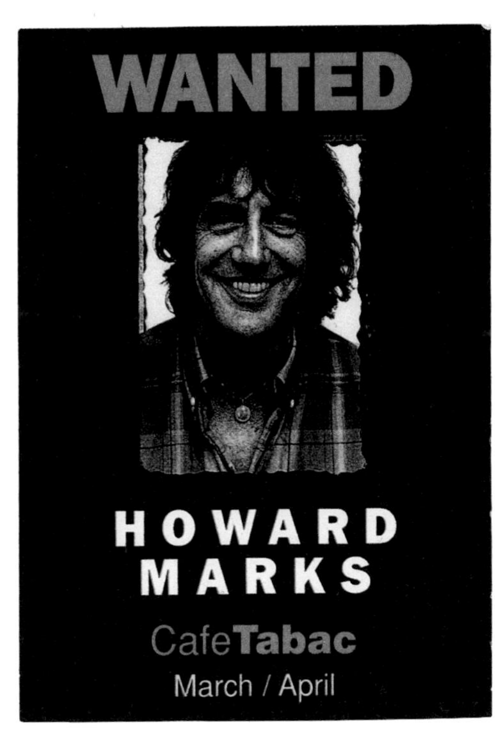

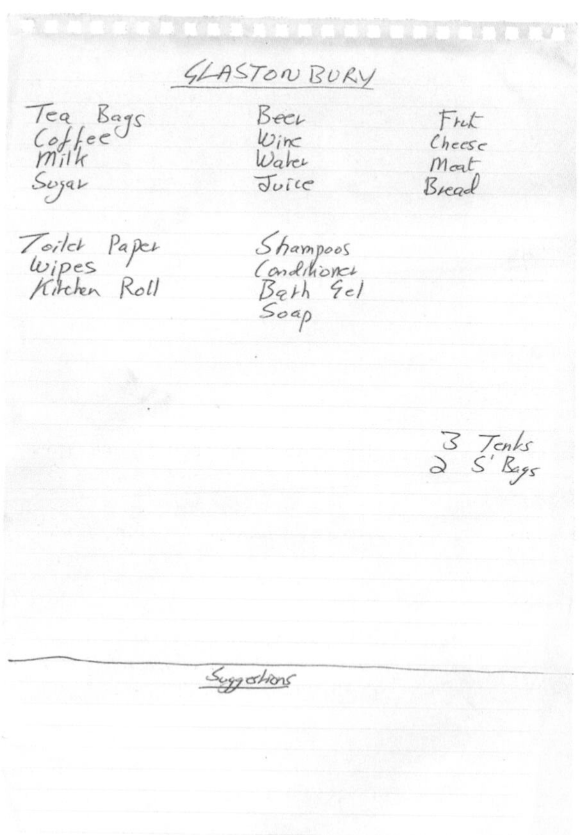

GLASTONBURY

Tea Bags
Coffee
Milk
Sugar

Beer
Wine
Water
Juice

Frut
Cheese
Meat
Bread

Toilet Paper
Wipes
Kitchen Roll

Shampoos
Conditioner
Bath Gel
Soap

3 Tents
2 S' Bags

Suggestions

(↑) Howard spoke at Glastonbury every year, taking his children to camp with him.

(→) Howard introduced his son Patrick to Patrick's favourite musicians at Glastonbury, including Norman Cook.

(←) Howard recorded 'Let me Grow More Weed' with PAIN, songs with Shaun Ryder of the Happy Mondays, Kermit Leveridge and Peter Hook. Songs were written about him by Super Furry Animals, The Clash and Stereophonics. In 2002, Sony released a compilation of Howard's favourite songs entitled 'Mr Nice: A Musical Trip with Howard Marks'.

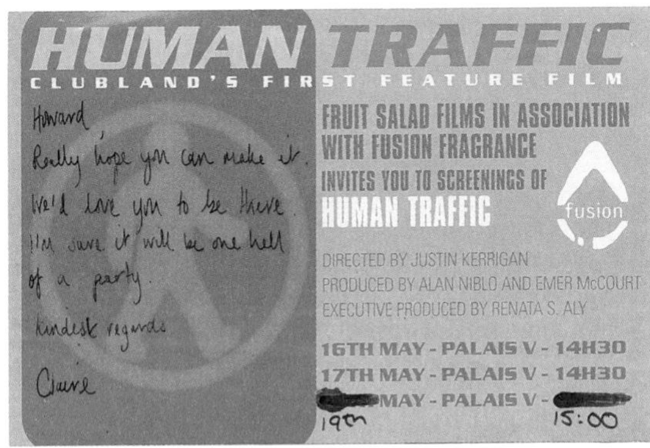

(↑) Howard explained spliff politics in a cameo role in the cult movie *Human Traffic*.

(↑↗) In 2010 a movie of *Mr Nice*, directed by Bernard Rose and starring Rhys Ifans, Chloë Sevigny and David Thewlis, was released in cinemas.

(↑) Howard was delighted to have secured a job that, at least as far as he was concerned, required him to smoke cannabis in public.

H.Q Reference No.

Control Section Reference No.
AS/DOB/2028/99(S)

香港特別行政區政府
入境事務處
Immigration Department
The Government of the Hong Kong Special Administrative Region

拒予入境通知書
REFUSAL NOTICE

日期 Date 3-5-99

*先生/女士/小姐 *Mr/Mrs/Miss/Ms MARKS DENNIS HOWARD
國籍/籍貫 Nationality/Native BRITISH CITIZEN
旅行證件號碼 Travel document no. 701171773
抵港時所乘搭*船隻/飛機的名稱 Arrived by *ship/aircraft VS 200
抵港日期 On (date) 3-5-99 時間 at (hour) 1530
來自(國家名稱) From (country) LONDON

上述人士(個人資料如上)已被當局根據入境條例第11條拒絕入境,*並被當局根據同一條例第32(1)條加以羈留。

The person whose particulars are described above has been refused permission to land in the Hong Kong Special Administrative Region under section 11 of the Immigration Ordinance *and detained under section 32(1) of the same Ordinance.

HK INTERNATIONAL AIRPORT SERVICES 為 being:

~~*(甲)運載該人抵港的*船隻的船長/飛機的機長~~
~~*(a) The captain of the *ship/aircraft in which that person arrived in the Hong Kong Special Administrative Region~~
*(乙)運載該人抵港的*船隻/飛機的擁有人、代理人或承租人
*(b) The owners, agents or charterers of the *ship/aircraft in which that person arrived in the Hong Kong Special Administrative Region
~~*(丙)下開*船隻/飛機的擁有人、代理人或承租人~~
~~*(c) The owners, agents or charterers of the *ship/aircraft specified below~~

*現必須遵照入境條例第24條的規定,以下開方式接載或安排該人離港:
*is/are hereby directed under section 24 of the Immigration Ordinance to *remove that person/make arrangements for the removal of that person from the Hong Kong Special Administrative Region by:

*船隻/飛機的名稱 *Vessel/aircraft VS 201
日期 On (date) 3-5-99 時間 at (hour) 2325
前往(國家名稱) To (country) London / Heathrow

又根據入境條例第33條的規定,在上文最後指明的*船長/機長須採取必要的步驟以防止該人在*船隻/飛機離港前進入香港境內。為達到此目的,該*船隻/飛機的*船長/機長可將他羈留在*船隻/飛機上。

The captain of the *ship/aircraft specified immediately above is hereby required under section 33 of the Immigration Ordinance to take such steps as may be necessary for preventing that person from landing from the *ship/aircraft before it leaves the Hong Kong Special Administrative Region. For this purpose the captain of the *ship/aircraft may detain that person in custody on board the *ship/aircraft.

被拒入境者簽名 Signature of person refused permission to land: refuse to sign MARKS DENNIS HOWARD

船長、機長或擁有人、代理人或承租人的代表簽名 Signature of captain or representative of owners, agents or charterers: HK INTERNATIONAL AIRPORT SERVICE

入境事務人員簽名 Signature of immigration officer: IO(A) W K LAI (Name in capitals)

*將不適用者刪去。 Delete as appropriate.

正本——白色——給被拒入境者 Original—White—for person refused permission to land.
第一副本——黃色——給船長、機長或擁有人、代理人或承租人的代表 Duplicate—Yellow—for captain/representative of owners, agents or charterers.
第二副本——藍色——給管制組備案 Triplicate—Blue—for retention in Control Section.

I.D. 122 (9/97)

(↑) Howard was not welcome everywhere. He was refused entry to Hong Kong.

(↓) Howard accumulated a large number of fines while touring the country with his one-man show.

Howard Marks
30 Wavenbarr Road
Kenfig Hill
CF33 6DE
UK

21st April 2012

Invoice

Dear Mr Marks,

The Head Housekeeper brought to my attention that you had been smoking in your room which you stayed in on the night of 20th April 2012. Since the smoking ban in Wales on April 2nd 2007, we have become a non-smoking hotel. There are signs in your room, and outside which displays this.

Below are details of the fine which have been incurred.

Item	Cost	Total
Smoking in a Non-Smoking Room (minimum charge of 1 nights stay)	£50.00	£50.00

A copy of the break down of your bill is enclosed.

Please contact us to make a payment as soon as possible.

Kind Regards

Emma Caple
Reception Manager

Hi Howard,
It's Louise from the ambulance service who picked you up a while back.
Please could you sign your book for my friend Ashley, who is a big fan of yours.
I have put in a stamped envelope with my address on if you will please post it back.
Hope you're now well.
It was lovely to meet you.
Thank you and take care.
Louise
x

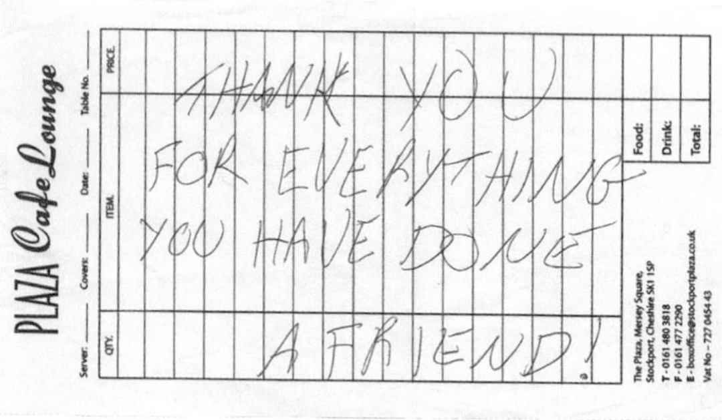

PLAZA Cafe Lounge

Server: Covers: Date: Table No.

QTY. ITEM PRICE

THANK YOU FOR EVERYTHING YOU HAVE DONE

A FRIEND!

Food:
Drink:
Total:

Howard made friends wherever he went and received thousands of fan letters, including several from ex-police officers. A detective from the Oxford Drug Squad, who claimed to have had dealings with Howard in the 1970s, wrote to thank Howard for *Mr Nice*, request an autograph and inform Howard that he now believed in the medical benefits of cannabis, thinking it should be available on prescription. Above, Howard agreed to pose for a selfie with members of the Metropolitan Police, at Notting Hill Carnival.

(↓) Hundreds of prisoners wrote to Howard, requesting everything from flutes, as Howard has noted on this letter from a prisoner in the Netherlands, to legal advice. Howard answered every one of them and did all he could to meet their needs.

WANTS A FLUTE SENT TO PRISON

Dear Howard & Family,

I hope this letter finds you well and happy. I hope it finds you full stop! I can hardly send it to Mr. H. Marks, Mallorca, so I've decided the best bet is to send it to your publishers, and hope they pass it on. I am from the fine city of Liverpool, which I miss very much! I am, or was, a musician by profession; although nothing special, I managed to get by. You won't remember me, although we met and chatted for twenty minutes in Liverpool, during your book promotion tour. I was the guy who gave you the fat, smelly "green" bud!! Somebody told me, that in your "LOADED" column, you thanked the Liverpool lads for their hospitality. I don't know if this is so, but if so you are more than welcome! Anyhow, it's been a while Howard, but I reckon it must be so much nicer to receive a letter from jail, rather than sending them!! I have a favour to ask of you, so please bear with the personal history a moment. Thanks!! Since my teens I have suffered from chronic anxiety, and depression. In and out of hospitals and shit! No sympathy required Howard, I'm fine at present. Last year though, things got real bad, for various reasons. My beautiful girlfriend, could take no more, and went back to New York. I can't blame her, although it fucked me right up. I embarked on a frightening binge of self destruction. I managed though to get it together, and took off back to Holland, in the hope of starting afresh. My life in England was filled with sad memories, and anyhow, the bailiffs had

0AI,97_01 Druk: DEMERSLUIS

TO MR HOWARD MARKS
ROOM 201

IT HAS BEEN ONE OF MY GREATEST PLEASURES MAKING YOUR AQUAINTANCE
HAVE A SAFE JOURNEY BACK HOME.

THE FRIENDLY BRAVO WAITER
TREVOR

SWALLOW ROYAL HOTEL
BRISTOL

Dear Mr Nice.

From those who know!
Enjoy your stay with us.

much respect.
Will, Dan
Room/Service.

WITH COMPLIMENTS

A SWALLOW LUXURY HOTEL
College Green, Bristol, BS1 5TA Telephone: (0117) 925 5100 Fax (0117) 925 1515

INVESTOR IN PEOPLE

I sent off for the application form.

CLICK

….AD LIB……….much like any other application form……

……………………………………………………………………..one strange question:

CLICK

"Any other names by which you've been known?"

….AD LIB…left one line…………………next:

CLICK

"Education, Professional Qualifications, and Other Training"

…………………………………AD LIB……………………………………………next:

CLICK

"Career History"

…………………………………AD LIB…………………………………………finally:

CLICK

"Reasons for Applying

Please say why you are interested in the appointment and indicate the relevance to the job of your qualifications and experience."

I then read out my answer which takes a few minutes…...……...…….and say 'I got a reply.'

CLICK

"Dear Mr Marks

CABINET OFFICE - ANTI DRUGS CO-ORDINATOR

Thank you for your application to this post. The selection team have carefully considered it along with all the other applications, and I am sorry to inform you that we were unable to include you among the candidates who were invited for interview.

(←) When Tony Blair's government advertised for the position of Britain's first Drug Czar, Howard was quick to submit his application. He didn't get the job but incorporated the correspondence into his stage show.

'Wondering in which direction I should next proceed to advance the date of re-legalising cannabis, I happened to be reading the employment section of *The Times*. It advertised a newly created vacancy in the Cabinet Office for the UK Anti-Drugs Co-ordinator, whose brief was to eradicate all illegal drug trafficking in the UK. Realising that by legalising all drugs, I could fulfil the brief easily and quickly, I wrote to the Cabinet Office. They sent me an application form, on which the following words appeared in large bold type: UK ANTI-DRUGS CO-ORDINATOR ALSO KNOWN AS "DRUG CZAR". I never thought I would have the opportunity of being promoted from a mere drug baron to a drug czar.

The salary was £75,000 a year, much less than an average drug baron's but not bad for a job with a built-in alias – I have always been fond of pseudonyms. There was also a £5,000 perk towards the cost of removing one's belongings from anywhere in the world to Whitehall. I could make good use of this to transport a container of my personal effects that had been sitting around in Kathmandu since the 1980s. I presumed there would be diplomatic immunity. Another page outlined the core requirements needed to fulfil the post. These included proven leadership qualities, negotiating and influencing skills, and the capacity for strategic planning linked firmly to the delivery of results. I found this encouraging as the authorities already had the proof that I used to be the head of the largest marijuana smuggling organisation in the world.

They were well aware of my successful negotiations with the *Mafia* and other international organisations, and knew that I had delivered well over a hundred tons of hashish. The page finished by stating that the successful applicant would require credibility in the drugs field. I felt I was in with a chance and wrote the following:

"My own experiences in the study of illegal drug transactions began at the University of Oxford in the early 1960s and were continued at the Universities of London and Sussex. Shortly after obtaining a Master's degree in nuclear physics and postgraduate qualifications in philosophy, I was recruited as an agent by MI6, the British Secret Service. I'm hesitant to detail here my drug-related work during this period, but presumably the Parliamentary Secretary for the Foreign Office is empowered to show you any relevant files. Suffice it now to state that for 20 years, I was intimately connected with illegal drug trafficking in the following countries: Wales, England, Scotland, Eire, Germany, France, Italy, Spain, Holland, Portugal, Morocco, Kenya, Lebanon, Pakistan, India, Nepal, Thailand, the Philippines, Hong Kong, Canada, United States of America, Colombia, Jamaica and Mexico.

In many of these countries, I worked closely with senior law enforcement forging long-lasting professional and social relationships. I have been granted unique access to many clandestine illegal drug processing plants.

I have held directorships of Panamanian media companies, Liberian record labels, British travel agencies, Dutch boutiques, Chinese publishing companies, Thai massage parlours and Swiss investment consultancies. I owned and managed a language school in Pakistan, not far from the Khyber Pass.

For the first half of the 1990s, I was employed by the United States Department of Justice, permitted to enter the Federal Bureau of Prisons' convict section, and allowed to teach incarcerated drug traffickers. I did that for seven years. I can keep down a job. At the same time, I posed as a marijuana addict and entered a drug abuse program to familiarise myself with the problems of denial and recovery.

I have written a book on illegal drug trafficking. It has sold over 750,000 copies in Britain, has been translated into six languages, is still a bestseller, and is available from all good bookshops.

I have written articles on drugs and crime for almost every national newspaper. I have appeared dozens of times on all major TV and radio channels as an expert on illegal drug trafficking, false passport acquisition and money laundering. I regularly give talks and lectures at rave clubs, music festivals and business conferences. I would gladly risk and even sacrifice my life right now to achieve the eradication of all illegal drug trafficking in this country. I am 100% committed."

I posted the completed application form to the Cabinet Office. I received a reply:

> Dear Mr Marks,
> Thank you for your application for this post. The selection team have carefully considered it along with all the other applications, and I am sorry to inform you that we were unable to include you among the candidates for interview.
>
> May I, nevertheless, thank you for your interest in this post and for taking the trouble to apply. I hope that your disappointment will not prevent you from applying for other positions which the Cabinet Office will advertise in the future.
>
> Yours sincerely,
> Colin Welch,
> Recruitment Manager.

Again, I was disappointed, but at least the door had not been closed.'

'I walked over Kenfig dunes to Sker Beach and thought of boats unloading hashish on to the sand, guarded and protected by RD Blackmore's mermaid, immortalised in his *The Maid of Sker*. The shore was deserted. Anchored in the distance were the massive, hundred-thousand ton, iron-ore ships that my father used to discharge after he left the sea and came to work ashore. The blast furnaces and chimney stacks of Port Talbot's giant steelworks still made most of the sky invisible. On the walk back we noticed the turrets of the buried city's castle just poking eerily through the sandy ground.' MN

Acknowledgements

This book would not have been possible without Dr Crofton Black, or Ben Weaver and Oliver Wood to whom Crofton introduced me. Much of the inspiration for its format came from the rare book and manuscript catalogues produced by Crofton, Ben and Oliver many years ago, and from *Negative Publicity: Artefacts of Extraordinary Rendition* by Edmund Clark and Dr Crofton Black (Aperture, 2016) for which Ben was the designer.

Oliver Wood helped me to get Howard's several hundred boxes of material into searchable order and preserved and protected for posterity, and also assisted me in identifying items for inclusion in the book.

Ben Weaver is a brilliant designer and his ability to work collaboratively with the author on both word and image, on item selection and narrative has enabled me to articulate my vision for this book and to enjoy the process of its compilation. I am grateful to No Exit Press for their willingness to work with him, and for being so quick to appreciate his talents.

I am very thankful for the editorial support and encouragement of Geoff Mulligan and for his brilliance at coming up with titles. Thank you to Judy Marks for permission to reproduce her telegram to Howard. Thank you to Jamie Peto and Charlie Ryall for being on hand to help me with last-minute transcriptions and even shelf building!

Most importantly of all, of course, has been the friendship and support throughout the production of this book from Linda, Tom Raikes, Rachel Reasbeck, Caroline Coon, Helen Wild, Anna Wilson, Niamh Eastwood, Ana March, Miriam Rius I Gironès, Ben Bowling, Arthur Irving, Cindy Curls, Tony and Siri Harris, Juan Carlos Torres Gari, Myfanwy Marks, Francesca Marks and Patrick Marks. Thank you all.

Special thanks must also be given to Fish for his loyalty, kindness and support and to both Fish and Marty Langford for their roles in safeguarding many of Howard's documents until we were able to find a home for them.

Amber Marks is a writer, researcher and barrister. She lectures on Law and Pharmacology, Criminal Law and Evidence at Queen Mary, University of London where she has authored several academic publications. Amber is a leading expert on drug law and advises governments, courts and NGOs in this capacity. She has performed stand-up comedy in a variety of venues and festivals and her book Headspace (a satirical account of her research into bio-surveillance) was described as 'astute', 'informal and engaging', 'wonderful' and 'funny' in the national press. Amber has written articles for *The Guardian*, *The Times*, *Wired* and *The Register.*